PRAISE FOR KEN CHURILLA &
NO ONE SAID IT WOULD BE EASY

I am kind of stingy/picky when people ask me who would I let do something for me or work along side of me. Being in the world of MLB baseball for so many years, you get to meet all kinds: those willing to help you and others who just want to be seen with you. Ken Churilla, I have to say, is the one you want on your side. He's creative and hard working—which is my favorite trait of anyone—but having good people skills tops them all. I know given a chance and challenge, Ken doesn't let you down. No doubt, writing a book on anything, he would be writing from his soul and heart.

—Ron Kittle, 1983 AL Rookie of the Year,
Chicago White Sox

Very few journalists are as passionate about music as Ken Churilla, and I've always appreciated how he approaches a story from the singer/songwriter's perspective. This book is out of the norm for him, and I'm excited to see how he tackles this tough subject.

—Gretchen Wilson, Country Music Artist

Having read countless memoirs, research, and instructional books about grieving, and supported many people on their journeys after losing a loved one; I haven't come across a book quite like this. *No One Said It Would Be Easy* is a raw, brutally honest account of one man's traumatic loss and his struggle to put his life back together. The mistakes and triumphs this man makes are lessons for all of us. Trauma happens to the entire family system, no one escapes cancer's path of destruction. The dying is certainly the most devastating, but the rebuilding is the most difficult. While not intended to be a manual about grieving, the author captures the range and intensity of emotions and the effect on the whole fa~~mily when a loved one passes~~ away from cancer. Self-help books tell u␣ ␣␣␣␣␣ balances those tenets with many "do no␣ ␣␣␣␣werful learning tools, so reading ab␣ ␣␣y's missteps, may really help a lot of ␣␣ ␣␣nt because it Normalizes such a broad ␣␣␣␣ ␣␣hinking dur-

D1411661

ing the grieving process. Men need to hear that their pain is important and the way in which they display that pain is "Normal." *No One Said It Would Be Easy* acknowledges the tremendous pain felt when losing a loved one to terminal illness. However, in the end, it is a story about courage and hope.

—Elizabeth Fazio, Psy.D. & Licensed Clinical Psychologist, Long Grove Psychological Associates

As a male whose wife had had breast cancer, and knowing other men going through life and family crises, I find this book to be helpful given its real and honest narrative. *No One Said It Would Be Easy* gives the reader a real sense of what is going on behaviorally and emotionally with this husband and father's struggle with his wife's battle with cancer. The book is also very real in highlighting 20/20 hindsight into various thoughts and actions. Raw and poignant insight into one man's psyche and actions as he deals with his wife's battle with breast cancer, I highly recommend this book as an effective therapeutic and cathartic tool not only for men but also women attempting to gain insight into a male's thoughts and actions. The entire journey is very effectively narrated as if the reader is sitting across the kitchen table from Tommy as he talks about his thoughts and actions.

—Dr. Frank Tantum, Retired Child and Family Psychologist and Lecturer, Cook County, Illinois

You often hear stories about battles with breast cancer and it always hits close to home when you are a women, as we all share that risk. On the other side of that coin are the loved ones who wage that battle alongside, shoulder to shoulder, and the fear, uncertainty and utter helplessness they experience facing such a harsh reality. *No One Said It Would Be Easy* is a sobering, well-written and brutally honest chronicle that stands as a "companion guide" for all men caught in this war of all wars. The Do's, Don'ts, and I Don't Knows are all captured here in a vulnerable tale that offers to shine a light in such inevitable darkness.

—Brandy Reed, Senior Publicist, RPR Media

No One Said
It Would be Easy

No One Said
It Would be Easy

*One Man's Journey Through
His Wife's Battle With Breast Cancer*

Inspired by a True Story

Ken Churilla

No One Said It Would be Easy

Copyright © 2013 by Ken Churilla

For information on sales, licensing, or permissions, contact the publisher:

Dunham Books
63 Music Square East
Nashville, Tennessee 37203
www.dunhamgroupinc.com

Trade Paperback ISBN: 978-1-939447-79-1
Ebook ISBN: 978-1-939447-80-7

Printed in the United States of America

DEDICATION

This book is dedicated to the millions of men who are forced into this journey. I hope you can take this story and in some small way, it helps you in yours.

CONTENTS

FOREWORD

WHEN IT COMES TO this dreaded disease, all bets are off. You can't predict when it will strike your life, you can't run away from the diagnosis and you can't stop the feeling of fleeting control. A thousand questions go through your mind and the strength and confidence you spent your life building all vanish with three little words: "You have cancer."

I know because I have heard those words not once, but twice in my life and with each time, my reaction was completely different. So was that of the people around me.

The first time I got the diagnosis I was in college and doctors found a tumor on my ovary. My Grandmother had died of ovarian cancer so naturally my mother began to over-mother, yet all I could think about was whether or not I could have children. It was before the days of in-vitro fertilization and egg freezing and back in a time when cancer could (and would) rob women of their fertility. My doctor's advice: "Try to get pregnant as soon as possible." That was a bit of a problem, as I didn't even have a boyfriend.

Fast-forward to four children later, a successful, happy healthy wife and mother is bowled over: cancer again. This time while nursing my baby girl I found cancer on my right breast. This time, I was worried. Now there were people who were counting on me, who needed me. Now there was a husband so scared he couldn't look at me. I didn't want to be a patient to him, a fragile sick person. I wanted to be his partner but that didn't seem possible now. As I journeyed through the multiple surgeries and treatments as my cancer spread, I made a drastic decision: I would keep my health to myself.

Yes, I lied. I created a distance. I told my husband and my petrified mother I was having hernia surgery when in reality I was having cancer removed. A year later when I finally confessed to my cover up, the two people who meant the most in my life were devastated. A mistake? Probably. But given the chance again, I am not convinced I wouldn't make the same choice. Cancer changes you.

This book explores those changes not just for the patient but for their loved ones as well. It reminds you in such a powerful way that you can't judge or even understand what others are going through and it lifts up those who have been there by saying however you handled your brush with cancer, you cannot beat yourself up. Leave the beating for the disease and choose to live!

That's the one gift that cancer leaves behind in all of its thrashing of your life: the desire to appreciate. We all say we want to live life to the fullest. We want to appreciate every person in our lives, shed the negative, embrace the positive and truly live. But rarely do we put that into practice. After the fear and self-doubt, after the battle and the insecurity, after the cancer if you are lucky you are left scarred and grounded.

And after reading this *No One Said It Would Be Easy*, you are left with the knowledge that you are not alone.

Thank you Ken! For me, and all of the scared spouses out there, this is a Godsend.

—Dina Bair, WGN TV, Anchor / Reporter

INTRODUCTION

AS I WAS WRITING this book, I wrote it under the working title *What About Me* because when it comes to breast cancer, everyone's focus immediately centers on the woman in the fight and if there are children involved, they share in that focus as well. The men attached to them however, seem to almost always be the forgotten party. Even though they are hurting and fighting right alongside their wives, typically they are counted on to just instinctively know what to do, help everyone along and keep the ship righted.

There seems to be countless books, support groups, and things of the sort for women going through breast cancer, but there is no manual for guys on what to do when death steals their wives. There is no road map on how to handle things or how to react.

I want to be clear; by no means do I intend for *No One Said It Would Be Easy* to be either of those. This is not a how-to book. As much as this book follows the thread of what Gina (the woman in this story) goes through, the reason I wrote this book was because of what Tommy (her husband) had to endure as a husband, as a father, and as a man. The purpose of this book is to provide you with a peek into his world, as a man who took every step with his wife and how those steps and their consequences affected both him and those around him along the way. I'll show you the mistakes he made. You'll see the situations he was in – some of which you may have already seen or some of which may lie ahead of you.

You'll see as you read through this book that Tommy's really just a regular guy. He wears blue jeans, drives a normal car and watches football like any other typical guy. He loves his wife and kids and would do anything for them.

At the same time, you'll see he's a hold-nothing-back kind of guy. As men, we have a tendency to clam up and not discuss our feelings with each other. There might be a close friend we occasionally open up to or confide in, but that's usually prodded along by a cocktail or two.

Typically as guys we keep our conversations limited to sports, business, and things of the sort. Guy things.

It's important to note that every situation is different. The woman in your life might be going through different procedures, you might have different circumstances, etc. As I said, this book isn't mean to be a road map, but instead I hope it helps to point out where some common turning points might be, either medically, emotionally, or just as life benchmarks.

Much like Tommy, I'm a hold-nothing-back kind of writer so I'm going to lay it all out here for you. I'll show you the road he traveled, where he took the turns well, where he put the car on two wheels and where he made mistakes and flew off the path altogether. As you'll see (or perhaps you already know), it's a long road and there are a lot of people that become involved.

If you're living this there will be times where you'll scream inside your head and not know where to turn. Hopefully this book helps you figure things out, not just how you handle any certain situation but how you handle yourself and your own sanity as well.

Here's to hoping your road is easier because of the pages that follow this one.

God bless,

Ken Churilla

1

AND SO IT BEGINS

THIS STORY PROBABLY STARTS the way that most of these stories do. Gina noticed a lump in her breast long before she did anything about it. It was December when she first noticed it, but having just given birth to our daughter Jackie, she paid no attention to it. Figuring it was probably something connected to the fact that while nursing a baby lumps are normal, she just discarded the thought. As time went by, the lump persisted, and it wasn't until early February that she did a self-breast exam and noticed one of the lumps was still there.

Her birthday was coming up on February 26th and I had a special night planned for her 35th birthday. Now I'm not the most sentimental guy, but I had a couple of special things lined up. I arranged for a babysitter, made reservations at a great restaurant, bought some roses and was going to surprise her with a song I hired a guy to write for us. The guy wasn't James Taylor or anything, just part of a service that took information from people's lives and worked them into a personalized song. I thought it was sweet and was damn proud of myself for coming up with such a romantic idea.

When the night finally came, I sprung the surprise on her. The roses were waiting for her in the car and I played the song on the way to the restaurant. I still don't know what her breaking point was, but she completely broke down, obviously overcome with surprise and emotion.

"Tommy, I found a lump."

If you've heard that line yourself then you know what I mean when I say it hit me like a ton of bricks. Not in a devastating way, but enough to wobble your head for a bit. I sat there listening to her tell me what she had found, but it wasn't really registering. It didn't faze me like you might think. I've gone back and forth about this a million times since then wondering if I was wrong for not being knocked out by the news. I mean, when you see this sort of stuff in the movies it's this huge poignant moment, with loud and dramatic music – yet it wasn't that. That will come later, but at this time it was just some news, albeit devastating news.

Like a lot of guys, I'm a fighter. Call it competitive, bullheaded, defiant, whatever. I heard what she said to me but I didn't look at it as something that could really change our lives, let alone take it. I just thought it was something we would deal with, get past, and then move on from.

I remember thinking that it wasn't anything that had been confirmed by a doctor. You know how that is when you have some sort of ache or pain, you don't really take it seriously until the doctor tells you to. Sometimes we dismiss aches or pains until a doctor confirms their malignance. You just kind of acknowledge it, put it on your To-Do list and go about your life until you can get in to see someone about it. That's kind of how I felt that night. I knew a lump in the breast is never good, but I didn't go jumping ahead to any conclusions.

We went to see her OB/GYN Dr. Arnold and he confirmed what we initially thought. It was indeed a suspicious lump and it needed to be seen by a specialist. They referred us to Dr. Jackson, a surgeon at a local hospital in Barrington, IL, but it would be five days until we could get in. I know that sounds like a quick turnaround to pull a doctor appointment, especially one that isn't your regular general practitioner or something, but waiting those five days seemed endless.

In hindsight, I learned a very valuable lesson right there. As we would come to learn, literally every minute is valuable in the fight against breast cancer.

We didn't really talk about it much in those five days. We didn't ignore it, but we didn't dwell on it either. Like I said, in my head it was just something we were going to have to deal with. Nothing more. It hadn't really set in and while I knew what the possibilities were, it was as if I wasn't allowing myself to consider it.

We did discuss the family though. She wasn't entirely close to her family and most of them lived in Puerto Rico, but we were close to mine. We didn't know exactly what to do about informing them of the news. We talked it over and eventually decided it was best if we told everyone immediately.

That was a hard discussion to have. We did it in the first day or two after the OB/GYN visit but before her appointment with Dr. Jackson. It was like going to them with bad news, without being sure whether we had any to deliver. We stressed to everyone that there was no confirmed diagnosis, but that we were concerned and thought that they should be in the loop. That kind of made me feel a little better about it, but again, I wasn't overly concerned at this point. Anxious, but not overly concerned.

Aside from that, we pretty much left it alone. Gina was a strong woman, so she dealt with it on her own which for me meant keeping my normal routine of blocking out the anxiety by immersing myself in work, which has always been my usual coping mechanism.

2

IT GETS REAL

THIS IS WHERE THINGS start to get tricky. The day finally came when Gina got to go to the doctor. We kind of knew what lay in store at the doctor's. Dr. Jackson was going to need to perform a core needle biopsy on the lump, which is a typical procedure at that stage. A core needle biopsy involves removing small samples of breast tissue using a hollow "core" needle. As much of a big step as it is, it's a fairly routine procedure.

I remember rationalizing with myself, thinking that if you can do the procedure at the doctor's office, how serious could it be? I mean, if it was that serious wouldn't they make her go to the hospital? Since the procedure was a routine one, Gina took herself to the appointment and I went to work. It was on my mind, but my way of coping was to ignore it. Distract myself with work.

She called me in the early afternoon with the news; the tumor was three to four centimeters in size.

You'll hear me say this often as we continue, but at this point, my naivety was probably my biggest ally at the time. I knew it wasn't good, but still I took it in stride as merely more family news, not much different than if my son twisted his ankle in a baseball game or if my daughter got a D on a test.

Gina told me the news but immediately afterwards said to go ahead and do what I had planned, so I did just that. She was a mentally tough woman. I talked myself into an okay sort of state, which in hindsight is probably what kept me from going into a panic. I finished out the day like I normally do. I wrapped up at work, went to play some basketball at the YMCA and then got home around 7pm for dinner.

For Gina, life was about checklists. She made checklists for everything. To-Do lists, grocery lists—you name it and she had a checklist for it. This was no different. When she got the news, she made a checklist of what we needed to do: who we needed to tell what, what doctors we needed to see, and in what order we would need to set up affairs at home. Now that she was armed with this news, it was just on to the next step.

My mom and I talk every day so she was the first person that I told. Her first reaction was panic. Obviously I was concerned too, but I didn't really understand why my mother was flipping out the way she was. Again, maybe it was my being naïve but I didn't quite grasp the picture. Not until we conferenced in my sister Robyn. Robyn is a critical care nurse but she had worked in oncology at Northwestern Community Hospital so she sees and lives in it every day. When I told her, she went right into professional mode. In the blink of an eye she went from being my sister to an oncology nurse peppering me with questions and blurting out terms I didn't know.

I remember feeling like my head was going to explode. You know, that feeling you get when you're flooded with information and terminology that you have no idea how to explain? That's when I felt the gravity of the situation for the first time, and it's a moment that I can honestly say I'll never forget. Don't get me wrong, I was still just as optimistic as I was before Robyn came on the line, but when she started breaking things down into laymen terms for me, the picture became a little clearer.

My wife might have breast cancer.

All of a sudden, I felt like we were part of everything I had ever seen with pink ribbons. Susan G. Komen, breast cancer walks…all of it. We could be a part of that now.

My wife might have breast cancer.

I kept repeating it over and over in my mind and no matter how many times I said it, it never seemed to lose its gravity. It's an odd realization when you find out you're a part of that. Cancer. The word even sounds ugly. And now we're a part of it.

I went to bed that night with a feeling I never felt before and to tell you the truth, I never really felt it again until after she had passed. It was an odd hazy process of trying to realize and grasp something that I never really considered possible.

3

THE FIRST FACE IT TAKES

DR. JACKSON SCHEDULED OUR next appointment for a week-night five days later, but this time I went with. At this point I felt like Gina and I were teammates lined up against a common foe. If you've ever played sports, you know the feeling. It was that kind of bond guys get in the locker room before a game or when they're walking down the tunnel towards the field. There was a sense of solidarity between us and there was an opponent we were going to face. We didn't know exactly what that opponent was or how powerful it would be, but we knew we were in for a fight and we were going into it together.

She drove herself to the doctor's office. I met her there since I was coming straight from work. The drive was strange for me. I tried to keep my mind off of it by paying attention to what they were saying on the radio. I'm a big fan of sports radio, and as any guy who listens to sports radio knows, you can really get lost in what they're saying if you want to. It's like sitting at a bar with a thousand other guys talking about what you think the Bears need to do about their quarterback problems, why the Cubs aren't winning or whatever. That helped with the drive over.

At one point I turned down the radio and said a prayer in hope for good news. When that was done, I called my mom just to talk and hear her voice. There's something calming in hearing your mom's voice. As I got closer to the doctor's office, for whatever reason it all started to become much more real. For the first time, I allowed myself to start thinking about a lot of 'what if's.' What if the news was bad? What would that entail? How would that affect my work schedule? Would I need to take time off? What was that going to do to our financial situation? How does our insurance cover all of this? As I said before, Gina was an incredibly tough woman. I didn't think anything the doctor could say would collapse her, so I didn't worry about holding her up. I was more concerned with the overall family well-being.

When I got to the office Gina was already in the waiting room. For whatever reason, I noticed the office had a very soft feel to it, which was odd because I never really pay attention to things like that. Our appointment was late, at 7pm or something like that, and we went right in. We sat next to each other, as teammates do, facing Dr. Jackson as he sat behind his desk.

We had prepared ourselves for bad news, at least I did, but I was still hoping to hear something good. Dr. Jackson looked at me first and our eyes locked in a surreal sort of way that I will never forget. To this day I can still see his eyes bouncing back and forth from Gina, to me, to Gina, to me.

Two words, "…it's cancer" was all that he initially said. That was all it took and I was immediately overwhelmed with emotion. I did everything I could to hold my composure but that feeling is one I will never forget. In an instant my head got hot, I felt light-headed, and tears came to my eyes. As I looked over at Gina, I could see tears had flooded her eyes as well. We weren't naive anymore so we were somewhat prepared for this result, but no matter how much you try, you're never truly prepared to hear those words.

The irony is amazing when you think about it. Here we sat side by side as teammates, yet across the desk sat Dr. Jackson. This man was going to be one of our biggest allies in what would turn out to be the fight of our lives, yet as the words slipped out of his mouth, the visual of that moment burned itself into our minds forever. As he told us the news and confirmed that horrible reality, his was the first face that this ugly disease would take.

He quickly went on to say he wanted to remove the lump for further biopsy and wanted to do it sooner than later. After that, he left the room, giving us a chance to digest the bomb he had just handed us. Out of instinct, the first thing I did was hug her. Gina was a strong woman but this was more than you could ever expect anyone to handle. I told her everything was going to be okay and that we were going to beat this. Things you just say not even knowing if you're right or not. Strangely though, even in the midst of that moment, I didn't think a bad outcome was even possible. I was thinking there was just a long road ahead of us.

A fairly positive and upbeat Dr. Jackson returned a few minutes later to inform us that he had scheduled surgery for a week later. He didn't say it but it was a lesson we would learn; time is never on your side when you're in this kind of a fight. And even though we were just informed of the news, this fight started long before we knew we were in it.

We only spent about thirty minutes in the doctor's office and even though we had been sitting the whole time, I was physically and mentally drained when we walked out. I walked Gina to her car wishing we hadn't driven separately. The car ride home for me was eerie. Neither of us called each other. I imagine it was because both of us were trying to digest the news. As you can imagine, I was down and upset but not in a 'why me' kind of way; I just felt completely unprepared for the news. Either way, I was getting myself ready for a fight.

Now it was my turn to start preparing checklists because I was getting ready for a fight. I immediately began to focus on her surgery. I know Gina is strong but sometimes that can be a hurdle. Even in the car, I was already worried about her mental state and what was going through her mind. I really worried about what we were going to tell our son, Jackson. The girls were young at the time; Amber was four and Jackie was only fourteen months, so they wouldn't understand anything anyhow. But Jackson was eleven years old.

Just as I was thinking about Jackson and what we were going to do with him, I pulled onto the street and the house came into view. We live at the end of a cul-de-sac so you can see the house as you approach. I saw everything differently that night as I pulled into the driveway. The saying goes that you don't truly appreciate something until it's taken away from you and that was the moment I knew that saying was right. I hadn't lost anything yet, but for the first time I truly appreciated how perfect my life had been: I was married to the love of my life, had great kids, and lived in the dream home she and I had designed and built.

Then in that same moment as I put the car in park, I thought about how cruel it all was that we were dealt such a shitty hand.

I must have driven pretty damn slow because by the time I went inside, Gina was already putting the kids to bed. We didn't discuss anything with them that night because we still hadn't talked yet ourselves. After the kids were in bed, I washed up and pretty much went right to bed. I was in a state of numbness and fatigue and I could tell Gina was too. We both just crawled into bed and I just kissed her goodnight. Even lying there, I didn't want to talk about it. Not yet. I just wanted to go close my eyes and go to sleep. Maybe I would wake up tomorrow and it would all just have been a bad dream.

4

COME OUT SWINGIN'

FROM THAT NEXT MORNING through the day of her surgery, I was still very routine in my daily ways. I went to work, kept my sales rolling, and maintained my basketball schedule at the YMCA. Without question, I slipped right back into my coping mechanism of immersing myself in work.

This was the point the 'why-me' questions started to sink into my brain, but they didn't derail me. I know some people who can get completely lost in self-pity, but I was able to shut out the bad thoughts pretty quickly when they started to invade my head. It helped knowing that our surgeon was one of highest regarded in his field. This, coupled with the fact that the lumpectomy was an outpatient procedure, kept me feeling somewhat safe because it appeared to be a fairly common surgery. Perhaps it was my naivety or maybe I was just talking myself off the ledge, but I still felt like things were in a secure zone. It's not in my nature to be overly analytical. All signs pointed to it being a routine procedure so I wasn't too worried.

I woke up on the day of the surgery a little earlier than normal. Sleep was still coming somewhat easily for me, but this night and day were a little more unnerving. My main fear was that the tumor, which was an aggressive type of cancer, had gotten to her lymph nodes. I was scared because once it gets into the lymphatic system it can metastasize (spread) to other parts of the body. I was worried, but optimistic. I kept telling myself the lump was just a setback and today would be our knock out punch. Dr. Jackson would remove it, and we would be good.

I felt different as I got my morning coffee, but not in an alarming way. I talked with Gina as we got ready, but kept it fairly light. I told myself it was for her but I'm sure subconsciously it was just as much for my own benefit. The drive to the hospital was quick, fifteen minutes or so, so I kept it light with jokes and whatnot. It felt like a normal car ride that we had taken a million times before. When I turned into the parking lot though, the air changed. It was like I was a boxer or something and I walked out of the tunnel and saw the ring. I immediately went into attack mode, or game face if you will. As we got out of the car and walked across the parking lot toward those big glass doors, it was as if I was walking in there with my dukes up. My blood started to run hot. My temples started to pulse. I could feel myself clenching and unclenching my fingers. I was ready for a fight.

After all the check-in procedures, I sat with Gina in Pre-Op. All I could do was hold her hand and be with her. It was a poignant moment, and even then, I recognized that. The more I soaked in the scene and our surroundings, the more emotional I became. It was too much. It was a lot like that when I pulled in the driveway coming home from our initial diagnosis; it caused me to step back and take a good look at what I had to lose.

I'm a guy who likes to be in control. I went into my line of work (sales) because it is commission based and I wanted to be able to control how much I made and how much I worked. I like to call the shots and control my own destiny. That said, I can honestly say this was the first time in this entire process that I felt at the mercy of others. I tried to take it in stride and remind myself that it was early and we still had the upper hand. Obviously in hindsight, I know now that you never truly have the upper hand when you're battling a disease like this, even though you always have to fight like you do.

As they wheeled her away into surgery, for some reason I was able to come down and calm myself. I don't know if it was my body going into autopilot or what, but I was able to return myself to some sense of normality. I checked in with the office, grabbed some coffee in the cafeteria and checked on the kids. I'm sure to any innocent onlookers who didn't know any better, I didn't appear to be a guy whose wife just went in to take her first swings back at cancer. And even though I knew that's exactly who I was, I didn't feel like that guy.

It was a fairly quick procedure, somewhere between an hour and two, so once I was done with my busy work I just sat in the waiting room. There was a desk with a phone on it and a nurse whose job was to answer that phone when it rang and then get the family of the patient who had just completed their surgery.

I tried to flip through a magazine but nothing was really registering. I re-read the same line in a *Sports Illustrated* about a dozen times, without taking any of it in. So I put it down and just sat there. Looking around me I saw a lot of families waiting just like me. I tried to read their faces to see where they were, but I had no clue. Hell, I didn't even know what I was looking for in their faces. Fear? Worry? Exhaustion? I saw all of it, but I had no idea how to place it on a timeline or anything. We were all just sitting there in the same room, but in reality we were each in separate worlds just waiting for that phone to ring.

The phone rang a few times and each time it did, everybody looked up with a look that I can't really explain. It was kind of a mixture between hoping it was for them and being scared to hear their name. After a few times, the nurse called me up to the desk and walked me back to Gina where she was in recovery. She had already woken up from the anesthesia and was coming to when I walked in. I started talking to her a bit. Not knowing what to say I just asked how she was feeling and threw in some mindless chitchat.

Thankfully, the doctor wasn't too far behind me, maybe about five minutes or so and told us the news together. He said the tumor was larger than they anticipated. They were able to remove the tumor but they couldn't get the negative margins. Negative margins are a circle region around the lump that is free of cancer. They try to remove this so they can get any cancer cells that may have gone undetected but built up around the tumor. They were unable to.

What he said next hit me like a bomb…he found a second type of cancer. To remove that PLUS attempt to get negative margins for both regions, he would have to greatly deform her breast. He recommended a complete mastectomy, which is the complete removal of the breast and some of the lymph nodes. He indicated that he didn't visually notice any spread to her lymph nodes, but we wouldn't know until the biopsy results came back.

I guess that's when I realized how serious this really was, more than I ever had before. Up to now, even when the news had been bad and made me more aware of the situation at hand, I had been looking at everything as if the glass were half full. I always felt like we could just go in, remove the lump, and be done with it. But standing in the surgical recovery room with Gina on a gurney having just come OUT of surgery, listening to our doctor say she needed to have her breast removed? That's the kind of news that punches you in the heart and weakens you at the knees.

I looked at her and in my mind it pained me immediately to know that the woman I love more than anything in this world was going to have to undergo another surgery…a major surgery…and this next surgery was not only going to change her medically, it was going to alter her physically.

All at once I was overcome with a multitude of emotions, each one just as overwhelming as the other: I was scared, pissed, upset, my head got hot, I didn't know what to do with my hands. I looked over at Gina and immediately I could see the fear in her eyes. For a brief second, I almost felt ashamed. There I was, reeling from this news, feeling all of these emotions, and I wasn't even the one this was happening too. I grabbed her hand and she grabbed mine and immediately my focus shifted to trying to comfort her and let her know that not only were we in this together, but we were going to beat this.

Inside my head though, I think that's when my optimism sprung its first leak. It wasn't necessarily in that exact moment, but we were still in the hospital when I started thinking about all the stories I had heard about breast cancer and what those treatments entailed. I didn't know much about chemotherapy or radiation, but I know the horror stories. I knew that it made you violently ill, caused you to lose weight and of course to lose all of your hair. It wasn't that I was worried my wife was going to look like a cancer patient. I was worried that she was going to have to go through all of this and there was absolutely nothing I could do about it. As a man, especially when it comes to your wife and kids, you pride yourself on being able to take care of everything and make things better. Yet here I sat helpless, with this disease staring me in the face, almost laughing at me, and there wasn't a damn thing I could do about it. Worse yet, I thought this was as bad as it could get. I would eventually learn that this was nothing compared to how helpless I would feel later.

5

LETTING PEOPLE IN

I WAS FEELING VERY overwhelmed and to be honest, I didn't know how to fight the feeling. I sat there with my thoughts and it came to me pretty quickly, I had two choices. Fight or flight. I know what you're thinking and you're right, there is no choice. The only choice is to fight. I started thinking about a lot of things at this point that I never really considered. Of course, I thought about our family and the effects this immediate future was going to have on us. We had three kids at home to take care of and try to explain what was happening to their mom.

I called my sister Robyn and again, she immediately went into nurse mode. She was pretty frank when she explained to me what we were in for. Again, I don't think I really digested it completely. I got it enough to understand what we needed to do, but I still felt like this was something we could dig in against and win. You've seen those movies where two guys get into trouble in a bar and end up back to back with everyone circled around them wanting to kick their ass, but somehow in the end they make it out of the bar safely? I know it's a crazy analogy but that's kind of how I felt.

The next surgery wasn't for a few weeks so we all tried to settle into our normal routines. I obviously went to work everyday and got myself back into going to the gym to work out or play basketball. Physically I got myself back into my routine but mentally, I was all kind of confused. I felt the need to discuss a lot of things, but Gina didn't really want to talk about things too much. She wasn't as communicative as I would have liked and that put me at a mental crossroads. I had so much I wanted to talk about, but how do you force a woman to talk about something like this when she's the one who is under fire? I didn't know it then but this would become a recurring theme for us; I needed to talk and she could not be communicative.

Even though she didn't want to talk about it much, she did feel the need to tell the kids right away what was going on. That kind of confused me. I mean, she didn't want to talk to me about it, but she wanted to tell the kids? I understood that she is their mother and was going to be laid up, there's no getting around that, but it bothered me that she was totally green light on communicating with the kids but yellow lighted on my road.

In any event we told Jackson first, within a day or so, and he took it okay. Better than I thought he would. He wasn't unaffected by the news but he wasn't devastated into instant death preparation either. He took a bit of time to process it and once he did, he had a hard time getting comfortable with it. He didn't go reeling into this uncontrollable kid, so I let her deal with him. After all, they were always closer to each other, so I kind of backed off and let the natural mother/son relationship take over. You kind of have to play the odds sometimes and forcing myself into that situation would have probably done more damage than good. It's not that I didn't love him and didn't want to be there to help him, but I felt the best way for him to swallow this was to do it with his mother's help.

Aside from that, I didn't notice any changes around the house but admittedly, I wasn't really paying as close of attention as I probably should have been. In retrospect, I think that for the first time, I went into a bit of a self-defense mechanism and mentally checked out for a while. The surgery wasn't for a while and I was part scared / part exhausted from this cancer cloud hanging over our heads. It's almost comical now that I look back at it. I guess they say ignorance is bliss because had I known then what I was in for, I probably would have felt immensely overwhelmed. More than I actually did.

I still wasn't researching much yet. Sadly Gina's situation had become more and more common so we were just following procedure. I was talking to Robyn a lot, but that was about it. I felt caught up in a fight where I didn't necessarily feel outmanned or underinformed, I just felt like time was against us. Obviously as anyone who has or is going through this kind of fight knows, from the minute you find out you're in it, you know that time got a head start on you. It's kind of like trying to win a marathon when the race started while you were still parking the car.

When it came to the actual removing of her breast, I never really considered the impending physical change or deformity Gina was facing. Not from my standpoint anyway. Sure I had questions, but for me that wasn't much of a big deal. I know this might make me sound shallow, but physicality is a huge part of being a couple. As a man who adores his wife and was still physically attracted to her, this is something that you have to think about. This might come across as superficial, but I'm not a huge 'chest guy' so it didn't really faze me from a sexual or physical perspective.

However, what did scare the shit out of me was that for the first time, mortality started to really enter my thoughts. I didn't share that with anyone but it really did. I talked with Gina about the checklist of things to do, but I kept my fears to myself. I dealt with them a little bit in conversations with my family, mainly Robyn, and those conversations seemed to simultaneously help and discourage me. It was like the more I learned about this damn disease the more I learned what an uphill battle it was.

I know now that Robyn always knew more than she let on. She was great at educating me and comforting me each step of the way but, like I said before, she's watched this disease beat up on women and families first hand for years.

I kept going to work as if nothing was happening at home. I was open about it to people at work, and to be honest that was more therapeutic for me than keeping it private. It would have driven me crazy to keep it all in. Like I said, Gina wasn't all that communicative about things so I needed some sort of release. As much as I love my family, sometimes you just need someone who is completely on the outside. I didn't go into details with everyone but I didn't keep everything hidden either. If they asked, I told them the big picture and kept people abreast of our situation. It's funny because I never worried about the pity factor. I was so consumed with everything it never even crossed my mind. It wasn't as if I was telling the kid who carried my groceries to the car, but I'm talking about people I work with and spend the majority of my time with. I felt blessed to have the friends I did.

I still wasn't paying attention to any differences with the kids. I felt like I was still just Dad at home. I mean, I was trying to keep life as close to normal as possible. Gina was still feeling pretty normal and had the house under control. At this point and admittedly maybe mistakenly, I figured the household was her reign and supporting it was mine.

6

SURGERY

ONE THING GINA had decided in this time was that we were going to need a little bit of help around the house with the kids. We settled on bringing Gina's mother in from Puerto Rico to help out. She was planning a trip to the States in the near future anyhow with Gina's sister so when this all fell in our lap, she changed her timing to be here for the surgery. For our sake, it was someone that we trusted with the kids. For the kids, it was a good chance to spend some time with their Grandma, which was something they didn't get much of a chance to do. So we flew her up and settled her into the guest room.

The night before the mastectomy, I was very out of sorts. It was like the night before a big game or something. I was both nervous and anxious all at the same time; it really felt like we were going into battle.

Throughout this whole process, any sexual intimacy had pretty much flown right out the window. There was a lot of stress and we were both continually exhausted, but to be 100% honest, I was the reason for much of it. I knew she was so concerned with what was going on with her internally, I felt hesitant. I felt like any attempts by me to focus on her physical body would cause her to dwell on the fact that her breast would soon be gone. It felt kind of like when you are trying to soak up the last few moments of a vacation. Even though you're having a wonderful time, there's that very present awareness that this is your last night with it.

Besides, I had so many other things going on in my head that sex was the farthest thing from my mind. I had a ton of fears, mixed with a good share of panic about what lay ahead. In my mind, I was always walking three steps ahead of where we were, but that's hard to do when you have no idea what the next step is. I didn't know if she was going to need chemo or radiation after this surgery, but what if she did? Were we going to need help around the house? Will I need to take time off? Luckily we were financially in a position to where those things were possible, but work isn't just income for me, it's a huge part of my personal being. It's my sustaining wheel. Not to mention I'm in sales and in my business, if you step out of the circle for a prolonged amount of time someone can and will slide in and form a new relationship with your client. One thing leads to another and then poof, all of a sudden you're competing for or maybe even losing a long-term client's business.

Again, I didn't share this with Gina. My job was to support her and give her some pep, which I did. I tried to liven that night before surgery with jokes and stuff like that. I tried to keep things light and normal. Was this the smartest thing to do? Who's to say? Every situation is different but for ours, I think I made the right decision. Lord knows I didn't always make the right decision and we'll get into those a little later.

However, the morning of the surgery was a different story altogether. I was able to sleep through the night but from the minute I woke up, I was a bundle of nerves. I remember glancing at her in bed, and she had this look about her. She looked so sullen about losing her breast and that killed me. I had no idea what to do or what to say. I remember thinking that it didn't matter to me one bit that she was losing her breast because that wasn't how I saw her. I was just happy that she was there and I felt overwhelmed by my love for her. I told her of this love as I hugged her, and while I know she believed me, I'm also pretty sure she didn't hear a word I said. She probably just chalked it up to me trying to comfort her.

She was quiet in the car and that drove me nuts. I don't know what I expected her to say and I can't say I would be different if the roles were reversed, but I felt the need to lighten the mood. Thank God for my sense of humor because that probably helped us both. I kept joking all the way until they made me leave her. I'm sure they weren't always funny jokes but again, it was my defense mechanism taking over. When we checked in, they took us to her room and informed me they would allow me to stay with her all the way up until the nurses came to take her into surgery. I watched her change out of her clothes into her hospital garb and it made me sad.

It's funny, you never really talk to God until you are either asking for forgiveness for something you did and simultaneously swearing that you'll never do it again, or you're asking Him to take care of someone or something for you. That said, I said a little prayer to myself, which I'm sure is something that everyone does at this point.

I kept trying to lighten the mood with jokes, which were probably as much for me as they were for her, with neither of us paying much attention to what I was saying. I was just kind of filling the empty air with noise at that point. It wasn't long until they came and got her, which I was thankful for. When you're sitting there waiting for something like that, minutes feel like days. I kissed and hugged her as they wheeled her away. I'll tell you one thing, there are few things that make you feel more helpless than watching someone you love disappear down a hospital hallway. I felt complete surrender and that's a feeling that throughout this journey, you have to learn to deal with. Trust me when I say that as hard as you try, it's never really possible. You never get to be okay with it.

And thus, my wait began. I was there alone as nobody came with me to the hospital. I didn't want anyone there because I felt like that would only complicate things for me. I would either feel the need to talk in order to keep the silence out, or I would just want to sit there and their conversation would annoy the shit out of me. So I sat there alone and soon enough, I slipped into my comfort zone. Instead of leafing through the magazines or staring at the TV, I did what I always do to escape. I went to work. I didn't actually go to the office but I checked in and made a few phone calls. I'm sure on the outside anyone who saw me walk in with my wife and then heard me on the phone talking about some client's order probably thought I was the biggest jackass on the planet, but that's what worked for me. I can bottle anxiety with the best of them and still when it comes to work, I'm able to focus like Michael Jordan on a jump shot.

As you can imagine, it was an excruciatingly long morning. Hours felt like days and all the while, I stayed in contact with my family. They were all concerned and wanted to know what was going on. Finally, the surgery was over and the surgeon came in to talk to me. He pulled me into a room and started to talk. I was so anxious just by the very sight of him I almost had to turn my mind off just so I could listen to what he had to say.

He got right to the point and I was incredibly cognizant of every word that came out of his mouth. He told me he successfully removed 24 lymph nodes and her breast. His initial thought was that things looked pretty good and he was very encouraged that it had not metastasized, but he was going to need to see the biopsies before he could make any real concrete assessments. Hearing that was a real sense of relief. The painful thing was that the results were going to take two to three days. Normally, that's not a long time at all, but when you're waiting on a report card like this, that sounds like an eternity and it feels like even longer.

At this point Gina was still in recovery, so I was still waiting to see her. The doctor hadn't spoken to her yet as she was in and out of lucidness from the anesthesia. I was so excited with the news and since I had some time, I got on the phone right away. All of a sudden, the glass was half full again. Things were back on the upswing. After I made my calls, I almost found myself skipping down the hall. I know, sounds kind of corny, but that's how happy I felt.

All that happiness was shot to hell when I finally saw Gina. She was still under some sedation and I watched them move her from the gurney to a bed. My God, the pain! That was such a tough sight to see. I actually felt her pain just by watching. I felt horrible for her. Cautiously I told her the good news and then left her to rest. The happiness was dulled by her excruciating pain. This was another one of those moments where you feel incredibly helpless. Here I had what I thought was the greatest news we could possibly hope for and even that wasn't going to take the pain away for her. I walked out of the room and instead of feeling the elation that I did only a few moments before, I was consumed with an odd combination of exhaustion, optimism, and anger. The exhaustion is self-explanatory, as is the optimism, but I was so full of anger that she was in such pain.

We had gone in early in the morning but it was late afternoon when I plopped my butt in the car. It was a tough ride home but I was looking forward to seeing the kids and just wrapping my arms around them. I picked up dinner on the way home, ate with them, and then put them to bed. It was just me and the girls, as Jackson was staying overnight at a friend's house. I called the hospital and checked in on Gina, but she was pretty out of it. She was on some serious pain meds, so we'll call it a less than spectacular conversation. It didn't matter though. As far as I was concerned, the sun was shining on our asses again. All we had to do now was wait for the doc to call us in a few days with the news that we were clear and our world would be normal again.

7

JACKSON

I GOT THE KIDS DOWN and then nuzzled up to a handful of cock-tails. Between the sheer physical exhaustion, the emotional roller coasters and the booze, I was finally out like a light. The next morning I woke up early so I could see Gina at the start of visiting hours. I wanted to sit there with Gina, but instead I ended up directing traffic; there was a steady stream of visitors and flowers from friends, family, and work colleagues. To be honest, the visitors were a welcome distraction for me.

I didn't know it yet, but Jackson was going to be an issue. It was easier to walk the girls through everything, but with Jackson being older and me not being his biological father, that was a harder road to navigate for both of us. It's funny (and a lot of guys with step kids have shared this sentiment with me as well); regardless of how long you've been a part of a child's life or how much you do for them, even if their 'actual' fathers don't do much for them, you never really measure up. I tried like hell with Jackson. I ran baths, made meals, tried talking to him and in a sense, tried filling in for Gina in the areas where she was very entrenched in his life. I'm sure part of it was him being a scared kid and maybe subconsciously being scared of losing the only 'real' parent he had left, but we had a hell of a time. Internally I was torn between wishing I could satisfy his needs more and wishing she could just get better so she could take this back over. I remember thanking God that this was only temporary because he and I were about to kill each other.

8

THERE'S NO PLACE LIKE HOME

AMIDST ALL OF THE craziness going on, the bed felt so empty. It had an eerie, creepy feeling to it. You know how it feels when you're traveling and you have to sleep in a hotel or a guest bed at someone's house? That's kind of how it felt. I think the main reason was because it had been years since I had slept alone. Sure, there were more than a million mornings where she had gotten up to start her day and I was still sleeping, but crawling out of bed alone is nowhere near the same as crawling into bed alone.

For some reason, that bed just felt ginormous. It felt like it swallowed me up. It was a feeling I never got used to, and that same unsettling sense came back after she had passed. But that's for later.

Lying alone in that bed was another one of those moments when I really realized how much I loved her. It kept running through my mind how much I was looking forward to her coming home the next day for a lot of reasons, and lying in bed alone put the exclamation mark on it. Just having her home would be so much better for the kids, for myself, and just for the normalization of it all. Even with her gone for just one night, I realized the truth of the saying that you don't know what you've got until it's no longer there.

I know I sound like a selfish jerk here, and I was. That's kind of the point of this whole book, and that's okay. As much as it is someone else who is going through the actual disease, it affects you too.

Here I was thinking she was going to come home and rescue us all, but she was really in pain. Since Gina was a housewife, she never really had anywhere she had to be on a regular basis. I don't intend for that to sound demeaning or anything because I don't mean it in that way. What I mean is she didn't have a job that required her to be there everyday, at meetings, client functions, etc. She wasn't tied down by the same kind of requirements I was with my job. She could be wherever she needed or wanted to be.

However, now that she had to start treatment, that was going to change. We didn't yet know what her treatments would be, but I did know that whatever those treatments would consist of she was going to have to deal with the after-effects of it as well, so our home life was about to change in a big way. The only thing was I didn't know how. After all, how could I? We had never been through this before. We heard stories from the doctor and my sister but they always ended with the words '…every situation is different.' Ever since we had gotten married, I had gone about my work life, she took care of the kids and the house, and it all worked seamlessly. Now for the first time, I was going to have to learn how to balance it all and to a degree, take over all of them. I was going to have to juggle her treatments, her reactions, work, the kids, the house, and everything else that went on in our lives.

I don't know if I did it right. In fact, I know that I didn't at first, but I like to think I was in a continuous evolution of progress. It was kind of like being a kid learning how to hit a baseball for the first time. The first few swings are horrible. I mean you miss everything, but you keep taking whacks at it and eventually you get better and better until you get to the point where you're making contact and getting some hits. Same goes for balancing your time and thriving both at work and at raising kids and running a home.

We were only a day and a half out of surgery and still waiting on the results, but I was operating with tempered optimism at this point because of the encouraging words that the doctor had said to me. I kept juggling all the possibilities I could imagine in my mind. If the news was good, if it was bad, if she was going to have heavy treatments, whatever I could dream up; I game planned it in my head.

When I picked her up at the hospital that morning it was pretty reminiscent of when she came home after her maternities. She was ready when I got there and I pretty much just wheeled her out and loaded her into the car. Granted, she looked more tired and beat up. To be honest she looked exhausted, but she was almost as anxious to get out of the hospital as I was to have her home. Just having her in the house was going to do so much for my state of mind. There was this calming effect that she had on me.

We talked on the ride home. Well, I talked. I know I've mentioned it before, but communication was a problem we had throughout this whole ordeal. It was always the 800-pound gorilla in the room. I would acknowledge something, she wouldn't want to, so I would back off. It frustrated the hell out of me and after it was all over, I really wished that was one thing I would have handled differently. I wish I would have pushed the issue a little more. I know she was scared and tired and fearful of the future. We both were, and even though this had been going on for a few weeks at this point, we were still kind of in a state of shock. It was all still sinking in. At this point, we were just kind of walking step by step. I was game planning, but I still had a Pollyanna outlook.

The kids met us at the door, which was awesome. It played out in front of my eyes like I was watching a movie. That night was a nice night. It was short because she was so tired, but it was nice. The whole family was back in the house, together. Plus we were still hanging onto the doc's encouraging words so things were looking up.

It was odd to see her with no right breast and I found myself glancing at it every so often. If she had just been some woman at the grocery store or something it probably would have hit me differently, but since it was her, I saw it in a different light. Robyn gave me a great bit of advice to make a concerted effort to focus on helping build her self-esteem. Even though Gina didn't tell me it bothered her, I knew that it must have. Besides, it didn't matter to me. This was my wife, I loved her, and that was that. It would have been no different than if she had a crazy scar on her cheek or some other form of visible deformity.

We met with the doctor within a few days to discuss our plan of attack with both chemo as well as reconstruction. Three of her lymph nodes were positive for cancer so the doctor wanted to start chemo in about three weeks. We wanted to get right into it because once cancer has spread to a lymph node, you already know it has metastasized. The odds of it spreading somewhere else in the body at that point are strongly increased so we opted to go after it with the chemo.

For the three weeks though, things went back to normal. I happily threw myself back into my normal routine of eleven-hour days at work and then a couple nights of basketball with the guys. Even though she was still dealing with the physical pain, she craved her routine as well and as soon as she could, she vigorously re-took her role as head of the household. But even with both of us happily reclaiming our former roles, things felt different. I would catch myself looking at her at various moments and became very aware of those dark thoughts that found their way into my brain. I was scared that I was going to lose her. I wondered how I could go on without her.

The kids still didn't know the severity of what was going on. They knew Mommy was sick and had to have an operation, so for now they felt like everything was over. Occasionally it would break my heart to see them playing with her knowing what I knew. Eventually we would bring them up to speed and not keep them in the dark, but at this point we felt like why scare them with something so severe when it could be over before it began? There were a lot of people who reached out. Cards and flowers were all over the house. Robyn was around constantly for me, which was nice. Not just that day, but she would call me or check in every so often and that helped me so much.

9

CHANGES TAKE HOLD

WE MET WITH A PLASTIC SURGEON for reconstructive purposes whom many people referred to as "the breast guy." We scheduled it for 9am and with the girls only five and two and a half years old, my mom agreed to babysit, but she could only watch them until 11am. We were running about five minutes late and we called to let them know, but apparently that was enough to push us way back in line, and we ended up waiting two hours as he went ahead with his next patient. At first this didn't bother me; why make everyone wait when he could keep things rolling along? But the more that time went by the more pissed off I got. Finally around 10:30am I left to go get the kids. My mom had to work and we had only planned on being there a few hours, so I had no choice but to bring them to the office. Again, we were blessed by their youth because they were so young they didn't know where we were going. I just told them Mommy had to go to the doctor so we were going to wait with her.

Finally, around 11:30am they called us in, but I got hit upside the head with another curve ball. The doctor refused to allow me in the room with her! As if I didn't already have a good case of the red ass with this guy. Rather than make a scene, I grudgingly agreed and sat back down with the kids. She was only in there for about a half hour so my mind bounced back and forth between feeling livid at this asshole and wondering what was being said.

When she finally came out, she was quiet. Driving home I didn't comment on anything because the kids were in the car, but about a half hour later after we had dropped the kids at the next sitter (we had to go to the oncologist appointment next) I exploded. 'What the hell' was the first thing I could get out and that was all it took for Gina to burst into tears. That freaked me out because I thought that my temper had broken some sort of barrier and pushed her to tears.

My regret quickly turned back to rage as she told me that during the examination, the doctor had grabbed her remaining breast. That didn't necessarily bother her as that's his job but it was the way that he referred to it as 'saggy' that cut her to the bone. Never in my life have I wanted so much to get in a car and go find someone with the sole purpose of beating the bloody hell out of him. What the hell kind of professionalism is that? Especially from the doctor who everyone calls 'the guy!' I took her into my arms and felt devastated for her. Needless to say, that was the last time we ever saw that jackass.

We moved on to our oncologist Dr. Smith to get his prognosis. As I mentioned before, three of Gina's lymph nodes were positive for the cancer. It was looking like four cycles every three weeks. Dr. Smith was completely the opposite of the plastic surgeon. The entire way he was great; he was instructive, educational, and a great hand-holder to both of us. Even still, I felt so bad for Gina. All I wanted was to be with her and make her feel better. Obviously it was hard for her but for me, it was a rough time going through this sort of thing and there truly was not a thing I could do. There was nothing I could do to make her condition improve, nothing I could do to make her feel better, and there was nothing I could do to really even take her mind off of it.

Even at this point, I wasn't being naïve but I felt like we just had a long, hard road in front of us before we could get rid of this thing. I still thought there was no chance of a dark outcome, just a long journey back to good. Sure, I knew she was going to lose her hair and I was pretty ready for that. I had seen her in baseball hats so it really wasn't much different than that. But between the medicine and the chemo she was wiped out. She didn't do much getting out of bed and who can blame her. I on the other hand, kind of overreacted and really freaked out. I was really worried about maintaining the house and I had this irrational fear of having to do it all myself. I tried at first, but I was all thumbs and that only angered me more.

My mother suggested the idea of a nanny. When I brought up the idea of a nanny to Gina she was lukewarm to the idea. I didn't really think about it as much as I should have then, but this house was her turf. This was the home she created and kept for her family and here I was asking her to allow someone else to do that. I convinced Gina that a nanny was something we needed, so rather than fight me she caved and we hired a woman for the duration of the chemo. We went through the hiring process together, calling a local agency and interviewing a few candidates. We ended up settling on Sofia, a Chilean woman. She was a good cook and had a very nurturing way about her.

Looking back we really didn't need her. I should have just sucked it up a little bit and figured out how to manage it. Not only did we not need the added expense, we just flat out didn't need her around. It was a luxury and one that in the end, I think may have started causing a wedge between Gina and I…but we'll get to that later.

I took her to chemo each time and that was exhausting even for me. I know that sounds selfish but walking in there and seeing not only Gina, but all those other cancer patients, was depressing as hell. There was always somewhere between six and eight patients getting treatments. I remember it looked like a bullpen at a baseball game, only these people weren't waiting to go into the game, they were already in it fighting like hell to win. As is my nature, I always tried to lighten the mood with everyone. I would clown around, tell jokes, stuff like that. I don't know if it was me trying to make them feel better or trying to make myself feel better.

That was the first time I really started to grasp some of realness of it. This was where it started to really sink in. You would look at these people and see it in their eyes. They were fighting, but still they possessed this obvious exhaustion. They had this clammy, kind of empty gaze fixed on their faces as the chemo pumped into them.

I would catch myself at times muttering 'why us,' and it wasn't just once or twice. I did it a lot even though I wasn't trying to. I wanted to keep a positive outlook but man, being in that room it was hard NOT to ask the question. I know the other people in the room were muttering the same thing under their breaths as well.

After a while, I got to the point where I would just drop Gina off and go into work while she was getting her treatment. When she was done my sister would pick her up and drop her off back at the house. I know that sounds like I was abandoning her but I never saw it that way. Gina was a fighter and often, she was a silent fighter. That might be the kind of thing that is different for other people. For us, it was the mental break that I needed.

Usually by the third or fourth day of treatment, Gina would be taxed. The first week was nothing much more than physically exhausting on her, but it was the second week where it really became apparent. That was when her hair started falling out and that was really rough on both of us. Don't get me wrong; if anyone could pull that look off it was Gina, but it was rough because it was yet another sign of reality. It was hard for me to see her take these different steps into cancer and even though I know this was the point where we were fighting it and driving it out of her body, seeing these things made it feel like it was setting in.

10

SOFIA IN...SOFIA OUT

AT THIS POINT, WE had settled into a routine. I took Gina to treatment and went to work, Robyn picked her up and brought her home and then Sofia took care of her from there. As time progressed, Gina and Sofia became quite close, so much so that I almost started to feel like a third wheel. They had their own ways about things, their own jokes, things like that. The air around the house got so thick you could cut it with a knife. I know this makes me sound like a nut, but I started to feel so extricated.

I started to wonder if I maybe did too much by deflecting too much. I think that maybe by trying to take so much on, I was actually working us backwards. To be honest things probably would have been a lot better if I would have just relaxed, stepped up, and gone for the ride, instead of trying to alleviate things by bringing in Sofia.

The weekends usually found a way to get back to normal, but I think that was only because Sofia wasn't around. As the summer wore on, it increasingly became just us. Our friends began to withdraw. They never said why but I'm sure it was because they were just afraid. People deal with cancer in a lot of different ways and a lot of that depends on who has it. I'm sure if it had it been a friend of ours I might have done the same thing in an attempt to respect their space, not knowing how to act, etc, but the fact that I was on the other end of the bridge on this one made it difficult to understand. It bothered me a lot because even though she would never verbalize it, I knew it bothered Gina.

We would go out occasionally. Typically the chemo would get to her on Thursday and Friday but by Saturday or Sunday she would have enough strength and be stir crazy enough that she would want to go out. We didn't do anything big, but we might grab a bite to eat or go to church or something. I wasn't really on the lookout for people looking at her strangely because she really didn't look all that different physically. The hair was really all she had to worry about but she had a wig.

Her chest looked normal because the doctor had given her a special breast prosthetic to wear. Much like they make prosthetic arms or legs, they make prosthetic breasts that fit inside the bra for women to wear until their reconstructive surgery.

Even though other people weren't, I started to find myself looking at her differently. Not with my eyes, but in general. The intimacy in our relationship at this point had gone right out the window. Not that I didn't expect that and Lord knows I wasn't pushing the issue. I mean she didn't feel good and with the state of her body and her hair, she sure as hell didn't feel feminine and sexy. I think I started sensing then that this had begun the distancing of us. It was not just because of the lack of intimacy, but that contributed to it. We would come back strong, but at this point we were starting to drift a bit. We were becoming teammates, but not much else.

I started to resent Sofia. This woman had truly begun to make me feel like an intrusion in my own house and Gina seemed to almost always agree with her. I began to feel very replaced by her in Gina's life. Chalk it up to jealousy or whatever but it began to really bother me when Gina turned to her to talk about something instead of me. I never did fire her, because I felt stuck with the verbal agreement that Gina and I had shared. That's not to say I didn't self medicate to make it bearable for me. I've always enjoyed a couple of pops, but I drank a lot more with Sofia in the picture. After work and even sometimes at home I'd pour myself a drink or three.

It continued this way until the end of the chemo run. When Sofia finally left at that point, nobody was happier than me to see her go. It was a rough adjustment for Gina at first and they kept in contact for a little while. To be completely honest, every time I knew they talked I would get that tinge of jealousy and all those doubts would surface again. One time I brought them up to Gina and that was a mistake. I should have used some better judgment there. You know that saying 'pick and choose your battles?' Well, let's just say that's one I should have just let sit within myself.

Eventually this would pass because Gina had always been the type of person who usually only gravitates to people who are in her everyday life. She was always somewhat of an out of sight, out of mind person. The stench of Sofia hung around for a while but eventually it faded away and life got back to normal.

1 1

HOW SPECIAL NORMAL CAN BE

WHEN WE WENT BACK to the oncologist we were optimistic. Gina had wrapped up her chemo treatments and even though she was pretty spent, we were feeling good about it. When we went to the doctor we got the two words we were looking for. CANCER FREE! That's not to say we were completely out of the woods. Not by a long shot. We still had to go every three months for an examination and a blood test and then complete body scans once a year, but as long as everything stayed the way it was then we were all good.

The funny thing is, I didn't really feel as excited as you might think. I was glad and happy and all that you might expect but this was something I felt was going to come anyhow. To be honest, it felt more like relief than excitement. It was as though the battle was over as opposed to a battle that we won. I know differently now of course, but at that point I just felt like it was the end of a long game that we were favored to win.

At this point, it was October and the next phase was going to be her breast reconstruction. We were going to have to wait a few months for the actual reconstruction surgery to take place. Because of the trauma that the body goes through, they like to wait before they try replacing a breast. Plus they have to do it in phases because the skin has to stretch. She had an inflatable implant inserted that worked to stretch the skin.

Things were rapidly improving in our lives. All the things I had looked forward to were coming to fruition. By Christmas, Gina's hair not only came back, it came back full and curly. She never had curly hair before so we joked and called it the VO5 Chemo Curl. But her hair was back, the cancer was gone, and she was looking good.

Life was looking up.

Even with things getting better for us as a family, as a couple Gina and I were at a difficult point. The cancer had not only taken a toll on Gina, it had punched some chinks in our armor as well. She felt that we weren't connecting emotionally and looking back I can see why.

Talking was one thing but communicating was another. There was only so much communication in Gina at any given moment and when that little well went dry, that was it. In our situation, Gina wasn't much of a communicator to begin with, and this situation caused her to retreat even more than usual.

I'm actually kind of upset that I didn't rely solely on myself at this point for a couple of reasons. In retrospect, had I tried to do it all without the nanny, I think I could have handled it. By having Sofia around and me leaning so heavily on her, it inevitably helped drive the wedge between me and Gina. While I was at work or playing ball, she and Gina were connecting on many levels. It got to the point where I would walk in the house from work and they would both be mad at me just for coming home.

At this point Christmas was coming and it was quite a sense of relief. Work had been uncharacteristically busy so that kept me consumed. Christmas was always her favorite season but this year Gina was putting even more of herself into Christmas. I suppose that was pretty easy to understand. She had just gone through so much and while we got the good news we were hoping for, for a while the thought had crept into both of our minds that maybe there would be no more Christmas. By coming out on the winning end, she felt a sense of rebirth both emotionally and spiritually. She had really found her faith throughout this ordeal, so this time of year took on a whole different meaning than in years past. I went along with it, the spiritual portion, really just for her. I was just glad to have her home and healthy so if that was what made her happy, then I was more than happy to join her in it. What I didn't know was that she was always seeking a faith that suited her. At this point we were attending Methodist services, but without me knowing, she was looking into a Christian Fellowship Church.

As Christmas Day finally approached, things were normal, but I had no idea how special normal could feel. We overdid it a bit; our holiday gathering was a little bigger than usual with all the aunts and cousins attending, but I guess when you shake someone that hard, everyone around them takes a deeper look inside themselves and realizes how important family is. It's kind of like when you're driving at night and you start to doze off. You pop back awake and for those next few minutes you are wide awake, but eventually you start to slip back to where you were. That Christmas we were all wide awake and aware of our family and I couldn't be happier. I had my wife, she was healthy, even her hair was coming back. We really felt like we beat it.

In past years we never really did anything big for New Years Eve, but as we turned the corner around Christmas this time, I couldn't be more excited for New Years. It wasn't that we were going to do anything huge, I just couldn't wait to get the stench of this past year off of me. Even if it really was only a matter of slashes on the calendar, just to be able to say that this all happened 'last year' was going to be a huge lift for me.

We kept the same game plan as before. We'd have a really nice dinner at the house with the kids and then turn on the TV to watch Dick Clark's New Years Rockin' Eve. At midnight we would toast champagne, kiss each other Happy New Year, blow in a call to Grandma and Grandpa, and then we'd all be in bed by 12:30am.

But this year, I remember laying down and looking over at Gina and being overwhelmed with the biggest sense of relief. Finally it was behind us! I knew we still had a lot of work ahead of us, most notably her reconstructive surgery, but for that moment, I just felt a huge sense of relief wash over my body. I could relax.

1 2

MISTAKES ABOUND

AFTER NEW YEARS WORE off (and that wears off pretty quickly), it was your typical long, cold winter. We started meeting with plastic surgeons again in January, and let me tell you, those guys are weirder than a four-dollar bill. I know this sounds unappreciative because these guys really do give empowerment back to women by helping rebuild their bodies and restore their femininity, but they are really odd guys. Creepy odd. They seem to look at people through a strange lens, almost as if they're model cars they can improve rather human beings.

They were all routine meetings for the most part, but it was all somewhat routine at this point. It was just the natural progression of things. Eventually we settled on a new surgeon and we opted to have him reconstruct her breast with a saline implant. Actually, it was more Gina's decision than anything. At this point I was going to the meetings but I had pretty much checked out mentally. It was wrong and I wish that I wouldn't have. Had I stayed more in touch with it maybe I could have broken through with her. I might have been able to pull more out of her and connect with her on a deeper level, but as they say in sports, that was a missed opportunity on my part.

Our surgeon was good but he was ice cold in the way of bedside manner. It was kind of offsetting to me but I let it go. Like I said, I was looking at this as the light at the end of the tunnel, so if this was who Gina wanted, then that's who we would go with.

She had her surgery in March and I was glad she was getting it done for a lot of reasons. I know this should have been the last thing on my mind, but there hadn't been any intimacy between us to this point and there were a few reasons for that. For the most part it was due to the lingering effects from the chemo, but she also wasn't feeling one hundred percent confident in herself since the mastectomy. She didn't feel sexy and I could see that. She was never self-conscious to the point where she would hide from me, but you could tell she didn't feel sexy or pretty when it came to initiating intimacy.

Through it all she had put some weight on, maybe thirty or forty pounds, so that created noise for me. Believe it or not, the breast thing didn't bother me because like I've said, I'm not a 'chest guy,' but the extra pounds, as shallow as it may sound, was hard for me to ignore. I don't feel like I have to defend it, it's not like I'm saying that I loved her any less or that I was thinking about leaving her because she wasn't attractive anymore. That wasn't the case at all. In fact, I still thought she was a beautiful woman but when it came to sexual arousal, the extra weight really was hard for me to deal with.

I know some of you are going to think I'm an ass at this point, but that's the point of this book, to point out the mistakes, and a big one is coming up right here. I started going out a little more at this point and I think it was because of that. The weight, the non-intimate bedroom, and the distance that had come between us; on a subconscious level it was eating away at me. Now I'm well aware that I'm not the chiseled hunk of man I once was either, but by playing basketball I keep in semi-decent shape. When I would go to the bar, I liked the attention I got. I didn't act on it and it wasn't going anywhere beyond harmless flirting and conversation, but it made me feel good.

I should probably come clean here on something pretty important. This book is intended to show everything that happened, even the mistakes I made and the parts I'm not proud of, and here's a big one. During my time at the bar I stumbled into enjoying a hit of Ecstasy every so often, and that might have been what was making me feel so good. I can't really tell. I'm sure it was a mixture of the two.

Today, I share the sentiments of any reader who might ask, "what the hell is that guy doing taking Ecstasy?" As a grown ass man, a father, a man whose wife was now a breast cancer survivor; what the hell was I thinking? To be honest, I don't know what the hell I was thinking. All I can say is that I was looking for some sense of an escape from the drama and the cloud of sickness that had hung over me for so long. The escape I had initially gone in search of turned into more than I bargained for.

What's sad is that I not only masked it and kept it from her, I convinced myself I was doing it all in the name of business. I was doing pretty well at work and I convinced myself this was all just me staying loose and building relationships with my clients. I know it sounds ridiculous and it is, but just like anyone who starts dabbling in that crap, when you're in the throws of it all almost anything can make sense if it gets you to your next time.

I know this sounds hypocritical but I was sensitive to Gina's situation so I never vented to her nor did I ever tell her about my feelings about what was bothering me. The extra weight, the non-intimacy, I never approached any of that with her. I figured with everything she had just been through she had real issues to deal with. I mean really, would you say something like that to your wife? That you had a problem with the extra weight she had put on? If you would then you are not only a braver man than I am, but a much smarter one and you have a relationship and a stream of communication that I wish I had with Gina. Here I was always bitching about her not communicating with me and I was doing the same thing. It wasn't the smartest choice I ever made and I'm sure it's part of what pushed us into marriage counseling the next year.

I wasn't alone though. Not that it makes it right but after our entire ordeal was over I was going through Gina's things and I found some of her journals. One of them had an entry from a year later that said, point blank, she felt better about her physical appearance but that she didn't feel we were as attached emotionally, which is exactly what I was feeling. Both the day I read that and the day you read this, I can't even begin to tell you how ashamed I am of where my head was then.

1 3

FAITH DIVIDED

FROM THE TIME OF her reconstruction surgery until about the beginning of November, life was completely normal. We took our family trips to Florida, I golfed in the summer, the kids played, she ran the house, and there was really nothing out of the ordinary to speak of. As fall fell away and Christmas started to creep up around the corner, Gina grew closer and closer to her Christian Fellowship friends. I went to a few services with her again, not because I really wanted to but just because it made her happy. In those few times I went, and this is by no means a slap to Christians everywhere, but the people of her particular congregation came across as very insincere to me. I like to think of myself as a guy who has a pretty good read on people, and these people seemed like phonies to me.

Some people think it's not important to be practicing faith together and for some it may not be, but given what we had just come through, I know it would have made things a lot better and we would have been a lot closer. I wish I would have been on the same page with her when it came to faith but she was going down this road and I just couldn't get comfortable with it. I'm a practicing Lutheran now, but regardless, I wish we had shared the same beliefs then. Gina was always searching spiritually and even though she didn't say it, our separate faiths were not good for us as a couple. To be honest, it drove a huge wedge between us.

She invited me to go with her to the Fellowship Christmas party that year. Now keep in mind I was raised Catholic but I'd been to a Methodist church as I fell out of Catholicism, so I figured I'd give it a shot. I had to meet her there since I was coming straight from work, so she got a ride from one of her Fellowship friends. I don't remember exactly why but for one reason or another I was running about twenty minutes late. When I walked in, they were all waiting for me before anyone would begin with the beverages and appetizers. What the hell?

It was a party! Instantly I felt uneasy, seeing as I was the object of everyone's stares. Then as I shook off my coat, they all gathered into a circle to pray and kick off the evening, which again, felt very uncomfortable to me. I was immediately on edge…and then I found out that there was to be no drinking that night! Even though this is a huge deal to me (I mean what holiday party doesn't come with a few cocktails) I shrugged it off and engaged myself in a handful of conversations with the various people there.

Let me tell you, these people seemed like phonies. Again, I'm not painting the entire Christian religion with a broad stroke, but this particular congregation was beginning to feel more and more like a cult. The weirdness of these people was overwhelming to me, cemented by mandatory forty minutes of holding strangers' hands and singing.

I remember looking over at Gina at various parts of the evening and wondering how the hell she felt at home with these people. I guess in a way I understood it. Here she was going through this crazy ordeal, diving into her faith to help her through it, yet at the same time questioning how God could put her through this. It's the classic tale of how people fall into cults and to be honest, that's what this was to me. She was sucked in at a very vulnerable time of her life.

When we got into the car after the party, it's safe to say we were of two very different mindsets as to how the evening had just gone. The first words out of my mouth where a sarcastic but serious 'What the hell?' and that I think it's safe to say that wasn't a good starting point. The scary thing to me was that in a sense we were right back where we were a year ago. The only difference was that this time instead of the nanny, she was investing her emotional closeness in these fruitcakes at the Christian Fellowship.

None of these deep connectivity issues ever surfaced until this damn disease entered our life. While I'm sure I made a lot of wrong moves and fanned the flames a bit myself, some of our issues formed from her reacting to things that she didn't understand and me reacting to her reactions. As time went on she got more and more invested in her beliefs. We would have good weeks together where life would be as it had been, but as Sundays approached I became the enemy again. Over the next few months she really began to change as a person. It got to the point where she would fight with me if I watched something like The Sopranos because it didn't fit her Christian beliefs.

We started spinning out of control and I thought it was ridiculous.

Of course, she thought I was ridiculous too, so in the spring we agreed to enter therapy. I conceded to her wish and we got a therapist / counselor. Who knows, that might have been a bad concession on my part, but I figured it would make her feel more at ease and I just wanted to get this shit aired out and get our life back on track at this point. I know a lot of people go through this sort of thing and I'm not saying it wasn't latent the entire duration of our marriage, but I firmly believe if we had never crossed paths with that damn disease none of this would have ever presented itself.

1 4

A SLIP BUT NO FALL

THE LAST THING YOU want when you start seeing a therapist is a surprise…right? I mean the whole concept is for them to put everyone at ease, let you relax, and then you can let the information and the resolutions flow. So imagine my surprise when I walk in to find out we are going to be 'interviewed' separately to start. What the hell? Granted, this was my first foray into the world of therapy, but I thought couples therapy was for couples, not two individuals meeting with someone separately. I was there to fix our marriage but the minute we got going this therapist wanted to go back to our childhoods and break us down from there. Really?

After the first session even therapy became tumultuous. We fought in the room, we fought in the hall, and we fought all the way home. It got so ugly that when we stopped at McDonalds she got out of the car in a huff and told me she was going to walk home. So there I was, driving alongside her, begging her to get back in the car. It was like a bad movie. All along I'm thinking this is what this disease had done to us. It felt as though it had made her so much more volatile and attacking. It wasn't even that she was asserting independence, it was more than that. It was more like a war and if you ask me, this therapist was not exactly a neutral party.

I agreed to keep going to therapy because I knew that we needed it, but I refused to go back to this quack. She made me uncomfortable and I didn't trust her, and for counseling to work you have to have trust. Gina succumbed to my wish on this one so we found a new therapist, someone we both felt good about. We found a guy that we agreed on and with that, we went to work on our marriage. This was the change we needed and I do mean we, not just I. He brought it back to a level that was about the marriage and us two both as individuals and as a couple. Ultimately, we started to mend our fences and he helped us start to communicate better.

Outside of his office, things were changing, but not much. I was still going out to stretch my legs and air out my head. I enjoyed having a few drinks and I enjoyed getting out of the house. Even though we were getting along better we were far from being 'good,' so the intimacy between us, both sexually as well as emotionally, was still a long way away.

Hypocritically, I strayed a bit. Now before you shut the book or judge me, know full well that I wasn't having an affair or anything, but I enjoyed the dance. You know what I mean. I enjoyed the flirtation, the feeling that you get when you know someone else finds you attractive. As men, it feeds our egos and puffs out our chests. I did make the mistake one night at the bar and while I didn't take it to any crazy unfaithful level, I did slip once and after a little too much to drink involved myself in a game of kissy face.

I believe that kissing is just as much cheating as sleeping with another person, and I'm not proud of what I did. If I had the chance to go back and live that moment over I would have walked out of the bar an hour earlier. Unfortunately life doesn't give us those opportunities. I struggled with the events of that evening a lot in my mind. Hell, I still do. While this is no justification or excuse, I know in my heart that I was struggling with a lot at that particular time. Gina and I were in such different places at that time. It felt as though she didn't even like me. As it turned out, she had depression issues that she needed to resolve and the effects of that depression were taken out on me.

I didn't know about the depression issues until much later. I found out on my birthday in September that in the late summer of that year she had started seeing a therapist on her own, without telling me. She put her on Prozac and that seemed to do the trick. It leveled her out, helped her keep her mind and her emotions in balance and ultimately it paid a great amount of dividends in our relationship. I started enjoying our time together and when she finally told me what she had been doing it made a lot of things clearer for me. It made me understand her better.

At this point in our lives, we were really just tackling issues and living life as a normal couple. I never really thought about the cancer thing anymore. As far as I was concerned, cancer was a thing of the past. In August, Gina's best friend's daughter had her quinceanera. (This is a Latin tradition when a girl turns fifteen years old.) There was a big party and obviously, we went. It's one of those deals that you really get dressed up for, almost like a wedding. I'll tell you what, Gina looked amazing that day. More beautiful than I had ever remembered. We walked into that party and I'm not kidding you, every guy there from eighteen years old up was ogling her. As a man, I felt like a big shot to have such a beautiful woman on my arm, but moreso, I felt so good for her. She was back. She had her confidence, her body, and most importantly, she truly had her life back.

That was probably the time that I really felt like we crossed the finish line. My family was healthy, my relationship with my wife was getting stronger by the day, business was good…life was good. I know I had not really thought about cancer in a while, I mean at this point it had been three years, but that night I can vividly remember looking at her and thinking, "We beat it. This race is over."

15

SECOND VERSE

IT DIDN'T LAST FOREVER though. In the beginning of November I was watching TV when Gina sat down and laid another bomb on me. She had found a lump in her neck.

She said the words and it hit me like a Mike Tyson uppercut. My head got hot, like it was expanding and was about to explode. I heard her, but I couldn't believe what I was hearing. My heart sank to the point where I literally felt like I was on the floor. This wasn't like before; I wasn't blessed with naivety this time. We both knew immediately that the cancer had metastasized. The doctor warned us this could happen but things had been clipping along so well that we didn't think it would. She had done everything she was supposed to do. She went to the doctors, took all of her meds, and went through all of the treatments. We thought it was all over.

People who have been affected by cancer will tell you that it is something you never get rid of. You learn to live with cancer. Even when you are deemed 'cancer-free' you never really are because from then on, you live with the fear of it returning. This news was the realization of my worst fear, even though I truly was naïve enough to think that it wouldn't be back again.

Immediately I was enraged. I was furious with God. How could He do this to her again? We had been through so much with the disease and all the problems that it brought with it, but we beat it. We took our punches and paid our dues; how could He come back and sucker punch us again?

We both cried and hugged, and I assured her that we would do whatever it took to fight it. I knew though, even as I was hugging her, that this time was going to be different. We weren't lucky enough to be ignorant this time around. At least I wasn't. I knew with the lump right on the neck that it was close to the lymph nodes and obviously this indicated the cancer had spread.

That was a long night. We sat for an hour talking, crying, and game planning. I had a few more glasses of wine and she had some as well. When we finally went upstairs, I remember looking at her as she was getting ready for bed and realizing for the first time that I could really lose her.

She fell asleep relatively quickly but I lay awake for a while. In one fell swoop, cancer not only came back in my life but it came back like a thundering herd of raging bulls. But that's the thing about cancer, it shows up in a hurry and punches you out. The first hit is always a sucker punch – fast, hard, and right to the head when you're not even looking. It blindsides you and sends you spinning in circles. Once it's in your life, it creeps around and moves very slowly.

I laid in bed thinking about a million things, my mind racing from every point it could find. I played out every what-if I could imagine. I thought about having to handle being Mr. Mom. I felt sorry for her, hurt for her, angry for me, worried for the kids. Do we tell them, do we not tell them? I hoped against hope that it would be benign. I re-traced my steps over the last three years feeling horrible about myself. I got nervous each time she went for her three-month check up, but I never went with. I figured it wasn't anything more than a check up, so why should I miss work? I would be in a hurry to talk with her immediately after she left the doctor's office, but I never went with, which I regret now. Seriously – what kind of dick was I? If I could, I would go back and change that too, but I can't.

At some point my mind must have tired itself out and I fell asleep. When I woke up the next day, it was a different kind of morning. I wasn't emotional or reflective like I was when I went to sleep. Instead I woke up in what I can only describe as attack mode. I went through my regular routine of getting ready for work, stopping for coffee, etc, but my mind was focused on our new fight. I called my sister Robyn right away and started peppering her with questions on how to fix this. I didn't want to feel that same helpless feeling that I had before. I didn't want to be at the mercy of the doctors any more than I had to.

Robyn cried when I told her the news and while that didn't surprise me, it did send a worrisome chill up my spine. Once she got a hold of herself and went into nurse mode, she started rattling off things to do. Armed with my checklist, I got off the phone with her and made a few more phone calls to let people know our new status—Mom, Dad, and my other sister Ellen.

Robyn called me later to tell me she had been speaking with a patient that day who she had grown somewhat close to and that patient was literally pleading with her to have me get Gina out of Good Sheppard and into MD Anderson in Houston for a second opinion. I had never heard of MD Anderson so I started looking into it. MD Anderson as it turns out is one of the world's leading cancer treatment hospitals.

When I got to work I got to my desk and dove right in. I'm able to compartmentalize pretty well and for me to sulk was only going to bring me down and cost me very valuable time and money. I engulfed myself in my work and plowed through my day. That's not to say I didn't talk about it; in fact I talked about it at work a lot. That's not the kind of thing you can keep to yourself even if you want to and man, I told anyone that would listen. It felt good to talk about it. It's not like I was telling people as if they were my best friend and I was leaning on their shoulder for support. It was more like me telling a story and the people in it just happened to be Gina and myself.

I didn't really think about getting off early because I didn't think Gina required that. In hindsight, I should have, because it was a healthy and strong Gina I was thinking of. I never really took into consideration the holes that something like this can punch into your psyche. I should have been a little more proactive at that point and been home for her. Even if she didn't want me there, I could have been in another room. I should have just been around her.

When I did finally head home, it was scarily normal when I walked in the door. I don't know what I was expecting, but I didn't expect that day to play out exactly as it had the last few years. She was just going about her business in the kitchen. I was happy to be home and happy to see her but there was no Hollywood moment or anything like that. Maybe that's because having been though this once, my confidence level that we would beat it again was at an all time high. Kind of like when a football team crushes another in one game, then has to play them again. Why wouldn't they feel like they were going to win? That's kind of how I felt.

I didn't do an abundance of research and I'm still not sure whether that was good or bad. If I thought I knew more than the doctor that wouldn't play out well, and if the doctor wasn't telling me what I wanted to hear or doing what I wanted him to, conflict would arise. I lived by trusting the doctors and trusting in the system. I figured that they were the experts. They'd seen this thing a million times. They should know what they're doing.

We decided not to tell the kids until the doctor visit so it was a pretty normal night. My brain was moving around a bit trying to sort out our game plan while I half listened to the kids tell me about their day. I do remember watching her more that night. For obvious reasons I paid attention a little more and I soaked it in. I would imagine that's just a natural reaction for a man when they feel like they have a chance at losing something. The sad thing is looking back I think this is probably the night I can honestly say I started preparing myself for the worst. I didn't know it then because like I said, my confidence was higher than it ever was. It was very much a subconscious thing and nothing I even really paid attention to until I started to think about this book, but going back I can see this is where I started to put up a little bit of protection around my heart.

16

HERE WE GO AGAIN

WE CALLED AND THE surgeon made room for us the very next day. I went with her and walking into that office, the memories came rushing back to me. It was like "…fuck, I can't believe we're here again." It was scary as hell that they took her right in and even then they didn't mess around, they got right to the point. The lump looked suspicious and he wanted to schedule surgery right away so he could remove it. Unlike the first time we sat at that desk, this time we were both more stoic as we took in the news. It was exactly what we were expecting to hear. I did feel that solidness between us again though. That unity of being a team in this fight.

The drive home was silent. I don't know what Gina was thinking but for me, my mind was just kind of there. I wasn't as numb or shell-shocked as I was before. After all, the doc had only told us what we already knew. The difference was that this time we walked out of the office with a date for the surgery. The way I saw it, we were moving right along on the list of things to do.

My head stayed pretty normal until the surgery. Life at home stayed pretty normal too. Everyone pretty much went about their regular lives, which was a blessing and yet incredibly odd at the same time. You would think we'd be a little bit more intimate as a family, or maybe we would have recognized that time as one of those moments where you realize how fragile things are and you do more together. But that wasn't the case. We just carried on as normal as can be.

The night before surgery was pretty normal too. I felt a tug of anticipation but didn't dare mention it to Gina. As far as I was concerned, this was just the next step on our To Do list and after this everything would be fine again. There was no reason for me not to believe this.

Getting to the hospital changed my line of thinking. I still felt confident but there's something about being in a hospital with the word 'tumor' and 'surgery' on your chart that can instill that glimmer of doubt. More than that, what returned in full force was that feeling of helplessness. I'm a fixer and a problem solver so to not be able to do anything was a hard pill to swallow. Once again, there was nothing I could do as an individual to help. I was at the mercy of this disease and our doctor's ability to battle it. It was like déjà vu. Were we really back here? Is the other shoe finally dropping? It's a worrisome feeling that wouldn't go away until the doctor looked me in the eye and told me the good news.

17

DEEP IN THE HEART OF TEXAS

THE SURGERY WAS A success, kind of. They got the tumor out but the pathology results this time were not good. The tumor was malignant so the cancer had obviously spread. I can't even begin to tell you how hard this news hit me. After all this time and all that we had been through the first time around, we thought we had beat it. We thought we had won, only to find out that we were back at the starting line again.

When I called Robyn to tell her the news, she brought up the MD Anderson again. Gina checked our insurance and everything pointed to it being our best play. I can't even begin to tell you how pumped up I was about this! The way I saw it, this was a new tool, a new weapon, and to be completely honest, what I felt was our best weapon in this fight. It was like being in a dogfight of a baseball game and then all of a sudden, you realize you have Derek Jeter or Babe Ruth at your disposal.

My parents and sisters agreed to help with the kids so I was pushing the idea like crazy to Gina. It took some convincing because Gina was pretty comfortable with the relationships we had. She liked her doctors, she liked Good Sheppard, and she didn't feel comfortable veering from that path. I on the other hand was the same as I always have been; I had a plan but if at any point something better came along, then that plan could change.

I found it odd that when we brought it up to our surgeon here he was a little bit on his heels. Actually, it pissed me off more than it worried me that he was hesitant. I looked at it like an ego thing, as if we were challenging his knowledge and abilities. Maybe indirectly I was but the way I see it, this was a shot of hope that we didn't have before. Eventually I won over Gina and we made our appointment at MD Anderson. Gina took care of all of the travel arrangements and literally a few days later we were on a plane to Texas.

Let me tell you, if you are ever in this situation MD Anderson is the way to go. From top to bottom, it was an amazing experience on every medical, personal, and comfort level you can imagine. The hotel is affiliated with the facility so as soon as we opened the door and entered the room, our itinerary was waiting for us right on the pillow. The hotel itself was beautiful and the staff really put you at ease. It wasn't like some sterile hotel room like a Holiday Inn or something like that. This was more like a luxury Hilton.

We made the best of our medically-necessitated trip and treated it almost like a vacation. That first night we had a wonderful dinner followed by some great intimate time together. Intimacy had been present in our lives again, but not as often and surely not like it was that night. Between the flight, the nice hotel and the nice dinner, that connection that had been missing for a while seemed to find its way to the surface. I have to say too, I felt like some sort of super-hero or knight in shining armor at that point as well. That had nothing to do with the sex, but here we were; she was smiling and feeling good and we were in a place that I had taken her to get well. It felt like I was pulling her out of this hole.

The next morning as we were getting ready, I was pretty amazed with Gina. She wasn't crying 'woe is me' or anything like that. She was astonishingly calm. Strong. As we walked the hall towards the facility, I even had a little spring in my step. This was a new chance for us, a new way to knock this sucker out of her body and out of our lives forever.

We had meetings all morning and then ate lunch together in the cafeteria. I couldn't keep from laughing because I could only imagine it was like eating at the U.N. There were people from every race and nation you could possibly think of in that lunchroom. That bolstered my confidence too, knowing that so many people traveled from all corners of the world just to come here to fight the same disease as us.

The next day was more meetings: Oncologist, Surgeon, Hematologist, Radiation Oncologist. You name it and we met with them. First we met with them individually and then after they all consulted, we all met together to come up with the best plan for Gina. Finally, I felt like we had a team of geniuses behind us. If you had asked me then, I would have told you that there was no way we could lose now. I was so impressed not only by the knowledge that they had but by the battery of questions that they asked. Another thing I noticed here that I hadn't noticed in any of our previous doctors was their bedside manner and their passion in what they were doing. That's not to say that our doctors back home weren't passionate about their work as well, but for some reason these people stood out head and shoulders above the crowd.

Now I was sure; it was only a matter of time.

I felt so optimistic I was practically skipping as we walked back to the hotel. On the way we passed a bar that had a drink special written on the board called the Cuba Libre. It was only a rum and coke with a lime but it sounded good so we stopped in for a cocktail. From there we went on to a great dinner and another great night of lovemaking. Two nights in a row now; this was unheard of not only in our situation, but as most married guys will tell you in general. The girls were eight- and five-years-old at the time, so we didn't see too much in the way of alone time. The second day we got our evaluation from the oncologist, Dr. Linden, and the news wasn't what we were hoping for. They found more tumors in her collarbone and one in her shoulder. Gina was in late Stage 3 cancer. What really shocked me was when Dr. Linden said our surgeon back home shouldn't have performed the surgery. As you can imagine, that news immediately lit a fire under my ass. Here we are, in one of the best cancer facilities in the country, and we're being told that our surgeon back home shouldn't have done what he did.

I felt vindicated about pushing Gina to come here but at the same time I was so pissed off and disgusted with our doctor back home. I was all ears at this point with Dr. Linden as he told us what he thought we should do going forward. He recommended more chemo, which immediately sank both my and Gina's hearts. Not only that, he mentioned something called Hypo-Chemo therapy stem-cell replacement. His main recommendation was four courses of chemo with Taxotere with each course being three weeks apart. The thing with Hypo-Chemo is that it calls for a three-month hospitalization because it kills all the cells, both cancerous and healthy, and depletes the immune system. It wreaks such havoc on the body that any small virus could kill you because your body can't fight it.

In addition to the tumors, Gina had something on her sternum that they couldn't quite identify. After her chemo was done he was also recommending radiation to go after whatever it was on her sternum. Needless to say, our trip had come to a grinding halt. Once again, this disease had reared its ugly head and not only stared us in the face, I felt like it had knocked us on our ass and was challenging us to get up and fight.

18

DECISIONS

THIS WAS A LOT OF information thrown at us in a very short amount of time and I had a million questions running through my mind. I wondered if I didn't understand the doctor correctly, if perhaps he didn't explain it well enough, because with everything he gave us, nothing seemed to have a clear advantage over the other. That was probably the most troubling part of it all. The problem with doctors I've learned (at least when it comes to this sort of thing) is that even when they're trying to outline specific plans of action they're always vague in their dialect on what can happen and how it can affect you. You would hope that by having all the information you could make an educated decision or at least play the odds, but at this point I felt like we were no better off than flipping a coin.

We opted not to do the Hypo-Chemo. Actually, Gina opted not to do it. We discussed it amongst the three of us and I was trying to be very careful at this point not to push my decision upon her. After all, she sat in the same room I did at MD Anderson. She heard the same information I did but at the end of the day, it was her body and her life. It was hard not to try and be that knight in shining armor again, but I had to.

Looking back, I have a feeling Gina was looking out for us more than she was for her with that decision. Logistically maybe she felt it was too much time away from home as all of the treatment could only be administered at the MD Anderson facility. Instead, she said she felt more comfortable doing the treatment of standard chemo with Taxotere at home in Illinois. Dr. Linden accepted her decision, but he wrote up a plan for us to give to our oncologist back home. As we shook hands with him and said goodbye, I couldn't help but feel like we were leaving something on the table by not following his lead. I respected her wishes and maybe I should have pushed harder here too, but instead I just thanked him for his time, took hold of Gina's hand

and walked out the door.

As we walked through that big hallway that stretched out over the highway my heart felt like someone had let the air out of the balloon again. "Here we go again," was all that I could think. I know Gina was dreading more chemo. She loathed the thought and to be honest, so did I. I tried to encourage her but inside I was scared. I'm a betting man but even I know going two for two against cancer isn't an easy task. It's not impossible, I knew that then and I know that now, but at the time I was looking at the glass as half empty more than I was looking at it half full.

We stopped at the lounge again before we went on to the room. It was still fairly early in the afternoon at this point and we didn't leave until the next day. While we were sitting at the bar, we met a woman whose sister was at MD Anderson with cancer. As we talked we learned that her sister's cancer had spread into the soft tissue. As we told her parts of our story, she adamantly warned Gina (and myself) about keeping it away from the soft tissue (i.e. liver, lungs, brain, etc). You might think after all we'd been through that day, having a stranger giving us advice would be too much, but instead, it encouraged Gina. It gave her fighting spirit a little boost.

That might have been the first time I saw how much support can come from being with one of your own. I used to see these walks against breast cancer but I always thought they were more of a way for corporations and people to feel good about themselves. I never saw them for the support that women and men like myself gain from being around the throngs of other people sharing stories.

We went to a nice restaurant and I noticed as we sat down how beautiful Gina looked. That hurt me more than anything because on the surface, she looked fine. Even she would tell you, she felt good. She felt healthy and strong. She didn't look or feel like a woman who had a deadly disease running around ravaging her insides. I spent most of the dinner trying to shower her with smiles. I felt so close to her right then, but that's the roller coaster that cancer becomes. Good news and bad news. Close and alone.

We started to talk some more about her decision to forgo the Hypo-Chemo, but I made a conscious effort to try and make jokes and change the subject. I think I even told her that we could talk about it later but after everything that just happened and knowing what lay in store for us again, I wanted to lighten her load and just make it a nice night out.

When we got back to the room it was tense. We made a few calls to my folks and my sister to let them in on the news. Nothing in too much detail but they were concerned and asked us to let them know as soon as we knew anything. After the phone calls, we didn't talk much. We pretty much changed clothes, crawled into bed, and watched a little television. The emotional exhaustion took a pretty heavy toll on her because she fell right asleep. I, however, didn't fall asleep very easily. I laid there watching her sleep, my mind racing as I could feel myself gearing back up into battle mode.

19

A WAR HAS MANY BATTLES

THE ONLY WAY I can explain the ride back to the airport the next morning is tactical. I launched right in, peppering her with things that both she and I were going to need to do and writing down a list. The list included everything, from finding a radiation oncologist to me getting a handle back on my work. I know myself well enough to know that the last thing I needed was both work AND health issues. Once we boarded the plane however, I thought it would do us both some good to just shut down and enjoy the flight as much as we could.

Once we got home and in the car, we spent the car ride from the airport talking about what we were going to say to the kids. That was going to be the hard part. It's not easy to stare two little girls in the eyes and tell them their mommy needs more treatment, but that's what we did. We softened the blow of course, but for the most part, we were pretty upfront with them. Jackson was a different story however. Gina thought it would be better if she spoke with him one on one. Truthfully that stung a little bit but I hid my hurt and told her that I agreed that would be the best approach.

As soon as those discussions were over and the tears cleared, we went about our usual nightly business. The anticipation of everything was eating away at my mind. Between work and her medical future, I felt like I needed to get moving.

The next day I was up early for work. I was so worried that having been gone for so long, things were might have fallen off track. Gina and I decided I was going to go in and focus on work today and she would take care of things from home. She called Dr. Smith, who agreed to meet with us right away that afternoon.

This is one of those points where again I got a serious case of the red-ass. When we were sitting with Dr. Smith, we talked a little bit about MD Anderson and handed him Dr. Linden's recommendation. He skimmed it, set it down on the table, looked us flat in the face and said, "…this isn't cookie cutter."

I know ego when I see it and this guy was getting into an ego battle with a doctor who clearly knew more about the battle with cancer than he did. I kept it in check and in a very nice but visibly irritated way, I told him he should take a trip down there. Furthermore, Dr. Linden's recommendation WAS the way we were going to attack this and he could either do it or we would find someone who would.

I'd like to tell you about what happened next but unfortunately, that part is a blur. I was so incensed that this guy would challenge what even he referred to as one of the best facilities in the world, I tuned out. I was done listening to this guy. As far as I was concerned I did my listening in Texas when I sat with the real experts and the marching orders came from there. In my mind this guy was a soldier now, and the generals were the doctors we had met at MD Anderson in Houston.

Dr. Smith wasn't happy with what I said, but he was obligated to do what we asked. He scheduled chemo to begin the next week, which was the third week of January. He also referred us to Dr. Sheldon as our radiation oncologist, whom we would meet shortly after, but even we knew he couldn't do anything until the chemo was completed. We went home with basically nothing more to do than wait for the next week to come.

I had a hard time coming down from that meeting. It was almost as if Dr. Smith's little ego trip put a chip on my shoulder, not just with him, but with all of the doctors back home.

The chemo schedule called for four courses of treatment every three weeks. As the first treatment approached, that 'here we go again' feeling took over me. It was a lot harder this time, because we knew what was in store for us. I knew how ugly and painful chemo was, and the worst part was that there was nothing I could do to protect her from it. We hadn't even left the house yet and I was already worried about when she was going to get sick and how fast her hair was going to fall out. I was already preparing myself and adjusting my game.

I thought I was ready for it but when it did finally happen, her pain was even more awful than the first time. There was absolutely nothing I could do for her but watch and hope all this agony was worth it. My parents and sisters wanted to help out so they would take the kids while Gina went through her treatments. They thought it would be good for me so I could focus solely on Gina, but to be honest, selfishly I would rather have had the kids with me. I don't know if sending them to Grandma and Grandpa's or to their aunt's house was the right decision or not. I wanted to shield them from seeing their mom go through all of that agony, but in those moments when Gina would be sleeping, I felt so helpless on my own. The diversion would have been good for me.

Pay attention folks, because this is one of those red flags. To fight the loneliness, I started to bury the sadness in alcohol. It's not smart and definitely not something I'm proud of, but this is one of those instances where I started to handle things very badly. It started with me knocking back a few cocktails at the house. That didn't really do the trick because the house would be too quiet for me. Gina would fall asleep around 8pm on the second or third night after treatment. She would just sleep. Since the kids were at my parents, I would sneak out to a local bar not too far from the house. Surprisingly, the company of the late-night crowd was soothing. Walking into the bar gave me such a feeling of normalcy and that was something I craved. These people didn't have lives that revolved around chemo and radiation and cancer and all that shit. They just had regular lives and I missed that. The problem for me was, I'm an intense guy and when I do something, no matter what it is, I do it to the fullest extent. I became a late night regular, which as anyone knows is typically the beginning of a slippery slope. As luck would have it (bad luck as it would turn out), a friend of mine that I knew through Gina would factor into this as well.

In the interest of full disclosure, I should tell you a little bit about my history with Charlie. A few years back, Charlie introduced me to the world of partying. I literally only did it one time when he broke it out at a party, but I didn't become a user.

I saw Charlie at various functions (barbeques, birthdays, etc), and we started to have that bond that people do when they are trying to run from something. Charlie was running from life. He was just one of those guys who always wanted to have a good time. As we got to be closer friends, he reminded me of that party, and I poorly decided to partake again. Was I thinking about my sick wife at home? My two little girls? No, on all accounts. I was ashamedly as selfish as I have ever been in my life, but with everything that was going on in my life and in my head it seemed like something I needed.

2 0

BIG MISTAKES

IT DOESN'T STOP THERE. I wish that was my only big regret but partying was only a part of my spiral. I know that doesn't paint me in a good light and where we go from here doesn't get any better. Not for a while anyways.

Soon the bar and the booze weren't enough of an escape for me. I went from going to the bar hoping he was there to calling him looking for it. I was careful, but that's always the case with guys like me. By guys like me I mean guys who have a life, people who have more to their lives than just junkies on the street. Not that we're any better than them, but we feel like we're more careful and aren't stupid enough to get caught. Like we aren't endangering anyone but ourselves and we're okay with that.

The truth is, and I didn't think about it this way back then, but I was endangering my kids more than I can even stomach to think of. Here were my two little girls, with a very good shot at losing their mother, and where was I? I was playing the role of the strong father and then sneaking off to party until the wee hours of the morning. It sickens me to think that I could ever sink so low. But this despicable chapter of my life doesn't end there. I had two separate lives at this point. In my public life I was a responsible, caring, strong husband and father who took care of everything. But when the sun went down and everyone went to bed, the moral compass pointed due south.

As the time went by at the bar, I met a wild couple who came out pretty frequently and always loved to party. As it turned out, they were swingers. I don't know if they already WERE swingers or if I was the first one they ever approached but they wanted to swing. Normally, I would have <u>never</u> run in a circle with these kind of people, but they were fun and like I said, they liked to party. We would find a way to hit it at the bar and one day we took the party back to their place.

For the first time in my life, I sobered up quickly, and something changed in me on the drive from the bar to their house. I pulled into their driveway not wanting to be there anymore. Like an ass, I walked inside anyway figuring I would just have a drink, find a way to bail and deal with it all tomorrow. After all, we didn't go over there with any set plans. I mean, when we left the bar it was flirty and all but it was left up to 'taking the party back to their house.' When I walked in there was a drink for me on the table. I grabbed the drink but what came next was a shocker, even though I was kind of expecting it in the back of my mind.

The woman slid in next to me and told me to relax as she rubbed the top of my head, then turned my face towards hers and slid her tongue into my mouth. My mind was in a fog and my body seemed to be going in slow motion. Then just like that, she was naked and starting to undress me and I had some sort of crystal clear revelation. I remember very vividly thinking, "My God... I'm 38-years-old with a sick wife and a family and here I am getting caught up in this shit? What the hell am I doing?"

In that instant, that crystal clear moment, I stood up and left. I heard them behind me calling out my name as I grabbed my coat and headed for the door but I kept walking forward, seeing myself clearer than I ever had before. I don't know if I was running away from them or if I was running away from me, but I got the hell out of there.

The drive home was the worst. When I walked in the door, Gina was passed out on the bed. I washed up and climbed into bed next to her feeling utterly sickened with myself. I watched her sleep and couldn't believe myself—what I had been doing and what I almost just did. Who does that sort of thing? Who the hell was I? The next day when we woke up, I felt horrible. Even though I hadn't gone through with the sex I wore the guilt like a heavy coat. I'd like to say that the guilt stayed with me for months but the reality of it is, all these years later that guilt still resides in me. I promise you, it's not my proudest moment. Looking back, I feel like throwing up every time the visions come back into my head.

But it happened...and that's the point of this book...and I'm sure I'm not the first guy who ran down the wrong road.

21

FIGURING OUT WHAT WORKS

LOOKING BACK, I CAN see clearly now the reason I was acting out like this was simply because I was lost. It's not an excuse; I know I was wrong and as much of a jackass as anyone could be, but I felt defeated. I never let on about how I felt though. As far as Gina or the kids or anyone was concerned, I was up for the fight and I was ready to win. Getting through the days was difficult, especially given all of the various regular life tasks that still abounded. I would drop her off at chemo and then go on to work. We had a prearranged ride for her to bring her home from chemo, whether it be my mom, my sister, whatever. It was hard to leave her, but we knew what we had to do to fight so it became more a matter of obligation than bonding time.

Being able to go to work was good for me. I was still able to just walk in that door and resume my old life again. Chatting coworkers and a ringing phone distracted me from the cloud of doom that hovered over the rest of my life. Getting immersed in my business and solving problems, dealing with clients; all of that really helped me to cope.

I knew that I needed an outlet and like most guys, I was hesitant about therapy. I tried to do it on my own and seek out my own therapist. I tried talking to my mom about my feelings but she just shut me down. She kept saying that it was not about me and that I was selfish thinking about myself when my wife was fighting off death. That's a hard pill to swallow, especially when it comes from your mother. She was right, but what about me? My life was turned upside down too and not just by the inconveniences of doctors and treatments. I was scared shitless that I was going to lose my wife. I was scared that my kids were going to lose their mother. On top of being scared, I was worried that I didn't know how to fill that role for them or for me. I didn't sign on for any of this, but this is the pile of crap that life dropped in my hands.

As you might imagine, throughout this entire period there was zero intimacy between Gina and myself. I'm not just talking about sex, I mean overall intimacy. Each day was literally about getting through the next sickness or the next treatment. I started to feel like we were just two people on the same team, not necessarily a husband and wife. I loved her of course, but that intimate connection had waned. If you ask me, the chemo killed it.

This period went on from January to early summer. Every three weeks (initially four) she would get her treatment on Wednesdays, be sick Thursday through Sunday, and then we would get a break for Monday and Tuesday. Mondays were the best because Tuesdays were always tainted with the looming doom of Wednesday, when it would start all over again. The kids were great with it all. They came to know the post-treatment days as Mommy's sick days and tried to do nice things for her these days.

Even though we knew it was coming, when her hair fell out it very deflating to both of us. It's one thing to know what you're in the midst of fighting, but when you see those physical changes, you can tell that you've taken a punch.

If you haven't gone through this, brace yourself, because this is a hard thing to go through. You watch the woman you love suffer so much while you and the people around her suffer for her. The worse thing is, there's no guarantee any of it is going to work. I started to live in the minute and in essence, built some walls between Gina and myself. I would help her, but from time to time I would escape to my bar and my group of friends that I knew were the wrong kinds of people to be around. They were enablers, but to me, they were the only people that saw it from my angle. Looking back, I don't know if they really saw it from my angle. Hell, they probably didn't see it at all. They just wanted someone to drink and if that was my reason then it was good enough for them. But they fed my needs. They gave me the affection I was longing for. They made me feel like I belonged.

22

THE ROLLER COASTER GOES UP AND DOWN

WE WENT BACK TO MD Anderson in April after four treatments were over. Again, we took advantage of the time and tried to make a mini-vacation out of it. What happened there however, was the last thing I expected.

The tumors were gone! After all of my doom and gloom, the tumors were gone! We were ecstatic with the news. The bad news was that he ordered four more treatments since they were working so well, but this was an easier pill to accept. It's odd, but I could feel the transformation take place in my head. As I sat in that leather chair, I felt my chest fill with air and I returned to a winning mentality. It felt a lot like a baseball game, when you're down by two runs and then all of a sudden your guy hits a three run homer to take the lead. We were back on top.

It was all I could do to maintain some sort of caution. As happy as I was, I knew it could come back. Not only did the doctor stress to us that even in the midst of this great news we weren't out of the woods, we knew for ourselves that it could come back from out of nowhere. It can always come back from out of nowhere.

It was hard to temper this kind of excitement so we told the kids and I told my mom and my sisters. I felt like I was in the dugout after that three run homer. Even though that other team is still just as dangerous, you feel like you've got the upper hand now. It is as if you are playing to win instead of just going through the motions and prolonging the loss.

The new treatments were going to take us into July and they beat her up equally each time. You would think that with the news and the brighter outlook that my lifestyle would have changed and I would have started making better choices, but sadly they didn't. Unfortunately my party habits didn't subside.

Gina and I still had these walls between us and even with the better prognosis that didn't change the fact that we weren't doing well as a couple. Our communication at this point had become almost nonexistent. Spiritually we had drifted apart. As lovers, we couldn't be colder to each other. At this point I had about as much intimacy with my wife as I did with the woman at the 7-Eleven down the street. None.

I still craved the belonging and the attention that my newfound 'friends' gave me, so I continued to go out. It got bad enough that a few times when Gina felt well enough, she would have to come and pick me up. There was even a time when Gina had to go out at four in the morning to gather me up and drive me home. It sickens me to look back on it now but I realize that I was reaching out for something. That doesn't make it right and sure as hell doesn't make it sit easier in my stomach. I called it my private stress reliever but in reality it was nothing more than a pity party for us all. When you're running from something and you're hanging with other people who are running, it seems ok. But to be blatantly honest, we were all acting like a bunch of losers.

The odd thing was Gina never knew about the drugs. I was good; I was able to mask it well. She thought I was just out drinking and letting loose. This was probably easily believable because I've always been one to enjoy a cocktail. But like anyone who dabbles in that shit, I was way too caught up with it. I was a 39-year-old man with a wife, a house, kids, and a great job. I was just relieving some stress. But if it was casual use then why the hell would I bust that shit out at home?

I've got news for you; do it once and you're hooked. Maybe not to the point where it takes over your life, and you might not even ever do it again. But knowing that you have the option will always sit in the back of your mind. Especially when you're in a situation like this, you're surrounded by temptation and if you fall into its trap, you'll find a thousand ways to justify it. You might be able to fool yourself, I sure as hell did, but you can't fool someone with an unclouded view. It's simple. Do it and you're hooked, even if it's just that devil sitting on your shoulder.

I broke her heart in August when she walked in the living room and caught me about to partake with my buddy. Rightfully so, she freaked out. The problem was I was so screwed up in my own mind (not high, I mean literally screwed up in my line of thinking) that I was acting like a teenager. I couldn't understand why she didn't just let it ride. I mean, we were adults, right?

The next thing she did was probably the meanest, but the best thing anyone could think of. Of course she kicked my friend out right then and there, but that wasn't it. She told the kids. When I was sleeping she told the kids what Daddy was doing. You want humiliating? Try waking up and having your six- and eight-year-old daughters and your sixteen-year-old son talk to you about what you're doing. That was the most humiliating morning I've ever had in my life. I was disgusted with myself.

They say that the devil has ways of getting his hooks into you. He tried and failed with the infidelity, but he took another swing and got me. Thankfully that hurt look in my angels' faces was all it took to win myself back.

2 3

FATIGUE FOR ALL

LIFE WENT ON, ALBEIT a bit more tense and cold around the house. Gina and I discussed things and eventually we worked it out. I don't know that she actually forgave me but she did put it behind us and that was probably the best I could ask for. Ironically, the guilt drew me closer to Gina again.

Radiation started in September and ran once a week until the end of November. I was encouraged that the tumors were down, but I had a hard time maintaining that winning attitude. I didn't feel like we had beat anything because I knew what she was about to go through with the radiation treatments. It was harder on me this time because not only did I fully understand what was happening, I knew how her body was going to react.

The kids were asking a lot more questions. They asked me some but mostly they went straight to Gina. I remember one day when Amber (who was nine at the time) asked me where we would run our errands on the weekend. I answered her honestly, with kid gloves of course, and I was shocked that she accepted the answer so well. It always shocked me, as it does to this day, that the kids were so well adjusted with everything. While Gina had a hard time communicating with me, she did a fantastic job talking with the kids. I can't take credit for it. She was the one who did the wonderful job of talking them through everything and cementing their faith.

I tried to be attentive to Gina during this period, yet at the same time I didn't want to overdo it. I didn't want to offend her independence and her basic person. That was hard for me, feeling like she did not want my help. I watched her fight through pain just so that she didn't have to depend on me. I can see now that I was thinking too much about myself here. She wasn't trying to make it without me, she was trying to keep her sense of self. But I was selfish and made it about me. I frequently left the house. I found a way to justify it in my mind by saying that it was in the name of business. I would stay at my buddy's office a lot. After all, we discussed business and he had a full bar. I drank. I laughed. I buried it all.

As the radiation continued and the physical effects were more and more in plain view, the more my outlook started to sink. I was getting scared that we were just spinning our wheels and that in the end, the other shoe would drop again and I was going to lose Gina.

There was one night in October when something inside of me snapped. I don't know what triggered it but I had this huge revelation. I didn't want it to be this way. I didn't want to keep carrying on the way I was, and I didn't want to be so separate from Gina. I felt like I was living in this God-awful movie and didn't want to be there anymore. I felt like we were going to lose, and I just didn't want to keep running and hiding, I wanted to take advantage of the time.

So I started to try and figure out how to do more together. I was already thinking about her birthday in February. Christmas was right around the corner and while I wasn't exactly counting on it being our last Christmas together, I started to move along the lines of savoring the moment.

As you might imagine, Gina was pretty deep into her faith at this point, which isn't unheard of with women in her situation. Many women reach to their faith when they are confronted with something like this. The problem was, I wasn't as spiritually laden as she was so it put us in very different spots. I was rooted in science and reality and while she was doing the duties science required and fighting with everything she had, she was looking more towards her spirituality to heal her.

As we went through the month, I started to entertain some morbid thoughts. This was the first time I actually wanted to talk with her about the dark side of 'what if.' We both knew it—she ran our house. The bills, the kids, its entire organization were all her turf. I knew then that if for some reason she didn't win this fight, I would need some things in line. That sounds selfish but trust me, it's not. I know this now, many years after the fact. There were so many things I wished I'd done then that would have made life so much easier now not just for me, but for the kids. Different things. I wanted her to show me how she managed the bills and things like that but more importantly, I wanted to start video recording her talking to the girls, teaching them how to put on makeup, capturing images of her reading on the couch or making dinner. Things the girls (and I) could go back to at different points in our lives if she was ever gone.

But how do you ask someone to help you prepare for life after they're dead when they're in the middle of fighting to stay alive? I didn't. I should have. I should have found a delicate way to approach it, but I didn't. Would I feel this way if she had lived? Maybe not. Actually, probably, because I know the consequences of not doing it when it doesn't pan out. Had she lived, we could have figured out how to deal with that.

When we were together and she was feeling good all I wanted to do was soak in the moment. Soak in the time with my wife. It was in the quiet moments at night when she was sleeping or while I was in the car driving to work that I would argue with myself whether or not to broach those subjects. In the end I just didn't have the stones to float it out there. I wimped out and figured she would bring it up in due time. Hardly the manly way about it…to wait for my wife to admit her impending death and prepare us for life after she was gone.

The radiation fatigued her, but she still ran the house on her own. We had a cleaning lady that came once a week but aside from that, she still had a handle on the daily affairs. Our communication was poor but I don't know if that was because she wasn't talking to me or because I didn't prod enough.

24

HOLIDAYS

HER RUN OF RADIATION treatments ended just before Thanksgiving. This holiday was easier on her, because we never hosted it. My mom took care of Thanksgiving every year and enjoyed making it a relaxing day for everyone. My mom's motto was "Just show up and relax." Nobody made a big deal out of our situation because we still thought we were winning this battle. The fact that she just wrapped up radiation was only more cause for celebration.

Everyone was celebrating, except for me. Even though I was still thinking about losing and was trying to soak in every last inch of every last moment, Gina had a different outlook. She saw it as a regular Thanksgiving. She didn't see it the way I did, thinking that this may be our last. In her eyes it was like every other year, and next year, we would be here again. She was still counting very much on her faith.

One of the things I decided in that moment of revelation back in October was to start cutting back at work. The holiday time is usually pretty busy for me, but this year I made it a point to be home more often. After Thanksgiving came and went we spent a lot more time doing things together not only as a couple, but as parents. I involved myself a lot more than I had in years past. We went Christmas shopping for the kids together, something that hadn't happened since God knows when. That was always just something I let her handle.

Things were feeling good. I felt good. As a couple, we were growing closer, and that meant the world to me. I started thinking about maybe doing some special things for her, like a trip for the two of us or something. The holiday came and went and we treated it much like we did Thanksgiving. It was just this year's Christmas and there would be another one next year.

As January rolled around, we were scheduled for Gina's next complete scan. She was both mentally and physically beaten down by the treatments and truth be told, so was I.

As we had hoped, the scan came back clean once again with no detection of any tumors. I was elated but with reservation. Actually, I think what I felt was more a sense of relief. I was more optimistic than before, but for some reason I still had it in the back of my mind that there was more in there, just hiding. Even though I still wasn't completely convinced it was over, I didn't spend my days waiting for more bad news. I didn't seek out any alternative treatments, because I put my faith and trust in the system. We had gone to the best center, we had seen the best doctors, followed their recommended course, and now here we were, cancer free again.

As I mentioned, I'd been thinking about taking her on a trip as I figured there was no time like the present. We had some friends who lived in Arizona so I thought it would be a nice surprise to take her there. I made all the arrangements. I booked us in the Hyatt Gainey Ranch, a spectacular resort in Phoenix. The room I put us in was way too pricey, but I figured after all she had been through and knowing what kind of curve ball life can throw you at anytime, it was well worth it.

When I sprung the news on her, she was beside herself with joy. I never really thought about it but over the last few years, any surprise she had gotten was bad news. The good news was always something that we were hoping for or anticipating. Never was it a surprise.

The trip was wonderful. We went at the end of February and it truly was five days of bliss. I soaked in every moment of her. She looked better than she had in what seemed like forever. I saw her for the beautiful wife, woman, and mother that she was. We spent time with our friends and we spent time alone. It was just a wonderful trip all around. While we were there I had made arrangements for Gina to have a surprise spa day. I wasn't completely sure about this decision, given what her body had been through, but it was one of the 'most right' things I'd done. She was in such a great place there and it really felt good on her body. I'm telling you, that trip was the most fun I'd seen her have in years. I know she had a blast because not long after we got home, she redecorated our bathroom in complete southwestern style. I noticed she had put a new photo up in a frame in our bedroom. It was one of us on that trip.

Aside from the upside of a bathroom renovation, the trip progressed our healing process. Our communication began to strengthen and I really began to feel like we were a couple again and that survived long past that trip. For the first time in a long time, that closeness continued once we had gotten home.

25

A NEW START

WHEN WE GOT BACK and settled into our life again, it was kind of a mix between a new start and a break from the normal that we had come to know. I guess you could liken it to a newly married couple that had already lived together. Things were different for us again. I was more in tune with her and she was more in tune with me. We both paid much more attention to the other's physical and emotional needs.

Sex had even started to seep back into our relationship. It was hard for her and I was well aware of that. She was taking Tamoxifen and that affected her a bit. Tamoxifen is an antagonist of the estrogen receptor in breast tissue. One of the side effects is a severe reduction in the libido. She also had issues with her physical appearance and to be honest, and even though I NEVER let her know, at times it would bother me too. She put on some weight, her breasts were different, and there were scars that were not exactly appealing. Things like that make a woman look different, but I loved her so it wasn't too much of a struggle. All I'm saying here is there were definitely things that I had to work on in my mind. All the same, I never let her know these thoughts of mine.

For the most part, other than sex returning to our bedroom, life became pretty uneventful and normal and believe it or not, that is what I craved. It was nice getting back to a routine in which my life (and wife) were not dictated by treatments, appointments, surgeries, etc. At this point all we had on the docket were some follow-ups with Dr. Smith once a month, and Gina started to handle those on her own. She didn't even really keep me up to date on the time of her appointments. I would ask her occasionally when her next appointment was and she'd tell me, but that was about it. After all, it wasn't much more than monitoring her. He kept an eye on her blood work and would do a digital check of her left breast to make sure that everything was okay. Her next full-body scan was set for six months later.

This is one of those lessons you don't really learn until you go through it but at this point, all you can do is learn to live with it… and that's what we did. We spent the summer like we had countless summers before. We took the kids to the pool, had cookouts, and went to the girls softball games. Jackson was working at UPS and going to Harper College, so he continued on his path with that. There was no more hovering around Mom.

My outlook on things had drastically changed as well. I wasn't looking at every day and every moment together as a gift. I didn't look at it as any sort of second chance or rebirth either. Sure, I could feel cancer constantly looking over my shoulder, but all I could do was pray every day and go about my business.

It's ironic I say I would pray because that's when faith became a real focal point in our relationship – so much more than even before. A new problem developed from all of this. Now that Gina saw herself as healed by the hand of God, she was a full on "born again." I was partially into my religion and I certainly recognized God had something to do with her recovery, but I wasn't as hell bent (no pun intended) on the idea that God saved her. In my eyes, God played a role, but without the help of those amazing doctors and their knowledge of science, we would be in a very different place.

2 6

SUCKER PUNCH

AUGUST WAS THE NEXT full-body scan and we went into it feeling pretty good. All the check ups had been good, even in July. She was still fatigued but we thought this was a lingering consequence of the radiation treatments. We just wrote it off as that.

I didn't know it then, but while radiation is known to fatigue you, it's not supposed to linger that long. I noticed the fatigue, but like I said, I just wrote it off as a residual effect. As time went on, I allowed my life and my senses to slip back to where they were before. I let my heightened attention to detail start to wane. I focused back on work. But something changed within me during the month of July. For no apparent reason, I started worrying again because I knew this next scan was going to be THE TEST! This was the one that told us if we were in the clear or if something was still out there hiding in the woods. Worry built up inside me as the test date approached, which I didn't share with Gina. To add to my anxiety, my work numbers were off for the year, which didn't bode well for me in salary or stature at my job. Suffice it to say, I started to really stress out and my temper with everyone got shorter. I pulled it all in and just lashed out. I barked at the girls and was irritable with people at work.

If I could pepper in some advice here, it would be to get yourself a counselor early and keep going even when you think you're in the clear. I had no reason to be barking at people like I was and nobody knew why. To be honest, I didn't even really have a reason why. What – because I was nervous? Even if I was, is that a reason to lash out at people at work? Work was down but I wasn't on the firing block or anything like that. Maybe if I had a therapist cooler heads could have prevailed and they might have been able to talk me down a bit. Besides, there was no reason to think the scan would go badly.

But as the test day came, I was submerged in the most negative outlook I think I have ever had. Still, because of my situation at work,

I went into the office and she went in for the scan by herself. I thought about going but there was nothing I could do. You don't get the results back that day so there was no reason for me to be there. Normally the results take two or three days, but we were able to get the results expedited so they were going to get them early that afternoon and call us at home.

I may have gone to work but I had a hell of a hard time concentrating. To quote Tom Petty, "the waiting is the hardest part." It's one thing to know the test is coming but waiting on the results—that's a killer. It felt like taking a final exam in college. Knowing the test was coming was hard, but the really difficult part was waiting for the grades to be posted. I was nervous but didn't want to talk about it with anyone because there was really nothing to discuss.

I was nervous and irritable and that was a bad combination that day. To make things worse, I had a client meeting as well. It was the kind where I would visit weekly, get the orders from all of the various departments, say my hellos, and leave. I had this client for about ten years so this was pretty much our routine. That day though, as I was walking out to go to another meeting, the purchasing agent called me in as I was leaving. He's not a pleasant guy on a normal day but because of my nerves, it was even worse that day. He said he wanted twenty minutes of my time, but I explained I couldn't because I was on my way to a meeting and then to see Gina about her tests. He whittled me down to five minutes so I agreed. We walked into his office and he handed me a letter of termination.

Again, this was a client, not my boss, so I wasn't being fired per se. But I was being replaced as their supplier. Now I understood business, but I also understood humanity. He could have waited a day to whack me, especially when I told him I could come back tomorrow and give him four hours if he needed it. But when I read that letter, especially with him standing over me just watching me read it, pure and unfiltered rage washed over me. I was so pissed at him, pissed at the world, pissed at the cancer, and I snapped. Fire leaped from my eyes as I balled the letter up and threw it like a fastball right over his shoulder. "I hope this makes you feel real good about yourself," I barked as I spun around and walked out the door dropping F-bombs under my breath and going on about what an asshole the guy was.

In hindsight, I know I was the asshole. I should have done a better job with my emotions but at that moment it was so damn hard. That's the thing about the waiting, it eats away at you until one day you snap and literally step so far out of character even you can't believe it.

I got home around 3pm because I wanted to be there when the news came. The kids had gotten home from school and were playing outside while Gina and I sat in my office literally waiting for the phone to ring. Even though we were at home, it felt like we were sitting in a doctor's waiting room. We passed the time with small talk about each other's day. Even though we both knew what we were waiting for, we were making a conscious effort to talk around the subject.

Gina jumped to her feet when the phone finally rang. I answered it, but I could tell immediately from his tone that the news wasn't going to be good. Even worse than hearing his somber voice, I could see Gina get so bug eyed with hope and wonder, focused intently on my face and trying to read every inch of it. I put him on speaker.

"We found something…" was the worst possible way he could have led off that conversation. At least that's what I thought.

As he ran down the list of what the scans showed, my heart sank lower and lower with each bullet point he listed. Tumor on the skull… tumor on the spine…tumor on the liver…spots in the hip bone…spots in the brain. Jesus Christ, they were all over the fucking place and he wasn't shutting up! As he was reading, it was all sinking in. I wish to God that I could forget the look on her face. Tears welled up in her eyes until there was no more room for them to fit and they started streaming down her face. We both broke down as he was talking.

Even though he didn't come right out and say it, we knew he was reading off a death sentence. He heard us breaking down so after he was done with his list, he waited a second to give us a chance to compose ourselves. When he did start talking again he kept stressing how shocked he was at the results. The one glimmer of hope he gave us was that he had one more treatment we could try to slow it down, so we obviously agreed.

As we got off the phone, Gina literally fell into my arms and we broke down again. She sobbed uncontrollably and all I could do was hold her. All I could think about was that the doctor just confirmed my worst fear: I was going to lose my wife. As I held her my mind went into a tailspin. All at once I started thinking about her dying, telling the kids and dealing with life afterwards. It probably goes without saying, but it was just utter and complete sadness.

This was hands down the worst moment of my life.

It may seem inhumane to deliver this news over the phone, but I'm honestly glad we were at home when it arrived. It gave us the chance to break down and be real. Had we been in a doctor's office we would have felt forced to compose ourselves before we walked into the waiting room, and I can't even imagine what the drive home would have been like. This was better.

2 7

BEWILDERED

MY MIND WAS SPINNING. I couldn't wrap my head around the fact that we went from completely clean in January to this, only eight months later. After we were able to calm down a bit, Gina went to the washroom to run some water over her face and I took the opportunity to call my folks and my sister to tell them the news. Thankfully my mom didn't break down into tears when I told her. Neither did Robyn, although she told me later that was the news she was pretty much expecting.

About an hour or so later the phone rang. It was our neighbor Jamie and her boyfriend Dale, a young couple that we knew. They happened to be in the neighborhood and wanted to stop by to say hello and hang out for a bit. Obviously they had no clue of the news we had just gotten. Here we were, standing in the ruins of our world that had just come crashing down, and just on the other end of the phone was this cute, young, full-of-life couple asking us if they could stop by for some smiles and wine. I had answered the phone on speaker and just as I was about to say no, Gina blurted out, "…Come on over." I looked at Gina with amazement.

When Jamie & Dale arrived we didn't tell them the news right away and I'm really glad we didn't. As the wine flowed the news ended up coming out, but looking back at that first thirty minutes or so we were just couples hanging out. More than that, that was the last time we were ever able to just hang out with some friends without a cloud of death hovering over their view of her. They only stayed a few hours but that few hours was such a blessing for us. I'm not saying it made things easier because it didn't, but it sure as hell made the night slide by a little smoother. I'm firmly convinced God placed them there to cheer us up and help us through that night.

We never did tell the kids that day. Between collecting ourselves before Jamie and Dale came over and drinking wine we didn't talk to them about it. It wasn't a conscious decision but something that just kind of transpired. When we finally went to bed that night we were somewhat at peace. There was no wallowing. I'm sure the wine helped. We talked about it a little as we were changing for bed. I know we discussed some of the options that the doctor mentioned and wondered about some others, most notably chemo. I remember that even at that point, she was hesitant about chemo again. I thought about really getting into the discussion but I figured it was best to let it go for another day.

We laid down in bed and for the first time, I held her knowing that she was going to die. Even though the doctor didn't say that per se, I knew what he had implicitly told us. I closed my eyes and took everything in. The way her body felt underneath my arms. The way her hair felt on my face. The way she smelled. I closed my eyes and let the wine buzz and all the beautiful things that were my wife lull me to sleep.

2 8

A LESSON IN PEOPLE

BETWEEN THE WINE AND complete mental exhaustion, I was out like a light for the entire night. Gina got up once or twice. By the time I had woken up, she was already up and milling around. When I did get up, I felt pummeled and it wasn't hangover pummeled either. It was waking up with the realization that yesterday was not a dream. I remember as I slid my legs over the side of the bed that even though I had spent the last few months preparing myself for this chapter, I wasn't prepared.

It was a Friday but I was taking the day off. After we got the kids off to school, we sat in the kitchen with our coffee and talked it over. True to form, I talked incessantly about how to tell the kids. We came to the conclusion that we didn't want to hide anything from them, but it would be better if we didn't tell them until Sunday. We thought maybe we could just enjoy this one last weekend without that cloud hanging over all of us.

Oddly enough, Gina did tell some friends. Earlier that morning, Gina had called our former neighbors Ken & Ari and told them the news. We knew them fairly well as their son was Jackson's age and we often crossed paths at football games, school functions, and things like that. They came by the house around 11am and we all ended up crying.

After they left, I went for a walk. I remember I could feel my feet going forward and the air against my face, but I was really out of it. My mind and my body were both still numb from the day before. The news was still settling into my brain and the last thing I wanted to do was start mourning my wife. As I walked around, a strange thought made its way into my mind. I realized that I was walking alone and it was a Friday. That may not sound all that unique, but for me to be home with no kids, taking a walk by myself, was very rare. I had this eerie sense of being alone.

Nobody else came over, including my family, which I thought was kind of strange. The phone rang more than usual, but nobody came over.

This is where I really learned the very valuable lesson that people react differently to this kind of news. Some call, some come over, and some feel so awkward they don't know what to say or do, so they withdraw. As word got around the neighborhood, various people stopped by to give Gina a hug and offer their help. It was nice but after awhile it got annoying to me. I just wanted to be alone with Gina and it seemed like every twenty minutes there was a knock at the damn door. But I didn't say anything. What do you say…please don't come tell my wife you care about her?

For the bulk of the early afternoon, we talked a little bit about it all, but for the most part we spent that Friday just processing it in our own minds. I can only imagine what was going through her head but my thoughts were kind of split in two. One part of me was trying to figure out what else we could do, if there was anything we missed, and the other was going to a place I had never wanted to go. I started thinking about how to handle her death. I thought about everything, from how to handle being a single dad and running the house to whether we should start videotaping Gina with 'messages' for the girls. You know the kind I'm talking about. Like her talking to a video camera to teach them things about boys, makeup, wishing them happy birthday, etc.

I didn't dare let any of those thoughts become sentences because I was so scared of what happened yesterday I thought it best to just leave her alone. It didn't feel like a good time to talk about that sort of thing, and I felt that the right instance would present itself. In reality, that <u>was</u> the best time to talk about it and I'm sad that I didn't bring it up. As it turned out, she never did bring it up and I never forced the conversation. So what are we left with? None of those things ever got accomplished and my girls are the ones who really missed out. But that's how things went from there on with Gina and me. We both knew it was a death sentence but we didn't acknowledge it as one.

Maybe that's because only one of us saw it for what it was. I'm sure this sounds bad but then again, I wasn't the one dying. I was looking at things from a realistic and practical standpoint and truthfully, from the standpoint of the guy who was going to be left holding the bag. It was almost as if I started making a 'To-Do' list of tasks for us to tackle before she died.

Gina on the other hand was praying for a miracle. Literally. She had already convinced herself that Christ was going to heal her. For her to have those conversations with me would mean she was surrendering to the fact that she was going to die, and she wasn't ready to give in. So who the hell was I to force that down her throat?

When the kids came home they still knew nothing, so it was business as usual in their eyes. It was surreal for me because I'm never home when they get off the bus. I'm always at work so I found myself standing off to the side watching them interact with their mother the way that they normally do. It broke my heart because it was like watching a movie where you already know the mother is going to die but the kids don't. As the days went on I found myself doing more of that, watching her interact with the kids. Part of me was watching it through sad eyes but the other part of me was studying her as she brushed Jackie's hair or helped Amber with her homework. I took mental notes, knowing I was going to have to step in and do that sort of stuff. It felt like I was watching her actions as if they had expiration dates on them. Morbid, I know, but that's what went through my mind.

The kicker was that she didn't *look* sick. She still looked ravishingly beautiful. Her insides must have looked like a war zone, but on the outside she was still the same beautiful, healthy-looking woman that we all knew. That night we took the kids out for pizza and I sat there mesmerized, just watching her with the kids. By the time we got home it was late so it was bedtime for the girls. Like always, Gina got them ready and into their pajamas, and once they were in bed, I went in to tuck them in. That night though, it was so surreal. As I did it, I could just feel my heart well up. I looked at these girls and felt so sorry for them. They were going to lose their Mommy and there wasn't anything I could do to stop it. I felt so much closer to them that night. I looked at them in such a different light. I felt like I had to be more protective of them than ever before.

That was the moment it started for me. Standing there in the doorway, watching them smile and then turn their heads onto their pillows; that was the moment when I started to pull away. Not from them, but from Gina. It was almost as if we went from a team of five to a team of four where we had to just take care of someone with us. It's hard to explain and I know its something you probably can't understand. I didn't even understand it until years later. Call it a defense mechanism, but part of me started preparing myself for her to die.

By the time I left the girls' room, Gina was already in bed watching TV. I tried like hell to do as she wished and keep everything normal. I got changed and lied in bed and again, I didn't force any conversation. Instead I stared at the TV with a million questions running around in my head. Is she going to fight this? Is she going to try the chemo again? Is she just going to give up? My head was screaming inside but I just lied there in silence. I left it alone, figuring she would bring it up at some point. Stupid move. She didn't say a word. She just fell asleep.

Saturday was more of the same, us trying to be normal but not really being able to pull it off. I kind of steered clear of her, thinking she needed space to sort out her thoughts, and she just kind of withdrew as much as I let her. You would think that there would be a lot of hugs and kisses at this point, but it was actually the opposite and that's something I regret to this day. In the way of our lovemaking, it had dwindled over the summer, and continued beyond that to be pretty much nonexistent. Again, I should have stepped up and initiated more, but for a number of stupid petty reasons, I didn't. I would rub her back at night but that was more just to ease the pain, because as we had learned, the cancer had settled into her spine.

That summer I had a standing Sunday tee time with some buddies for golf. The guys were close friends: my cousin, a good friend, and my neighbor. You can imagine that after keeping all of this in for two days, I was ready to explode. As we were warming up I started yammering on to the guys, telling them everything. My God, it felt so good to just talk about it and get it out there. By the time we hit the first tee, I had gotten it all out of my system. We talked about it throughout the round and by the time we hit the turn, I felt much better. The back half was almost like normal life again, just being able to escape the real world and knock a golf ball around.

We were planning on telling the kids the news later that night. My car was a convertible so I decided to keep the top down for the drive home. The sun and the wind on my face felt nice, even with the knowledge that I was driving home to a much different Sunday afternoon. The kids were outside playing as I pulled in and the sight of them snapped me back into reality.

It was later that night when we finally told them. We had come to the conclusion that we really only needed to tell Amber and Jackson. Jackie was only six-years-old and probably too young to understand it. In retrospect, that was a bad decision because for whatever reason, we didn't count on the kids talking about it between them so much. In the end, it wasn't as if she felt left out or slighted, but I think it might have been better if we had just included her in the conversation.

We called Jackson and Amber into the family room. As I sat there waiting for them to come down and get situated, feeling the pressure building up inside my head. It was almost as if it were on fire. Now I know what it was like for the doctor that first time he called Gina and me into the office to deliver us the bad news.

We told them together, kind of trading off back and forth. We were honest, but we tried as much as we could to smooth out the rough edges for them. We told them the cancer had spread to their Mommy's brain and skull and liver. We said there was still one more treatment we were going to try, but things weren't looking good and there was a chance that Mommy might not live through it.

The wonderment in their eyes was enough to kill you. Amber broke down right away. I put my arms out and pulled everyone in for a group hug. There were tears and hugging and so much love there, but my head and my chest were on fire. Jackson handled it all differently. He was the kind of kid that internalized everything. Through the windows of his eyes, I could see the rage building. Gina sensed his pain right away and made an immediate effort to connect with him. I held Amber as she cried, but I watched as Gina walked with Jackson out of the room, which I have to say, frustrated the hell out of me.

There was a special intimacy to their relationship that didn't include me. I don't know if it was purely a mother / son thing or if bloodlines had anything to do with it but at this moment more than ever, I felt like a third party in that group. Nevertheless, I wasn't about to voice my concerns. I just manned up and tended to my quivering Amber, who was still sobbing uncontrollably.

It took about an hour or so for everyone to get their cry out. Once everyone was pretty much all out of tears, we all washed up and tried to have a normal Sunday family dinner, but as you can imagine, there was nothing normal about it. I didn't know how to behave. I hadn't the slightest clue. Not only was I dealing with my own grief and confusion, I then had to worry about the girls' anguish, and about Jackson. I know it sounds stupid, but I was pissed at him, and it bothered me that I was angry.

Dinner was more silent than ever. We didn't want to belabor the conversation, especially since we didn't tell Jackie, but nobody could bring themselves to talk. I tried to break the ice a few times but even I didn't know what to say. In my mind I was screaming, but my voice was nowhere to be found. All anyone really heard that night at dinner was the eerie clinking of forks and knives as they banged against the plates.

After dinner we all hung out in the family room and watched some TV. It was such an awkward gathering. I watched Gina and the kids more than I did the television screen, and the whole time it felt like I was watching a movie. My mind was racing as I was trying to come up with some sort of game plan on how I would go forward. I didn't want the rest of our time to be like this, reacting to every day like we had just been punched in the gut. I wanted to be a step ahead of the action. Here I was, watching my dying wife with our kids, knowing full well that while I wanted to remain hopeful, I was looking at a disappearing picture. I knew that at some point in the not-too-distant future, I was going to be smack dab in the middle of a new reality—one that didn't involve a dying wife. I was going to have to raise these kids on my own, and when that time came, I damn well wanted to be in front of the curve.

Bedtime that night played itself out comfortably. Gina went with the kids to get them ready, and I went up afterwards to tuck them in. Sitting alone, waiting for my part of the routine, created a peculiar moment for me. The silence was overwhelming. This wasn't the first time I had sat there by myself with everyone upstairs getting ready for bed, but there was something different about it this time. I could feel it on my skin.

I took a few deep breaths as I walked down the hall. In retrospect, I wonder whether they wanted to talk about it. It's not that I didn't know what to say, but I really didn't want to discuss it anymore. It was a little early in the game to be just sick of it all, but I was. As it turned out, Amber was crying, so I comforted her and did what any Daddy would do in that instance; we talked about Mommy and I told her we were going to fight real hard. I didn't stay in there too long though. I felt like the longer I stayed in there, the more she would want to talk about it, and at this point the best thing for her was to fall asleep. I poked my head in Jackson's room, but he had already started to internalize everything, so I just said goodnight.

Our own bedroom that night was hard for me. Gina and I spent the evening laying there, talking. At first the conversation was pretty surface. In fact, it was so surface it was almost comical. If you were watching that scene as a movie you would be asking "…how can they NOT be talking about it?" But we weren't. I finally brought up the chemo treatments the doctor had suggested and I was shocked to hear her say that she didn't want to do them. Not only was I shocked, I was confused. How could she not want to fight? I wanted to fight. I wanted her to stay alive, how could she not want to? It was as if she just told me in so many words that she was okay with dying. I asked her if she really meant that and when she said yes, despite how deflated that made me feel, I surrendered to her decision.

My head was swimming with things I wanted to talk about but didn't dare bring up. Again, I figured I'd wait for her to prompt me on when to start talking about final preparation-type things. Things like finances, house affairs, and maybe some video-taped messages from her to the girls for me to give to them as they got older.

But we didn't talk about any of that. Instead we just lied there with her head on my chest, talking about nothing and me worrying about how I was going to prepare for the fallout that was inevitably coming.

29

FAILURE TO COMMUNICATE

FROM THIS POINT FORWARD is where the train really came off the rails. It happened pretty easily and nobody really noticed how far off the tracks we were until it was over. In short, and you'll see this unfold, our communication broke down more as each day passed. As much of an asshole as that might make me sound, it was a pretty even mix of Gina's lack of ability to deal with things and me not forcing certain issues that were important. Every time I felt the urge to bring something up for discussion, I choked it back down with the reminder and excuse that she was the one going through this, and compared to that, my feelings were minimal.

The thing is, they weren't. If I can give you one piece of advice, it would be to remember that your feelings aren't insignificant. Don't trample on her feelings or wishes, but don't be scared to bring things up or force some conversations. Don't let things go unsaid.

Find a way to communicate about how to handle the end when the end is coming. You can still fight and you can still hope, but you have to figure out how to handle the end WHILE YOU STILL CAN! I gave Gina all the space in the world, but all the while I was wishing she would reach out to me. As you'll see, everything ended up getting pushed off and at the end of the day I was left standing in the ruins with a lot of questions and very few answers.

A black cloud had found its way over the house, settling in every facet of my life. It took over my relationship with Gina, the kids, my work, everything. I could feel myself starting my own death march. You remember the movie *Dead Man Walking* where Sean Penn is led out of his cell for the last time as they walk him down to the execution chamber? That's how I felt when I woke up on Monday, and from that day on, every day was like another step down that hall. Even the sunny days that peppered themselves in there had a black tinge to them.

Gina had retreated to her Bible and reading scripture. I figured that was a pretty normal reaction. Think about it; how many times have you ever prayed to God the minute you got into trouble? I know I sure as hell have. The thing here was while Gina was always very into her faith, I wasn't. I think Gina's faith was part of the accelerant for my pulling away. At the time when I should have been pulling her and God in closer, I was starting to put some emotional distance between us. I've said it before, but I think it's just in my nature as a defense mechanism. I started preparing to let her go.

I don't think she ever knew this. Through the final moments I did everything I physically could for her. I handled whatever she wanted and was there to support and love her every step of the way. After all, I still loved her very much. That never waned. I started to feel the tension battle within myself of wanting to spend every last second with her, and at the same time wanting to distance myself from her and the whole death-tinged world that surrounded us. I felt bad about it, I really did. I felt ashamed for wanting some distance.

I guess the only way I can describe it is if you think of a relationship that just peters out. It begins to wane, and even though you still love each other you become less and less emotionally attached. This is how it was with me. I was becoming less emotionally attached, yet was still very much in love. Looking back at it now with a clear head, I know that I should have been tougher. I still carry a sense of guilt for having secretly desired this increasing amount of space.

Amazingly, as those first few weeks moved past us, the kids adjusted fairly quickly to what we were going through. Luckily school and their sports provided them all with distractions and kept their minds from really settling in on it. At this point Gina still felt pretty good, so she handled them for the most part. The home routine was still somewhat normal, so I was usually gone to work before they were awake, and their mother was the one at home when they got out of school.

I found myself paying close attention to them though, much more than I ever had before. Not in the sense that I never paid attention to my kids, but I began eagle-eyeing them for any problems. Obviously Gina handled them much more closely than I did because she was with them more on a daily basis. When the day came for Gina to go back to the doctor, she and I talked and she reiterated that she was still very much against the idea of chemo. I couldn't blame her, even though hearing her say that hurt me more than I can put into words.

Mornings had gotten to be so sad around the house because I would find myself almost daily looking at Gina as if she were a museum exhibit. I mean I would literally stare at her knowing that she was going to be gone. The appointment wasn't until later in the day so I went to work for the morning with the plan that I'd come back to get her for the appointment. That's probably the best thing I could have done. It was a nice step away from my cancer-clouded house to be able to go and focus on work. Routines are great in the sense that they allow us to compartmentalize and really escape. Whenever I would get to the office, it was like a switch went off and everything at home was gone. Not that I ever forgot it, because trust me, it never truly leaves your mind, but for a few hours I could at least operate as a normal human being. Going home was never fun. It's hard to explain but my mind used to struggle with itself at this point. Part of me would be excited the day was over and I was able to go spend time with my dying wife, but at the same time, part of me dreaded it. Talking to my mom or my sister was equally as sad. Every conversation pretty much centered around Gina and how she was feeling. I couldn't blame them for being so concerned. I'm glad they were, but at the same time it felt like that was all I talked about with them. With anyone. Cancer had taken over everything in my life, including my conversations.

Driving home to get Gina for the doctor's, I began to feel as though we were going through the motions. Have you ever been on a team or part of a group that consistently lost? Like every game that you went into you knew you were going to get your ass kicked? That's what it felt like. I never communicated this to Gina but everything we were doing now felt more like we were checking things off of a To-Do list as opposed to living life. Even my focus at this point was shifting from being strong for her to being strong for the kids.

Walking into the doctor's office even felt different at this point. It wasn't like before when I would be able to walk in with a sense of hope or optimism. Now when I walked in with Gina I still felt like we were a team, but a losing one. We sat with the doc and it killed me to look across the desk at him. You could see the sadness in his eyes and that just made my heart sink even further. I don't know why. I knew what we were walking into but even still, when you're going through this your emotions become a roller coaster.

As he started talking, the picture got even bleaker. By the time he was done I felt like I had just been beaten down. For the first time in my life, I felt like quitting. Looking across the desk at him I knew that there was no way we were going to beat this. Even worse, there wasn't much we could do to slow it down. He outlined a treatment plan for her that if all things went well, might give her another twelve to eighteen months.

You know how it looks when a boxer is wobbling on his feet just before he gets hit with that roundhouse knockout punch? That's how I felt, and hearing the words "maybe a year or a year-and-a-half" was the knockout punch. We weren't talking about a business contract or a cell phone plan; this was the outline for how long my wife had to live. My heart hit the floor with a thud. I felt nauseous and lost and defeated all at the same time.

When Gina looked at me, it broke my heart. She looked at me with a look I don't ever recall seeing in her. She was a smart woman and tougher than nails, but I could see in her eyes that she was hoping against hope this might somehow give her a chance to live and now it was outlined pretty clearly—that wasn't going to happen. Deep down she was still praying for that miracle where someone would tell her she had a shot, and she was looking at me with eyes that wanted that someone to be me. My eyes welled up with tears and it took everything I had not to cry. All I could mutter was that I would support her in whatever she wanted to do.

Surprisingly the doctor convinced her to go ahead with the treatment plan. I felt a mixture of excitement and disappointment wash over me. I knew what she was looking for and I could sense that his urging her to take the treatment was something she was twisting into hope.

Walking out of there truly felt like 'dead man walking.' Even though we had a new plan, it wasn't like there was any sort of renewed energy or hope. We both knew it wasn't going to fix anything but it might buy us some time. I remember being unfathomably mad at a lot of people. My anger was for pretty much everything; God, Karma, doctors, you name it. If I could look at it, I blamed it. It comforted me a little that she was going to have some more time with the family, but I suspect that's pretty natural. Even when you have a sick pet or an old grandparent, you always want to postpone death.

There wasn't a lot of conversation in the car but I could just see in her face that she finally heard what he said. She understood that this was only going to buy her some time. She mumbled that she wasn't looking forward to the chemo but that was about it. For my part, my mind was swimming with thoughts about the end. I was thinking about preparations and what we needed to do as a couple. This was the first time I even started what I call 'dark daydreaming;' I started to think about things like the girls weddings without their mom. As time went on I would find my mind going to this place, to future events that their mother would not attend. Christmas, prom, Mother's Day, and all of those special life events.

I felt sorry for her so I kept my mouth shut but looking back, I wish I hadn't, because that was the moment where it couldn't get any worse. It wasn't like I was going to kill a good day and I'm not saying we should have dove right in, but if ever there was a window for me to say something like "…maybe we should start thinking about some things to get in order," that was it. The end was literally just outlined right in front of our eyes, and we still wouldn't address it. My God, I'm such a pussy.

The kids were home and expecting us because we told them we were going to the doctor. We all sat down in the family room and it was like experiencing bad déjà vu. I mean, we had already done this once. I could see it in the girls' eyes—that hope against hope that things were going to be okay for Mommy. It's moments like this that really try your backbone as a man.

There's a fine line between being truthful and scaring the shit out of them, and we tried to be very cognizant of that. As a parent you want to cushion the blow but at the same time, you don't want to sell them a bag of goods when you know what the reality is going to be. We wanted to be honest and truthful but at the same time we candy-coated it a little and told them that Mommy was going to try another treatment but that there were no guarantees.

I got a little scared because the kids didn't cry at all. Not that I wanted to see them cry, but I paid close attention to their eyes and they seemed to be digesting the news as if this was one more shot. I didn't know what to do. I didn't know if I should interject to make sure they understood fully or if I should let them ride it out and not squash their optimism. I quickly chose to ride it out, recognizing that reality would set in soon enough and they would have the rest of their lives to try and understand it.

As I watched this transaction of information, my mind drifted back to me. Once again, as I looked at Gina I thought to myself that this wasn't what I signed on for. I was only 39-years-old and I was watching my wife tell our children that she was dying of cancer.

30

FADING IN PLAIN VIEW

AT THIS POINT SOME things started to happen. The Lymphedema began to show through with the swelling of her feet and her right arm. Lymphedema occurs when a clear fluid builds up in the body and typically it happens in an arm. When they remove the breast, they take lymph nodes. Lymph nodes help move fluids through the body and without them the body can swell. At this point her swelling wasn't very noticeable. Aside from that she looked and felt pretty normal, which was probably what still made it so hard to swallow. It was almost as though I couldn't believe she was dying. Not that I wanted her to look like a cancer patient with the sunken eyes and the frail body, but in the back of my mind I knew that once the chemo began, Gina's appearance would once again change.

I began to see her differently at this point. Visually, I saw her as more beautiful than ever and I appreciated her more than I ever did. I kept soaking in moments that before this whole ordeal I took for granted just like every other husband does. But I found myself often seeing her through a cloud of frustration and anger. I was mad at life, at God, at Jesus, and the more she didn't want to try and prepare for a future without her, the more angry I would get at her as well.

Ironically, as I sat there all focused on Gina's impending death, my birthday was swiftly approaching. Forty is one of those milestones I think guys look forward to more than women. Maybe we don't look forward to it, but we embrace it much better than women do, that's for sure. If anything, it's an excuse for us to be able to have a party and celebrate. Now if this doesn't speak volumes about the love my wife had for me, nothing does. There she was, dying of cancer, and one of her main concerns was throwing me a fortieth-birthday party. To be honest, I wished she wouldn't have worried about it and let it go by. I never said anything about it because I could see this was something that was very important to her. It wasn't that I didn't want the party; hell, I'm always up for a good party. But with everything going on it really gave me a guilt complex to be celebrating my life while I watched Gina lose hers.

I will admit it was nice to finally have something to look forward to again. Gina had started her chemo treatments, but I'm convinced that having that party to look forward to helped her through it. It still roughed her up but not like before. She bounced back much faster this time and by the time the party arrived, she looked absolutely fantastic. The party was at the bar in the Holiday Inn not too far from the house, and she did a fantastic job. I had such a mixed bag of emotions running through me all night. All of our friends were there and on the surface it was a great time, but to be honest as much as it was my birthday party, it was almost like a going away party for her as well. Morbid, I know, and that wasn't our conscious intent, but everyone (myself included) showered her with attention and kisses and love. I remember at one point leaning against the bar looking around the room, thinking how lucky we were to have all these great people in our lives. I felt a twinge that it might be the last celebration we would ever have together and as it turned out, it pretty much was. We had a great time though, laughing and dancing all night. I still have a picture from that night in my office. As much as I was against the idea I'm so happy that she threw it. We made some great memories that night that I still think about and smile.

It wasn't long after that night that the reality of everything started to push its way through her body. The cancer had spread to her bones and her skull, so she was increasingly experiencing excruciating pain, which mostly came at night. More and more often, I would wake up to an empty bed, and every time I did, the reality of what was taking over slapped me in the face. When I noticed she was gone, I would get up and go to her, but as I did, I couldn't help but think that death was creeping closer. Every time I walked down those stairs in the middle of the night, I felt like I was starting to lead two separate lives. On one hand I was trying to maintain a sense of normalcy and take care of things (her included), but on the other hand I felt like I was preparing myself for my wife to die.

31

ONE MORE (GOOD) TIME

UP IN LACROSSE, WI they have a great Oktoberfest and just after we had gotten the news, Gina and I had made plans to spend a weekend up there. I really pushed for us to keep those plans partially because I needed to get the hell out of dodge, but more so because I knew this could very well be the last time she was going to be able to get away. She was deteriorating and I wanted her to be able to milk a little bit of fun and a few more smiles out of life. She liked these kinds of things so I really wanted to make this trip fun for her.

Living in Chicago that time of year can be tricky with the weather, but luckily it was beautiful out. I blasted the song "Beautiful Day" by U2 as we pulled out of the driveway, and it really was. It was so beautiful in fact that we were able to take the top down on the convertible. I had done a little research and found all these back roads we could drive down, so between the warm air, the top down, and the beautiful fall colors all over the trees, it really was magical. I would glance at her every now and again just to see her looking out over the passenger door, and it really made my heart feel good. We both loved cruising in that car. It was one of those things that was always able to clear our heads from whatever kind of day we were having. Those drives were always fun, but they didn't compare to this particular day. I didn't know it then, but this weekend would be the last time that car would have that effect on us. After she died I still took the car out with the top down, but it was never the same.

In addition to it being the last time for us cruising, it was the last time we would ever be intimate with each other as well. After we got to the hotel, we had a nice dinner with a couple glasses of wine. We were both smiling, laughing, touching each other. We were like a young couple on our honeymoon. I was geared up and ready to go as any guy would be, but as soon as we got back to the room and got going, things went bad.

I had conjured up this idea in my head of what this event was going to be like and it turned out to be nothing like I had imagined. The actual act of sex was difficult because she was having so many physical problems. She was dry, which was perfectly normal given the treatments she had been receiving. I was very aware of how delicate she was and was worried about her pain. I didn't know what to do so I offered to stop, but she kept pressing for me to keep going. I knew she was doing this only because she wanted to please me and make a nice memory for me, but my heart was breaking. I could tell she was in pain and there was no way she was enjoying any of it. To be honest, neither was I, but I couldn't just stop because that would only hurt her more. I soldiered through but that's really all it was.

This will sound odd, but the second that we were done I had a very strange feeling. You know how after sex you both lay there for a second? Well that still happened, except this time it came with a strange sense of finality. I knew instantly that was the last time it would ever happen.

The rest of the weekend went by fine. The festival was okay, but mostly it was just nice to have a weekend with Gina. Living with this heightened sense of awareness, there were a number of times where she would catch me looking at her, but she would just smile. I didn't play the role of the puppy dog though. I had thought about this a lot and I figured if I was going to make her smile, my turning into a giant pussy was not going to do it. I wanted to keep things normal. I was never a puppy dog before and turning into that now would just insult her.

32

YOU CAN'T ESCAPE REALITY

THE MINUTE WE GOT back home reality was waiting right there for us. It wasn't anything in particular, just the normal difficulty in returning from a nice vacation to your normal routines of work, kids, etc. That's how it was for us, only we also knew that somewhere in there, Gina would die.

I noticed pretty quickly that things were starting to change with Gina. She was sleeping in much more often, so that meant I was getting the girls up and off to school before I headed in for work. Her patience was getting shorter as well. She had angry quips and her tolerance for their antics was much less than normal. I noticed it but never addressed it. I figured her pain was increasing so she was just irritable. Besides, how do you tell someone in her situation to lighten up?

I started to pour myself back into work again. I don't know what it was, but I looked up at work one day and started to really freak out over my stature there. My numbers were down which was very much understood by my bosses and colleagues, but unacceptable to me. I was having such a hard time balancing my head and adjusting my thought process, so everything I acted on became a string of knee jerk reactions. When things got bad at home, I pretty much dropped everything at work and focused solely on that. Now with these ugly numbers staring back at me I went the complete opposite direction and started obsessing about work, so much so that I started spending more time there than I should have. It helped me cope with my situation for sure, but I should have been at home more.

It's easy to see now, but while I thought I was thinking clearly and had good vision, it couldn't have been more clouded and my mind couldn't have been more jumbled. I bounced from problem to problem like a pinball. I wish I would have just stepped back and taken a look at the big picture the way an even keeled coach does. He doesn't freak out when his team is losing and he's got crazy off the field problems.

He doesn't run from place to place and give everything half of the attention it requires. No. He steps back, evaluates what he needs to do, figures out where his time and energies are needed, creates a game plan and then executes that plan.

The worst decision I made was to continue partying. It was more like self- medicating really. I still liked to stop off on the way home and have a few drinks, and I was still partying to take the edge off every now and again. I was cautious not to get caught by anyone. Gina, the cops, work, you name it. Nobody knew except whom I wanted to know.

This is the part where I should introduce a very important part of this story and of my life. Mark is one of my very best friends, a fraternity brother from college whom I've stayed close with ever since. He's one of those guys that I've been close with for the last twenty-plus years. He's my right hand, my "Luca Bratzi" (bodyguard for The Godfather). He's the guy that always had my back and was often thinking clearly for me and my family when I couldn't. When I told him about what was happening with Gina when we were at NIU's homecoming, he stared me straight in the eye and said, "Tommy, I'm single and I've got time. I'll be with you every weekend while she's going through this and whenever else you need." And he never let me down. Not in nearly two decades of friendship before this, during this, or after this.

At this point it was late October. Our community always has a big family-oriented blow out for Halloween and this year, given the future we were facing, I thought it might be fun to do a big family dress up. I hadn't dressed up for Halloween since college, but Gina thought the idea was fun. The girls were excited too, since they never before had seen me embrace the idea of a costume. I dressed up like one of those goon monsters from the old Three Stooges shows and led the little kids' parade with Jackie and Amber. It was fun marching around with all the neighborhood kids and parents. It allowed everyone to forget about things for a little while and to just feel normal again.

After the parade we all went trick-or-treating. I took the girls by myself. Gina stayed home but that was normal. I usually took the girls around the neighborhood and she stayed back to hand out candy to the trick-or-treaters at our house. I can't tell you what a great day that was. The kids at the parade, the trick-or-treating, it all felt like a welcome sense of normality and it really put a smile on my face to see the kids having fun. I watched them the way you watch a movie after you've already figured out the ending.

There was an adult party afterwards that I went to. Typically Gina and I would both go, but she wasn't feeling up to it. I initially wasn't going to go, but a neighbor talked me into it. I also kind of felt like it would make Gina feel better if I went, so that I didn't miss out on something just because of her. I also knew the booze would be flowing and it was an excuse to get out and self-medicate, and that's what I did. I got hammered. As you know, alcohol is a depressant, and while initially I was enjoying myself, after a while I started noticing that all around me were nothing but happy couples. It really bothered me to see everyone have someone and know that my wife was dying. I remember feeling like I had to get used to this but that's when it also occurred to me that I really should be making my way home. It wasn't as though I didn't belong there, but I felt guilty about not being home with Gina.

Had I known the shit storm that was waiting for me when I walked through the door I would have stayed and had a couple more drinks. Gina was pissed at me for going and rightfully so. I shouldn't have left her home to take care of the kids when she was in so much pain. Especially with them so hopped up on their candy sugar high. Jackson and I got into it that night as well. I was no longer incredibly drunk, but I wasn't exactly sober either, so I fought back with him pretty hard. Nothing physical or anything, but we were pretty vocal and mean. This was really the instance where he and I started falling apart. The ordeal with his mother had drawn him very much into his relationship with his church. Jackson himself was becoming a very right-wing Christian and taking on what I view as their very judgmental ways. One of the big problems he had with me was my drinking and that was the root of many of our arguments, including the one that night.

Now I'm not going to bag on any religion or anything like that. People see God the way they see Him and that's fine. I felt that this particular church, however, was really doing Jackson and our family a lot of harm and a big disservice.

As we headed into the holiday season I remember wondering how were we going to handle it. Gina was starting to deteriorate at a much quicker pace. The tests showed a quick blip of help from the chemo, but you wouldn't have known it by looking at her.

Thanksgiving came and went with no real fanfare. We went to my mom's like we did every year, and everyone tried to make Gina feel as comfortable as possible, but it was difficult for them to divert their attention from her situation. She wore a wig, which probably helped put everyone at ease, including her. We didn't make too much of a big deal out of it. Even though we knew what we were up against, we didn't treat it as if this was going to be the last one.

I didn't really discuss it with the kids and tell them how to act. How do you do that? I wanted them to act naturally with their mother. As it turned out, they did their normal thing that day as well, playing with their cousins and not glomming onto Mom. Even when we ate, my brother-in-law said Grace, but he kept it general, giving thanks that we were all together, making no reference to Gina specifically or her situation.

I was different though. I admit, I kept catching myself glancing over at her, and every time I began to think of the situation's finality, the fact that next year, it was probably just going to be the girls and me. Nobody said it so I don't know if I was the only one thinking this would be the last Thanksgiving, but if they were, they didn't treat it that way even when we left. When we saddled up to leave, there were no tearful goodbyes or explicitly solemn reactions.

That next week Gina and I were talking about Christmas and it was obvious that I was going to have to help more than ever this year. She wasn't driving much anymore and the fatigue was really getting to her. There were a lot of days where she was so tired that even when the kids got home from school, they were kind of left to fend for themselves.

Now we've got a decent-sized house, and traditionally, Gina would go all out with the Christmas decorations, so much so that it would usually take at least a week to finish. I offered to bring everything down from the attic but she insisted on helping. I'm not sure if she really wanted to help, or if that was one way she could prove to herself that she was still capable. So we did it together, but she fatigued easily and had to take breaks often. Sick or not, nobody likes bringing all that shit out of the attic, so I would keep on working putting things either where she told me or where I remembered her putting them before. It was nice and I'm glad I did it, but at the same time I loathed every minute of it because it happened with such a looming stench of death.

From that night on there was a pit in my stomach that really stuck in my gut that it would be our last Christmas together. It didn't matter if I was at work or home or in the car, that's all I could think about. That's not an easy thing to digest. We had been together for sixteen years, and after that one, everything that I knew as Christmas would cease to exist.

This leads me to my next quandary that Christmas: her gift. What do you get for someone who is about to die? It's not like you can buy them something they can use in the spring or summer. I had no idea how to ignore it, address it, and work around it all in the same motion. My neighbor Holly came up with the idea to make a video montage of all of our old home videos and have it set to music. It could've been the worst idea in the world because it was so retrospective, but that wasn't how I saw it. I thought this would be perfect because it would show Gina how wonderful our life together had been, what a wonderful family she had built and raised. I looked at it more as a tribute to our family and our great memories.

I liked the idea but didn't know how to make it happen. As luck would have it, I was talking about it to a friend of mine who just happened to do that sort of thing. He didn't do it professionally, but he had a lot of Mac products and software, and liked to tinker with it at home. He offered to put it all together for me in a video that we could watch on our TV.

That next week, which was the first week of December, we went back to the doctor to see how the chemo was going. You could look at her and see it wasn't doing much, so even though we knew going in it wasn't going to be a great visit, we were hopeful he would tell us that we had this inordinate amount of time. It turned out we were right; the chemo wasn't really helping at all. I can't say that was any surprise, but the surprise was what the doctor said right after that. He told us that we should get our affairs in order because she might have six months left to live.

33

TIDAL WAVES

IT NEVER GETS EASIER to hear and you can never prepare yourself for a statement like that. Even if it's what you expect to hear, it still jelly legs you. When he told us that he was anticipating she had five or six months left, the cold reality really hit us both. There were tears, but nobody really broke down. I can't even tell you the despair I felt when we walked out of that room.

This is going to sound selfish, but I was awkwardly quiet as we left and walked towards the car. Even though I was expecting bad news I had a hard time grasping it. This was the first time I left there with absolutely no hope of anything. At least before there was something to hope for, some sort of chance, even if I chose not to grab onto it. When we finally got in the car, I lost it.

You'll learn that you'll have moments where tears come like a tidal wave and there is no warning that they're coming. This was one of those moments. I started crying uncontrollably. I was so out of sorts that Gina actually started calming me! I wish I was stronger at that moment and that I would have handled it better, but you never know what your mind and body are going to do when you get that sort of news. Here I was, the man of the house and the big strong husband, so out of sorts that my dying wife was consoling me!

When we got home that afternoon, we sat down and talked to the kids. They were already pretty aware of the situation even though I don't think they completely comprehended it at the time. The next thing we did was call her family not just to tell them the news, but to make arrangements to bring everyone in. And when I say everyone, I mean everyone: Mom, Dad, her three sisters, one of which had two boys. I flew them all into Chicago and put them all up in a hotel not too far from the house.

That night was a hard one. We lied in bed and believe it or not, there we were, dancing around it again. We lied there and talked about nothing. To be honest, it was probably better because I don't know if I heard a word she said and my guess is she didn't hear me either. While I have no idea what was running through her head, all I could think about was the fact that my wife was going to die.

I spent the next few days freaking out about the unknown future that was lurking in front of me. I spent more time worrying about the imminent death and destruction it would leave, instead of dealing with the present. Think of walking through a haunted house. You don't look around at where you are, but you are scared shitless of what is going to come out of the blackness two or three steps in front of you. That's what I felt like. I wasn't looking forward to it, but I was so focused on it that it consumed me. One thing I did was decide that I was going to work on her timeline. After all, she heard the same news that I did. I didn't want her to feel like I was hustling her into death by pushing for us to take care of everything, but I promised myself that I would work on her timeline.

I started to formulate some things in my mind. First I figured if the doctor was telling us five or six months, then we weren't going to make it to summer. Since I had nothing else to look forward to, I knew full well that every minute from there on out was more than precious, so I started looking at dates. The first big date coming up was Christmas. In past years I'd spend a lot of time at the office around now. I always had a lot of year-end deadlines so I would work and she would take care of all the shopping and gift-wrapping on her own. Not this year. I pulled back considerably from work and focused on Gina like a kid with a new puppy. It was tough getting in the Christmas spirit, but I tried with full force. We did it all together. Shopping, decorating, wrapping presents. You name it and we did it together, and I have to admit, I'm so glad we did. I'm embarrassed that it took her death sentence for me to embrace it like that, but I'm glad I at least did for that year because I loved it. I wish we would have done it more that way.

Those next few weeks leading up to Christmas I spent with one focus: her. I was able to fight off the depression and 'finality' of it all, but I didn't do it alone. That battle was won with the help of some booze and other mind-altering substances every now and again. It wasn't an everyday thing—I limited it to Fridays—but it gave me something to look forward to and it really helped me shake off the feeling of death. I know it sounds shallow and shitty and you're right, it is. I'd advise against it to anybody reading this, but I have to be honest and say it got me through.

I know I'm talking pretty much about me and not the kids but that's because at this point Gina still pretty much handled them. Jackie was only six-years-old so she was still pretty oblivious to the whole situation. Amber stayed a pretty normal course but Gina eased through those waters with her. Jackson was the one who was really struggling. He was visibly upset and wasn't coping well at all, and there wasn't much anyone could do to help him. He loved his Mom.

34

CAN'T FIND THE RIGHT TIME

GINA STARTED GOING to bed earlier as the fatigue started wearing her down more and more. I'm not necessarily an early evening guy but I would go to bed with her. I can't tell if it was to help make her comfortable or if I was just trying to soak up every second with her that I could. It bothered me because I would fall asleep easily, but as tired as she was, the pain in her bones would keep her up. I can't tell you how many times I woke up in the middle of the night only to find her downstairs. Let me tell you, there's not a more helpless feeling than looking over the banister and seeing your wife in her housecoat rocking back and forth in pain and knowing that there is nothing you can do about it.

As time goes on, you learn to live with the reality. You never seem to fully digest exactly what you're in the middle of, but you learn to get through each day. I still wondered to myself how I was going to pick up the baton when I really had to do it. I prayed a lot at that point for strength. Strength for me, strength for her, strength for the kids. It always gave me some comfort and to be honest, I think God answered my prayers a little bit there because the girls were handling it relatively well.

I was pretty good about not outwardly focusing on the finality of things and I'll tell you, that's not an easy thing to do…especially when it's the first thing people around you want to talk about. Understandably they just want you to know they care and are there for you, but their well wishes and sad glances don't let you escape from under that cloud for even one second.

At this point we were about a week past our damning doctor's visit and Gina still wasn't overly concerned with her affairs yet. We hadn't really been talking much about things because again, I didn't want to make her feel as though I was hurrying her into the grave. I decided we would get through Christmas, and then begin to figure things out.

The problem was that I could never plan the right time. I could never bring myself to force the issue and I really wish I would have. At that point, you obviously have her feelings and emotions at heart, but the reality is once you get to this point—days don't get better. Every day things get just a little bit worse and the longer you wait, the worse she is going to feel. Each day makes it harder for her to handle and harder for her to do. Like an idiot, I missed my window. I should have done it when it was fresh so we could ride out the rest of our days and not have it weighing on my mind twenty four hours a day, seven days a week.

It was a bizarre time for me, trying to be happy while I was mired in despair. Given the fact that it was Christmas, it wasn't hard to bury it in booze.

35

FEELING LONELY AHEAD OF THE CURVE

BY THIS POINT YOU could easily see her deteriorating. Her legs and feet were starting to swell a lot and she was in pain all the time. She was really starting to feel self-conscious about it too even though she would never admit it. It was hard for me to watch her deteriorate into this geriatric, carcass of her self. She never was one to bitch and moan although truth be told, I wish she would have. That was always one of my problems with Gina from the day we met and it went down right to the very end....You always had to read her mind. I talked with her about it a million times...to the point where she would call me "Tina," because my desire to talk and communicate so much was like a woman's.

That's probably what fueled my anger so much. I know it sounds crazy as I sit here and talk about how much I love her and how much I was enveloping her, but I was angry. Even today, I'm still angry. I wasn't mad at her per se. Our communication disconnects still eats away at me, but in general I had this non-directional anger. I was mad at life in general and I sure as hell was mad at God. In the midst of the holiest of seasons, that is supposed to be all about family and religion and kids, God was taking away my wife and cheating my kids out of their mother. I won't go as far as to say I denounced God, but I was angry as hell, that's for sure.

You might feel this way too and that's okay. It's okay to be mad at God but at the end of the day, that's where most of us ultimately go for comfort.

What was worse was that Gina was falling deeper and deeper into her faith, but she wouldn't share it with me. I think it was something she felt was personal between her and God and there was no room for anyone else. I tried to involve myself but she was pretty steadfast about keeping me out so I didn't pry. I was hurt but I didn't pry.

Even still, I tried to make the best of it. Our relationship had grown stronger probably in part due to my heightened sense of appreciation for her. I didn't treat her with pity, but I did treat her with much more adoration than I had in years. As a couple, our love had grown strong again. Physically we were shattered. Her body was shutting down and she was in so much pain that sex was completely out of the question. I also started to shy away from physically touching her. I didn't hug her or hold her though I wish I would have. I thought it was too painful for her but to be honest, it was also awkward and uncomfortable for me. Imagine trying to hold your wife, the same woman that you've held for years, and not feeling comfortable doing it because you might hurt her? I pansied out when in reality, I should have forced myself through it more.

She wanted to be upstairs in bed almost continually at this point. She would fight through the early part of the day the best she could when the kids were home, but even that was getting to be difficult for her which in turn made it difficult for me. Even with her still home and with us, I was already starting to feel like a single dad. Worse yet, I was already starting to feel lonely.

36

MERRY CHRISTMAS WITH LOVE

CHRISTMAS EVE FINALLY CAME and I was fighting to feel festive. As the day crept closer, my sisters and I talked about what the family was going to do. Traditionally we had Christmas Eve at my sister's house. We settled on the fact that the easiest thing to do was to still have it there. This way Gina didn't have to do anything to get ready for it and in her mind, it would be keeping with the normal course of things.

We never really did anything on Christmas Eve morning, so until about noon it was pretty much like any other day. When the time came to get the girls ready, I watched Gina do it. Part of me watched through the eyes of the somber husband, but part of me was taking mental notes. I was kind of making a mental checklist of what this process required. Dresses and tights and shoes and hair pins and…the whole thing started to really scare the hell out of me. For a very brief moment I entertained the thought of asking if I could help, but my better judgment took over and I didn't. I would cross that bridge when I came to it.

We went to my sisters around 3pm but Gina was feeling absolutely horrible. All the same, we loaded the girls and our normal bag load of gifts into the car and away we went. The ride over was pretty normal but once we arrived, a strange feeling set in. It wasn't so much as strange as it was awkward because everyone was trying TOO hard to make it normal. There was no direct conversation about Gina. There was the occasional '…how are you feeling?' but that was it. Instead we just tried to keep it normal and for me on Christmas Eve, that meant a few drinks. Our family is a drinking family and that was a welcome excuse for me. I didn't get crazy because I was going to be driving home but it sure did feel good to take the edge off a bit. I was a little worried about how the gifts were going to go, but that went fine. It was nice to have all these kids in the room to focus on. You could tell Gina felt that way too.

Dinner was probably the most awkward time of the evening. When we said Grace, there was no mention of her or her illness, but you could cut the tension in the room with a knife. It was almost as if everyone was waiting to see if my brother-in-law was going to work something in. He didn't, and everyone seemed simultaneously uneasy and relieved that they didn't have to acknowledge it either. I didn't say anything because I didn't want to make Gina any more uncomfortable than she already was. As it was, she was very self-conscious about her appearance. Bringing it up would be like shining a spotlight on her. But sitting next to her already felt strange, like I was sitting next to a ghost. It sounds horrible and it sickens me to say that, but it's true.

When it came time for us to leave at the end of the evening, it wasn't a big deal. We always spent Christmas Day together at my mom's so it wasn't like this was the time for any sort of tearful goodbye. After all, we would all be together again in less that twenty-four hours. When we got home, I did more than I ever have. Normally when we would get home from my sisters I would fall right into bed, but this year I did more work than ever on that infamous Santa night. I helped the girls put Santa's milk & cookies out, put them to bed, came back downstairs and got the gifts out of hiding to put underneath the tree. At one point when I was trying to make them look pretty like magazine pictures I had seen over the years, I stood up and realized this was something I wished I had done all those years with Gina.

All the while, Gina was resting in bed because she was both in pain and worn out. Her body was so run down that a normal night of visiting was equal to running a marathon for her. We had wrapped the presents in the weeks leading up to Christmas. The last gift I put under the tree was the one that I had for Gina. It stopped me for a moment, but I put it under the tree and then went right up to bed. As I turned off the lights and went down the hallway, I found myself in a strange state of excitement. Shockingly, I was genuinely excited about waking up with Gina for Christmas Day. I wasn't dreading it, I wasn't focused on it being our last Christmas, none of that. I was excited to give her the gift.

As I had mentioned, my buddy had put together the video montage for me. When I picked it up from him it was only about a week before Christmas. Naturally I saw it when I picked it up, but that was the only time. He and I watched it in his conference room at his work. It was about twenty minutes long and at the end of it, we were both crying our eyes out. I can't even imagine what people must have thought when they saw the two of us go into the conference room for what they could only think was a normal business meeting, only to see us emerge half an hour later as though we had a cry fest with each other. But it was perfect. I couldn't have dreamt up a better gift.

When Christmas morning finally came, it felt very normal at first. The girls woke us up around 7am and were jumping up and down, all excited about Santa. I was my usual groggy self as I made some coffee, and the girls ran off to wake up Jackson. It was strangely normal and joyous. I remember noticing that for the first time in a long time, there was no "death aura" hanging over the house.

As we tore into the gifts, the kids went first. I really enjoyed watching them but I was watching Gina too. You could see a little sadness and despair in her eyes. After the kids opened all their gifts and I did mine, Gina was the final one. We had wrapped the video in a big box. So there was this huge box in front of her and you could feel the anticipation building. The kids were all giggly and I was nervous as hell. My heart was racing a mile a minute. When she finally opened the box the look on her face was priceless. It was utter and total surprise.

The TV was in the family room, so we all climbed onto the huge pit couch and gathered around Gina. I put the video in and came back and sat next to her as it started. If ever there was a picture to see, it was that one. Everyone was together on the couch all in our jammies as one big family.

It started with our wedding day and went on through our life together. Vacations, the kids' birthdays, first bike rides, parties…all the things that as parents you videotape through the years. Everyone was welling up as the years rolled by on the screen. They were all watching the video but I was watching Gina and the kids. I could tell by her face that she was truly touched by it and I can't tell you how happy that made me feel. It was the greatest gift we could have given her. I felt so in love with her in that moment and that's a feeling that I cling to even today.

The last part of the video was Christmas from the year before and I had that part set over the Louis Armstrong song "What A Wonderful World." The last image showed Gina giving Jackson his lettermen's jacket and hugging him. Everyone was sniffling throughout but when that scene came on, we all surrendered to a bawling hysteria.

She reached over and hugged and kissed me in a way that she hadn't done in a long time. It was a true love embrace and to this day, I can still feel it on my fingertips.

I hadn't intended on creating that moment, but it turned out to be the catalyst that our family really needed. It broke a lot of the tension and silence over what was going on. Everyone had been holding in so much emotion and that video was the wrecking ball that knocked the walls down. In a sense it kind of brought her back from being a living ghost to being Gina and Mom again.

That went on for about half an hour and then the kids brought us back to the moment. They tend to collect themselves much quicker than adults, which again was a blessing. We moved back to normal Christmas morning with me putting together toys, and them playing with their new presents on the floor. But that moment, that magical hour, really lifted Gina throughout the day. I imagine it very easily could have gone the other way and regressed into a death march, but it didn't. You could see it in her eyes; she felt loved.

At that point, it was only 9am and it was already a great day.

3 7

ONE FOOT IN TODAY, ONE IN TOMORROW

WE TREATED THE EXTENDED family portion of Christmas Day the way we did Christmas Eve…the way we always had. It was never a big production, pretty much just dinner at my mom's, but it was always nice and it was something I always looked forward to.

I'm not sure of the exact moment but at some point as the morning slipped away, so did my cheeriness. I tried my best to block out the ugliness, but it kept picking at my brain that this was the last Christmas. I put on a bold face, but I went through the day pretty much with my guard up. Out of the corner of my eye, I kept an eye on the girls. I wanted to make sure they didn't slip into sadness that would taint their Christmas, their last Christmas with their Mom.

I started feeling a little better as we walked through the door of my mom's house. My family had been a source of strength for me, and I was thankful for that. Sometimes it was something they said and sometimes it was just being able to sit with them and not talk about anything. They had a very calming affect on me.

This day, however, had the potential to be disastrous and if I were smart, I would have talked to my family before that night about how to treat things. Last night was one thing, but today was the actual holiday and if there was any day that people would dwell on Gina, today would be it. With so much going on it slipped my mind to lay down some ground rules for the situation with them, but God love my family, they were appropriate throughout the entire evening. That's not to say they didn't show the love. It was more evident that night than it had been probably in years but it seemed to come from a place of thankfulness and genuine love for our family than of pity or despair. Nobody dwelled on the issue at hand and I know that made Gina a lot more comfortable.

My sister Robyn and Gina stole away for a bit and that was actually kind of nice. They had become close throughout this whole ordeal because Robyn's such a great nurse and to be honest, it made me feel good that Gina had her to turn to. But sitting there, watching them from across the room, my brain began to flash-forward to the next year. It was like watching a movie, knowing that it was never going to be like this again. Like I said, I spent that evening with one foot in the present and one playing out scenes and being scared shitless of what lay ahead for me. I was able to filter myself though. I had a lot of things that I wanted to say to my mother or sister or whatever, but I didn't.

Leaving had this unspoken weirdness to it. At least for me anyway. We gathered up the kids like normal but when everyone was giving their goodbye hugs as we walked out the door, I slipped back into "movie watching" mode. It appeared as though Gina felt it was normal, not like it was her last Christmas, so I made sure I appeared that way too. But I sure as hell didn't feel that way. Any sense of normalcy left me early that morning.

I held a lot in that day. Once we got home, we put the kids to bed and that was a real out-of-body experience for me. I kind of stepped back and let her do it, but it was painful to watch. She was struggling both physically and emotionally. We tried for a normal goodnight, and thankfully, the kids were oblivious to the magnitude of the moment. They were in their beds, gave us both kisses, told us they loved us, and wished us a Merry Christmas one last time.

When we were finally safe in our bedroom and the day was officially behind us, I felt the pressing need to talk to Gina about a lot of things. The problem was I didn't want to spoil what had up until this point been a great holiday, so I didn't press the issue. I just kept the sadness buried. Besides, she was all fired up because tomorrow was the day her family was scheduled to fly in. I wasn't fired up about it. I wasn't a big fan of her family, but seeing her so genuinely excited and looking forward to something, it was hard not to be excited for her.

That's kind of how it was at this point. I was much more in tune with her…much more than ever before. I was much more attentive to her needs. I tried to make her comfortable and take care of things since I knew she would never ask. I'd get her pills, rub her back, and rub her feet. That was always big with her. Her feet were so swollen you could see in her eyes how good it felt to have someone rub them. It always scared me because she'd become so frail and riddled with pain I was always scared I would hurt her. But you just play it by ear and end up finding your groove, figuring out where that line is between pleasure and pain.

That night, we went to bed in two totally different frames of mind. I lied there recapping the day's events and put a dark bookmark on it, knowing I had just experienced my last Christmas with my wife, while she was excited for her family's arrival the next day.

3 8

THE NEW YEARS BALL DROPS

THEY WERE SCHEDULED TO arrive late morning and planned on staying through New Years Day. It had been so long since she had seen them. Her sister Camilia and husband Juan were here about a year-and-a-half before, but outside of their visit it had been years. She hadn't seen her sister Anita in years and I had never even met her sister Natlalia. Her mother and brother Tomas were all coming as well. She was excited not only to see her family, but also to show off her family and home to them. She was proud of us and the home we had built. With the exception of Camilia and her mom, none of them had ever seen our house. They knew our old house but they didn't see what Gina called her dream house. Ironically enough, they all resented me for it. Maybe it was rooted in jealousy or maybe it was because they didn't like me, so to see us doing well just further incited their disdain for me.

I arranged for a shuttle van to bring them from the airport to the house. Not that we didn't want to greet them, but there were so many of them and with luggage it would have been impossible for us all to ride together. They arrived at the house and watching her with them made all the headaches and the outlay of cash worth it. I say outlay of cash because I was the one footing the bill for all these people, for both their round trip airfare as well as their hotel bill. I know it makes me sound like a miser and a bit of a jackass, but even when you are doing something for the right reasons, when you are paying for people who you don't like it's still a tough pill to swallow. But I did it with a smile on my face. After all, it was all for her.

The week between Christmas and New Years I pretty much disappeared. I worked a lot and let Gina enjoy her time with her family. I also allowed myself to enjoy my time WITHOUT her family. I didn't pull a complete Houdini however. I spent a little bit of time with the family and one day I took my nephews to Sports Authority to buy them some baseball equipment.

The crazy thing about New Years is that very few people think about it until it's right around the corner. You're so focused on getting through Christmas that once you do, you realize, hell, New Years is less than a week away! Making New Years plans was a struggle for me. Knowing full well this was going to be the last one, I wrestled with a lot of different ideas. Part of me wanted to stay home with just our family and part of me wanted to really do it up big. Gina was pretty non-committal on anything. Whatever we did, I wanted it to be special, but at the same time, I felt like I should keep it as normal as possible because to do anything outlandishly grand would have made Gina feel even more conspicuous. It's weird, not knowing if you should ignore what's staring you right in your face, or grab its hand and dance.

In the end, we went to the Holiday Inn where her family was staying. They had a typical all-inclusive New Years Eve package that was very geared towards families. They had a fabulous indoor pool and in Chicago, come January 1st it's usually pretty brutal, so to be able to get into a swimsuit and fart around in the pool was something that both the kids and I were looking forward to. Our friends John and Colleen got a room and came along to celebrate with us. They have a daughter (Sarah) who is restricted to a wheelchair so it was a nice thing that we could all do together.

We spent most of the evening at the pool. The kids splashed around and the adults lounged in beach chairs nibbling on snacks and drinks. It was actually pretty nice. Gina was in some pain but she was soldiering through it as best she could. I could tell she was really trying to make this work for me and I was trying to make it normal for her. As the evening progressed, the kids played themselves into a tired mess, so by about 10pm we made our way to the room. By this time Gina was in some serious pain, so she decided to take some pain meds and hang out in the room with John & Sarah. The kids lied down and within minutes they were fast asleep.

The hotel planned a celebration for the stroke of midnight but at about 11:30pm I looked at Gina and could plainly see she was hurting too bad to do anything. I didn't want to miss the celebration so I went next door and knocked on Colleen and John's door to see if they were going to go down. He was going to stay with their daughter but Colleen joined me and we went down to the celebration.

And thus we enter another chapter of my bad judgment. I didn't find out until later but Gina was pretty hurt by my selfishness there, and I can't say I blame her. Not to defend my actions, but at that point after having been with her family for so long and having had too many drinks at the pool, I had to get out. Should I have stayed in the room with Gina? Absolutely. I can't even imagine what must have been going through her mind as the clock struck midnight on what we both knew was her last New Years. We were ushering in the year in which we both knew she was going to die, and there she was…in a hotel room…without me.

As for my dumb ass, I was having a good time downstairs. Colleen wasn't in the same situation as I was but having a daughter in Sarah's condition meant sacrifices for her as well, so getting out and being able to cut loose was a treat for her as well. The booze lifted my mood and helped me forget for a bit the gravity of everything staring me in the face. Colleen and I were having a good time and while there was nothing to insinuate that it was anything but completely innocent, Gina's sisters thought I was flirting with her. I chalked this up to the fact that they hate me, but I can now see where they had a right to be pissed. It was completely innocent, but here I was, out celebrating the New Year while my dying wife was in our room. We didn't stay long. In fact we got down there around 11:45pm and were back in our rooms by 12:30am. When I came back in I gave Gina a New Years kiss and laid down in bed. I was exhausted from all the drinking and dancing so I fell asleep pretty easily without any thought of this being the last New Years with her. I was drunk and just zonked out.

Gina's family was pretty shitty to me when we met for breakfast in the morning. Like I said, I don't blame them now, but at the time I chalked it up to us not liking each other. The one thing that did put some pep in my step was that they were all leaving that day. When we left the hotel, we all went our separate ways. They got on a shuttle to the airport and we got in our car and went home. I was happier than hell to wave goodbye, but it was sad watching Gina saying goodbye to everyone. I mean, everyone there knew this was really goodbye. Given her condition, this was almost certainly the last time they would ever see her alive. Gina was pretty quiet for the rest of the day. She did, however, mention that she was hurt by me for leaving her alone for the stroke of midnight.

If I can offer you one piece of advice – actions speak louder than words. My actions said some pretty shitty things that night and I hurt her pretty bad. I have to say, I felt like a complete ass. Still do. I think I apologized a hundred times but it didn't matter. After a while, I left her alone. Luckily New Years Day is made for guys, so I just kind of tucked myself away on the couch and watched football.

3 9

NOT LONG NOW

ALL I CAN REMEMBER about January of that year is my swollen, sunken, pain-riddled wife walking through the house. The cancer had spread so much it was literally eating away at her. The pain was unbearable and her body had become so weak that she needed a cane to get anywhere. Her legs and joints were swollen, her belly was filled with fluid, and her face was what they call "moon face" from the steroids to help manage the pain. It hurt me to see her in this condition because she was such a beautiful woman. I don't mean that to sound shallow, but she was such a beautiful woman even six months before. She saw it too. I tried to reassure her all the time of how much I loved her and how beautiful she still was, but to see her reduced to this tore at me every time I looked at her. It tore my heart out and the worst thing was knowing there was absolutely nothing I could do.

It made me nervous to see her going through this. Remember, we weren't doing any treatments, so any meds she was taking at this point were strictly for pain management. It's nothing I would wish on anyone but once you go through it and watch it unfold like I did, it really makes you understand how cancer patients end up with morphine addictions.

The weak economy was playing a role in January's typically rough work cycle. I tried to come home earlier from the office as much as I could. I even started to let go of some of my extra-curricular activities like basketball with the guys and stopping off for a drink after work. That's not to say I didn't need them for my own sanity's sake, but I made myself a promise after the New Years Eve debacle that I wasn't going to worry as much about my own head and my own sanity. There would be plenty of time to do that after she was gone and every slash on that calendar was a stark reminder that day was not far away.

Even with my newfound dedication, my selflessness was tested. Gina's temper was getting shorter and shorter. Not just with me but with the girls too. For the first time I could ever remember, she and the girls were genuinely not getting along. Hell, she gave Amber the silent treatment for two days over something so trivial I can't even remember what it was for.

I don't know how, but I could sense at this point that we weren't too far from the end. I didn't necessarily think she was going to die right away but I could tell she was getting worse and anything I needed from her was going to be harder to get. There were still a lot of things I needed to learn from her just to keep the house going in a forward direction once she wasn't here. Things like the bills, her sense of organization, things about the kids schedules and doctors and such. We still hadn't covered any of that.

Finally, I mustered up the strength to ask her to teach me some of these things. To be completely honest, I was scared as shit to ask her. I had played out a million approaches and finally went with a soft, "When you're ready to show me, I'd like to see how you do it." She was receptive, though I could see in her eyes that it hurt. How could it not? In so many words I was asking her to prepare me for life after her death. She knew it and I knew it.

Even then, it took me asking multiple times before she would sit down and show me. I don't know if it was because she felt like if she didn't do it then she wouldn't die or what. All I know is it must have taken some building up to for her because all of a sudden one day, she sat me down at the kitchen table, covered it with piles of bills and other important documents, and we went over it all.

If the words "sticker shock" mean anything to you then you know exactly how I felt. It wasn't as if we were in a bad financial situation I didn't know about, we were still okay, but whoa was she spending money! In hindsight I can understand. For a woman who always took care of everything to suddenly be confined by pain to her house and then her bed, she felt as though she needed a purpose, so she bought things. QVC and Home Shopping Network were her vices and they got to know her (and her credit cards) very well. She bought all sorts of things. Jewelry, clothes, gifts for the girls, gifts for other people. She just shopped. What could I say? Like I said, I understood…even though for the first few seconds I looked at the credit card statements I was instinctively filled with anger. But I swallowed it back and brushed it aside and I'm glad that I had that self-control. Especially now, looking back on that day. I could have really hurt her feelings had I lost my cool.

Throughout that month, the 'casserole ladies' of the neighborhood kind of took over. Our friends around the neighborhood knew what was going on and how she was deteriorating, so they would bring over food. That was a Godsend. With as much pain as Gina was in, dinner for the most part consisted of the girls and me at the table with Gina laying down upstairs. She didn't come downstairs as much anymore, as she was getting too weak. Jackson was working at UPS and going to school so his schedule was all out of whack. Plus he was a real S.O.B. at this point. I haven't mentioned him much in the story recently because he really distanced himself from the family. If I didn't see his dirty laundry every now and again, it's like I wouldn't even remember that he lived there.

As the month progressed, there was somewhat of a changing of the guard around the house. I was starting to handle things more and it was a big adjustment for me mentally as well as physically. I fumbled around a lot. I freaked out a lot. It might not sound like much, but it was exhausting to work all day, and then come home to run a household and take care of a dying wife, two little girls, and a son with a chip on his shoulder. I know there are people who do that everyday and let me say, I tip my hat to them.

Come the end of January I knew I was going to need help. There was no way I could handle all of this on my own. My friend suggested I get a nanny through a licensed service. I talked it over with Gina and she reluctantly agreed. I say reluctantly not because she was going to have to give up some responsibilities, but because it was just one more telltale sign that she was breaking down. As it turned out, Gina's best friend had a sister Nona who was available. That was nice because there was already a familiarity and comfort level with her. We felt like we could trust her.

In hindsight, I wish I would have held out and worked at it a little harder. Not that I didn't try, but I didn't give it 120%. I should have taken the lead at this point with a lot more things. For example, I could have figured something out to make for dinner and then taken it upstairs for us to eat in the room with Gina. I wish I would have talked with the girls more about what was going on as it was happening. I regret not getting them some professional help right then to help walk them through it all. To this day the girls went through very little professional counseling. Jackie did eight weeks of grief counseling after Gina died and Amber did one, but I really wish I would have made them go for longer. But we'll get to all that later....

40

THE BALL STARTS TO ROLL

JANUARY 29TH **WAS THE** day that we finally took Gina to the hospital. She had been deteriorating on a fairly regular basis but when I woke up in the morning, I knew today was that day. She was practically immobile.

I had gotten the girls off to school and right about that time, my cousin Crystal and her husband stopped by. She was shocked by how bad Gina looked and convinced me to call my sister Robyn. As she and I described Gina to my sister, Robyn convinced me that I needed to take Gina to the hospital.

Gina didn't want to go and I can't say I blame her. Even though nobody said it, we all knew that this was a one-way ride to the hospital. She fought me and my heart was breaking so badly I would have given in to her, but they convinced her and she reluctantly agreed. They helped me get her to the car because she was too weak to walk. I hate to describe it this way, but it was like getting a crippled ninety-year-old down the stairs. The only problem was that it wasn't a crippled ninety-year-old, it was my forty-year-old wife.

We loaded her into the car and I took her to the hospital. It was a very surreal ride. My head was spinning, yet I had this unreal calmness to me. Gina was very focused on her pain and that was all she talked about on the drive there. I did everything I could to drive softly, avoiding anything that even looked like even a crack in the road. Once we got there, there was no waiting to be admitted or anything like that. I pulled up and boom, they took her right in, got her right into a room, and made her immediately comfortable.

Now for the problem. As of January 1st, Dr. Smith was working in Libertyville and only his partner was at the hospital where we were. Now his partner might have been a nice guy and he might very well have been a good doctor, but I didn't know this guy. Dr. Smith was our doctor, not him. To top it off, this new doctor was being very elusive with information, which really chapped my ass.

Mind you, all of this was happening while the girls were in school. On top of this doctor pissing me off, I was trying to figure out what to do with the girls and Jackson. I had game planned that no matter when the day came, I wanted them to be with their mom when she passed. At this moment the girls were at school and Jackson was at Harper Community College. Neither was too far but when you don't know exactly where you stand, ten seconds can be the difference between saying goodbye or not.

I wanted information from the doctor as to where we stood. When he finally told me what I needed to know, I decided not to go get the girls. We were close to the end but this wasn't it. There was no need to disrupt their day. Their world was going to be turned upside down soon enough. I called Jackson on his cell to let him know what was going on and figured I would get the girls after school. Between working nightshifts at UPS and then going to school for the majority of the day, his schedule was all over the place. He and I were still having our problems, so he was shitty to me on the phone. At this point he had delved so far into his newfound religion that he thought of me as the Anti-Christ. I didn't want to fight so I let it roll off my shoulder. I gave him the update and he said he would come by on his way to work that night.

I spent the next few hours just sitting there with Gina. She was in a lot of pain and they had given her a good amount of morphine, so she had no cognitive skills whatsoever. At some point a woman dressed in business attire came into the room and asked me to step into the hall to discuss hospice options, which believe it or not was something I hadn't prepared for. I hadn't really given hospice any thought but when she said this to me I kind of figured it was part of the whole hospital process. I wasn't aware it was a separate entity unto itself.

That conversation took about fifteen minutes and was bizarre. My head was spinning. Who does this kind of meeting in a hallway? And at that time? I guess in hindsight that's the best way to handle it, and because of Gina's rapid decline, it makes sense that it had to go down this way instead of going into their building for a preset meeting. I was also under the impression that hospice was something similar to transferring your hospital room to your house, with a bed, nurse, etc. I was shocked to learn that what it actually was, in our case anyhow, was transferring a hospital bed, but the nurse would only come a few times a day and that was more to administer pain meds. There were no real check ups or medical procedures. It was basically keeping her comfortable while she waited to die.

A few hours later as school was ending, I went to pick up the girls. I think I cried from the minute I closed the car door in the hospital parking lot to the minute they climbed in. As they got in the car, I told them that I had to take Mommy to the hospital because she was in a lot of pain. They asked me if we were going to be able to take her home and for a split second, I didn't know what to say. I told them maybe and that seemed to make them feel better.

When we arrived at the hospital the girls were visibly nervous, so I tried to calm them down. Before we went to the room we stopped by the gift shop and the girls bought Gina some flowers. Standing there watching them pick out flowers made my heart break in so many ways. It was breaking for what I was going through, it was breaking for what they were going through, and it was breaking for what they didn't even know was about to come crashing down on them. The tears just kept coming and I was really worried I wasn't going to be able to keep it together. Reality was setting in fast.

Walking them down that hallway was very surreal for me. As soon as we got to the room, the girls bolted and ran to her side to hug her. Seeing that broke my heart and tears began to well up again. Gina was lucid so she knew everyone and what was going on around her. That night felt simultaneously like the longest and shortest one of my life. When the girls were hungry I took them down to the cafeteria to eat dinner. They were obviously scared to be there. Jackie didn't quite understand but Amber got it. She knew what was coming, but she held strong.

We talked over dinner and I can't tell you how scared I was at that very moment. I was scared as their father for what they were about to go through. I worried for their emotional loss and how they would handle it. I worried about keeping the house together and being able to raise them right and give them everything they would need and were about to lose. I was scared as a husband for what I was about to lose. I was scared to be alone. I was scared of having to walk back into that house without her. Even though we had been distancing from each other, when it came down to it, she was more than just my wife. This woman was my best friend. She was my everything—and, to this day, she still is.

The walk back to the room was a long one. It was weird; even though we had only been there less than a day it felt as if I had been there for months. Maybe it was the lighting, maybe it was the weight of the situation, but I was already sick of the place. I wasn't happy to be there but I knew we had to be; just by looking at Gina, I could feel her pain.

I don't know what came over me but when we got back to the room, I gave up. I remember it clear as day. As I stood looking at her lying there with the girls by her side, I started praying for God to take her sooner rather than later. I felt guilty as hell as soon as the thought entered my brain but anyone could see that it was over. Somehow the cancer had ramped up its speed so much that in roughly one month we went from all sitting on the couch on Christmas morning hugging each other to this.

Word spread pretty quickly amongst our neighbors and friends. Some even made their way to the hospital. I witnessed the shock in each of their faces as they came in the room and it killed me every time. The last time most of them had seen her she was markedly better. The weird thing was that I didn't feel the total closeness between Gina and me that I thought I should have. I was certainly heartbroken over what was going on, but Gina just seemed to shut me out. I tried to be loving and comforting and affectionate, but she wasn't responding to it at all. Granted she was on a ton of morphine and pain meds, so I'm sure her unresponsiveness was due to the heavy dose of drugs and her mind being so flooded and freaked out. But still, I felt hurt. For all we had been through and as much as I loved her, as she lay on her deathbed, I felt like the woman I considered to be my soul mate didn't consider me hers.

All I wanted at that point was to get her stabilized so we could take her home. You could see in her face that she didn't have long but I didn't want it to end here. It felt too cold and routine. That was another one of those things we never discussed but I felt that if she was going to go out, I wanted her to go out in the house she built with the family she loved.

41

DRY RUN

WE STAYED UNTIL VISITING hours were over. The nurses had been checking on her regularly, so they kept me abreast of what we were looking at in the way of time. The nurses convinced me that she was stable and the best thing for me was to get a good night's sleep. I was torn leaving, but with all the pain medication, she would be fast asleep all night. Besides, I felt like the girls were going to need me more than ever. They were shaken pretty badly, so I wanted to be there for them.

The ten-minute ride home from the hospital was chock-full of me fielding and deflecting questions from the girls. I wanted to be honest with them, they deserved that, but I didn't want to tell them that their Mommy was going to die. As we drove that night, I remember feeling very lonely in the front seat, but at the same time, very, very close to my girls.

I also remember how utterly shitty it felt to walk into that house with just the three of us. It was absolutely awful…as if it were a dry run of what my new life was going to be. I know I had been trying to prepare myself for these sorts of things but seeing the finality barreling down on us was spooking me. As we took off our shoes in the foyer I whispered to myself, "…Get used to it because this is what it's gonna be like."

I got the girls ready for bed fairly quickly and then sat in their rooms with them. They were ten- and seven-year-old at this point and each had their own room, so I had to alternate. It was the right decision to go home with them. We said prayers and talked. About fifteen minutes after I tucked them in, I saw them both standing at my door wanting to sleep with me. They would do that from time to time when they were scared, and I could tell they were scared. So there I was, lying in my bed with my two girls, with them sleeping and me just staring at the ceiling. My mind was racing in fifty different directions. Part of me couldn't stop thinking about Gina and what was going on with her. I kept trying to picture what was going on and how things looked in her hospital room. I started thinking about what preparations I was going to need to make, like hospice, getting her home, where to put her, etc. Part of my mind was on the girls sleeping next to me and on the imminent change that was about to hit their worlds. For the first time, some panic started to set in, not as much about Gina as about being a single Dad with two little girls and Jackson I know I've said it before, but I was so worried that I wouldn't be able to handle it all. To keep the house in order, to give them the love of a father and a mother, to be nurturing, the important things. It was all very weighing, very saddening. I don't know that I have ever been as depressed as I was in that particular moment.

The next morning the girls seemed a little better as they got ready. I checked in with the hospital and it looked as though Gina still had some time and would be coming home for hospice, so I sent the girls to school. That morning I spoke on the phone with a woman about hospice care. To be honest, I figured that this would be something the hospital would arrange or at least offer some assistance with. Today many hospitals are starting to hire Nurse Navigators whose job is to help patients and their families down the line from the moment of their diagnosis through hospice, but that wasn't the case for us. It would have been nice for someone to give me a heads up that this was something to think about, and maybe include some sort of referral service or something. You would think this would be something maybe even Dr. Smith's office would have prepped me for.

I was shocked, however, to learn how minimal it was. When I got to the hospital, Gina was in a lot of pain. She was coherent however, so we discussed it. She didn't want to die in the hospital and I didn't want her to either. She handed me a sketch she drew of my office at home and how she wanted it to be set up for her hospice bed.

I know some people might find it eerie to have their wife die in their house, like it would stain or taint that room. I have to admit, as much as it seemed like the right thing to do, part of me worried about her dying at home. It wasn't a memory I wanted nor was it something I thought the girls could handle. I mean, how was I supposed to go into my office and work knowing that was the room that she died in? And what do I do about it? Do I express these concerns to Gina or do I swallow my tongue and deal with it? I didn't want the house to be a funeral parlor but at the same time, it was in essence my wife's dying wish. It would be an easy decision if it was just my own insecurities holding me back, but I was also worried about the girls. The house was completely her. She decorated it, she ran it, and she raised a family in it. I wasn't sure if it was right to denigrate all of that with their last visual of their mother being her dying and then wheeled out of the house with a sheet over her.

It felt like a catch 22 situation. If I said something, I was being a good dad trying to protect my girls, but at the same time, I would be an asshole of a husband if I denied my wife her dying wish. I had no clue what to do.

The day was long. It was nice spending all that time with her and I was trying to soak up every minute, but good God, sitting in a hospital just drains the hell out of you. I took a lot of walks through the hallways and even tried to get some work done when Gina would doze off. It wasn't my best work but it was nice to force my focus elsewhere. I went to get the girls at 3pm and to be honest, I really needed that break.

The rest of the night was pretty much a repeat of the night before, except that the girls were less scared this time. Jackson came by the hospital to visit and took the girls home for me so I could stay. I stayed with her until the end of visiting hours and the nurses were forcing me out the door. I took that as kind of a good sign, thinking that if they thought things were bad enough, they would have let me break the rules and stay.

4 2

BOOM

ALLOW ME TO PAUSE here and mention something. A lot of times women in this situation are out of their minds on medication. They drift in and out of coherency and at times they say things that make absolutely no sense. My advice at this point is if you hear something you don't understand or something that hurts you to the core, try to remember that. It won't be easy, I know, because to this day I wrestle with what Gina said to me that night.

When I was getting ready to leave things still felt pretty normal. It was snowing out so she told me to be careful driving home. There she was on her deathbed, and she was thinking of me first. My heart melted. But then when I told her I loved her she looked right at me and said, "Tommy…you still don't know me."

Nothing has ever taken the wind out of me like that statement did. Ever. I was completely taken aback and didn't know how to take it. When I asked her what she meant, she just shook her head and repeated it. I didn't know if it was the morphine talking or if she was being unabashedly honest with me. Either way, I walked out of the hospital in a mixed daze of anger, hurt, confusion, and fear. With all of those emotions in the mix, anger was the one that seemed to win the battle and rear its head. How dare she throw that out at me! How dare she challenge me to read her mind. What the hell did that even mean?

As I turned up our street, a chill washed over me. The air felt stale and still. When I walked in the house, it was different than it had been the night before. This time I could feel her absence. I was still fuming at Gina's comment as I undressed and got ready for bed. But I calmed down enough to start running through the logistics of the hospice arrangement. I didn't get too far though; instead I took a Tylenol PM and zonked out.

The next morning I got up and got the girls ready for school again. They were adjusting pretty well at this point to Mommy being in the hospital. I wasn't going into the office at this point (obviously) so after dropping them off at school, I went straight over to see Gina. On the drive over, I was still obsessing about the remark from the night before and how I was going to address it. I was still thinking about it, when I walked into the realization of a nightmare. My sister Robyn stopped by to see how Gina was doing, and she was talking with the nurse in the room. Gina had taken a sharp turn for the worse overnight.

I stood there staring, utterly stunned at how bad she had gotten in just eight hours. Immediately I was disgusted with myself for not staying, but I quickly shrugged that off and got my mind in the moment. Being a nurse that deals with this sort of thing on a regular basis, Robyn has seen this play out, so she knew exactly where we were. She explained to me that there would be no moving her now and that hospice was no longer an option. It was imminent and in so many words, she told me it was going to happen that day.

My mind started racing a million miles a minute. My head got hot and my shirt collar felt as though it swelled so much it was choking me. I couldn't move. It was as if everything around me was a moving blur but I was moving at the speed of molasses. I just sat next to Gina and stared at her. Tears were welling up in my eyes but they wouldn't fall, so literally everything was a blur. I looked at her but talked to Robyn. The first thing I asked was if I should go get the girls but Robyn said no. She could read her breathing and even though it would most likely happen that day, it wasn't going to happen in the next few hours, so she thought it best to leave the girls at school.

I'll say this, thank God for Robyn. I realize most people don't have a nurse for a sister but if you have anyone you can trust to be with you in that situation, I advise you do. Someone that can keep a cool head and grab the wheel when you freeze because that's exactly what Robyn did, and I am forever grateful for that.

Robyn left the room, only to appear a short time later with a pastor who happened to be on the floor. He came in and held both my and Gina's hands and prayed. Gina was so unresponsive and limp I had to focus to see if she was alive and breathing. Robyn left while the pastor was in the room and started making some phone calls for me. She called my folks and my younger sister. I imagine they called some friends because once again, word got around in a hurry and people filtered in and out all day. I just sat with Gina the entire time. I didn't move. I don't even know if I got up to use the washroom that day.

A lot of that day is pretty vague in my memory. I know I sat and held Gina's hand the entire time, only letting it go so I could get up to kiss her on the forehead, but I really don't remember most of the other events that took place. I do remember asking her to hold out for the girls and Jackson to come say goodbye. The morphine was pretty strong and she was pretty incoherent, so I don't even know if she knew anyone was in the room.

Robyn went and picked up the girls from school. I don't know what she told them but they were already crying when they entered the room. They went right to Gina's side and started talking to her. They were so adorable and scared, and that's when I almost lost it. All I could do was hug them and answer every question that came out of their innocent little mouths.

Little by little the room filled up around us. By 4pm everyone was there in the waiting room. My entire family was there, the girls were there, and some friends and neighbors had come by. I couldn't really focus on it at the time but I was so thankful I had some people there with me and if you have any say so at all, I suggest you do too. It was a world of help at a time when all I could feel was despair. The only person who hadn't come was Jackson. I tried to call him and I'm sure everyone else did as well. She never regained consciousness that night with the girls there. I let them come and go between the room and the waiting room. After all, the floor was full of cousins, aunts, grandparents, you name it. My mom had pretty much taken over watching the girls so I could focus on Gina.

It felt like a dream. That whole day, from the moment I walked in to the hospital, felt like one long, slow moving dream. As much as I was prepared for it, I wasn't prepared for it at all. She was in so much agony, I began praying to God to take her quickly and peacefully. I felt a little guilty about wishing for my wife to die, but if you could have seen her agony. As the night waned on I became more and more intent on watching her chest rise and fall. I saw it get slower and slower, almost to the point to where a few times I felt my own heart stop because I thought she had stopped breathing.

The night dragged on slower than anything I had felt before. It was agonizingly long, but it seemed peaceful. When 11pm came I had my sister Ellen take Amber home for me. Jackie had asked me earlier in the night if she could stay, so I let her. She went to sleep in the waiting room with my mom while I stayed in the room with Gina. Jackson was still at work at this point. At this point it was pretty much a vigil in the room with people going back and forth between her room and the waiting room. There was a ton of people there.

I just sat there talking through the entire night. I don't know if she could hear me or not. I know she was still physically alive, but with all the pain meds and edging that close to death, I have no idea what kind of mental functionality remained. Regardless, I let it all out. I told her how much I loved her. I told her I would take care of the kids. I told her everything I could think of, knowing full well this was going to be the last time I would ever talk to her.

Her breathing slowed so severely and had become so shallow I thought she had died. I just looked at her and felt this feeling rush over me that was a mixture of relief for her and sadness for myself. Oddly, I didn't freak out like I thought I might. I can't say the same thing for everyone else in the room. I can't say what was going through my mind right then, but I just froze. I thought I had just witnessed my wife and best friend die.

An instant after that however, I saw her chest rise ever so slightly and realized she wasn't gone. THAT was a weird feeling. It was like getting a dry run on watching your wife die. I kind of brushed it off in the moment and everybody around me seemed to as well. We were all so intently focused on the present moment that we couldn't be bothered to think back to what we thought we had just seen.

We all let our guard down and collected our breath. Some retreated back to the waiting room while most of the others stayed right where they were. My mom went to check on Jackie and once she saw that she was fine, she came back into the room.

Then about fifteen minutes later, without any warning or fanfare, it was over. It wasn't like in the movies where there's this big moment or anything like that. It was that simple; one minute she was breathing and the next she just stopped. I saw her chest go motionless and when I looked up at the monitors, I knew. My body seemed to know as well because unlike a few minutes before when I thought she had passed, this time I just let go. The tears came rushing out as I collapsed onto the side of her bed. Every bit of strength and energy and emotion just came rushing out of me. My legs went limp, I couldn't hold my head up, and I was exhausted with sadness and relief. You would have thought I had just run a marathon.

As you might imagine, when her monitors started to flat line the nurse's desk was alerted. As all of this was happening and everyone was hugging me, I saw the doctor enter the room. My head started spinning into what felt like a whirlwind as I watched him approach the other side of the bed. It was like an out of body experience watching him check Gina for a heartbeat. Then at 12:15am on February 1st…just short of four months after we were told she had six to twelve months to live…he pronounced my wife dead.

43

I LITERALLY DON'T KNOW WHAT TO DO

I WISH I COULD TELL you the details of what happened right thereafter, but I can't. I honestly can't remember what was going on around me. One distinct memory I do have though is telling Jackie what happened. It happened so fast and without fanfare that without any buildup, we didn't think to go wake her. Then as it happened we all got swept up in the moment and nobody went to get her.

When I did go get Jackie, she was furious. My mom had woken her up in the waiting room and while she didn't tell her what happened, she could tell her mom had died by everyone crying. I know you might be thinking that I robbed her of her mother's last moments and you may be right. But part of me was glad she was sleeping because I didn't want that to be her most pressing memory of her mother. Seeing her walk down that hallway though, my already broken heart shattered into a million more pieces. I scooped her up and gave her a huge hug and a kiss. I told her that Mommy died but it was okay because now she was heaven and in peace. She wasn't hurting anymore.

As you would think, she immediately started crying, but what kind of caught me by surprise was the anger that flew so quickly. She was mad right away that nobody woke her up. I have to be honest, I don't know what the right call was to make. Would I do it differently if I had the chance? I don't know. I really don't.

I'll say this, I thank God I had the support around me that I did that night. To have my mother and sisters right there with me was a God-send, not only to help me but also to help take care of the kids. For that brief moment in time, I wasn't the sure-footed, brick-spined father. I had been reduced to a sobbing heap.

My best friend Mark had called Jackson almost immediately after Gina passed and told him what happened, then he took off for the house to go get him. He didn't want him driving in that condition and I love him for thinking straight when I clearly wasn't.

Everyone had left the room. As I stood out in the hallway with Jackie, I considered taking her in but then thought it would be better if waited for Jackson and we went in all together. So Jackie and I just held each other and told each other that we loved each other. My heart was breaking in so many ways both as a husband as well as a father. After a little bit, I took her back to the waiting room to sit with my Mom, and I walked back to the room. Once I got there though, I didn't know what to do. I stood in the room; I went out of the room. I was a man with no country. I felt scared and awkward going up to Gina right then. Just an hour before I was sitting in there holding her hand, but then sitting there felt taboo, so I just looked at her from the doorway. She looked so peaceful, finally, but to be honest, she looked like she was just still sleeping.

Once Jackson got there, we all hugged and walked in together. Here we are, I thought. This was how it was now. We had finally started what we knew was barreling down on us. I didn't keep Jackie in there long. I'm not sure why but at that moment my protective nature kicked into high gear and I didn't think it was right for her to just sit in there crying over her dead mother for a long time. I gathered her and Jackson up to walk them out, but Jackson wanted to hang back for a minute. I understood. After all, this was his mother and he was much older than Jackie. He understood this on a whole different level. So I patted him on the shoulder and Jackie and I left the room, giving him the chance to do his thing. When he was done he came to the waiting room and sat with Jackie so that I could go in alone.

This time I felt comfortable walking up and sitting with her. As I sat down, that familiar thought went running through my mind that this would be the last time I was with her. This was the first time I had seen someone just after they passed so she didn't have that look people normally do when you see them at a wake or a funeral. Even still, I just started pouring out. I kissed her and talked to her as if she could hear me. I told her how scared I was to be on my own and how much I was going to miss her. For the first time, I told her a lot of the things I wish I had said when we were still at home and she could hear me. I think back to that a lot now and it still eats away at me. It kills me that I didn't push forward on the preparations and I didn't tell her these kinds of things when I knew she could hear me and appreciate them.

Walking out of the room I felt the finality of it more than ever. It was almost a dreamlike feeling, like you finally know where you are going to be. As I headed towards the waiting room, it was as if my emotions had run out and now my brain was moving on to the next thing. I was already thinking about tomorrow and what to do for funeral plans.

As I got to the doorway of the waiting room, I saw the kids there with my Mom and sister. Everyone was still there and I can't tell you what a comforting sight that was. They all waited for me. But standing in that doorway, it hit me. I didn't know what to do next. Nobody from the hospital had come to the room and explained anything to me. Was I supposed to wait for them to come take her? Was I supposed to just leave? Where did I find out any information on what to do next?

Not long after, a hospital rep came up to me, offered her condolences, and asked me out into the hall. There she explained that I would need to wait just a bit longer for them to enter some of Gina's details into the medical certificate of death. They also needed some information from me like which funeral home we had decided on, since the funeral home would be contacted to pick her up. Thankfully, my mom and I had discussed this the night before. She actually brought it up to me that I would need to make some decisions but she would be happy to take the lead on making any arrangements as I tended to Gina while she was still here. It was in this conversation that we settled on a funeral home close to the house.

After I filled the hospital in on everything they needed, we were free to go. So there we were, less than an hour after Gina had passed, walking out of the hospital. Thankfully we didn't have to pass her room again to get to the elevator and that was just fine with me. I held Jackie close to me as we walked, and as I looked in at other people's rooms, it was as if each one was its own separate movie. I was oblivious to it before, being so engulfed in my own drama, but now I felt this irresistible urge to look in each room as I slowly walked by. It was odd but everything felt so distant. Like I was walking but I couldn't feel my feet hit the ground. To be completely honest, I could barely tell that I was moving.

44

HOME ALONE...BUT NOT REALLY

MY SISTER ELLEN WAS the one to break the news to Amber. They had left the hospital only about an hour or so before Gina died, and it was a forty-five minute drive to Ellen's house. There was no way they were going to make it back in time so I made the decision to just let her tell her. Amber was ten-years-old and knew it was coming. Should I have brought her back that night? Maybe. Do I regret not having the conversation with her myself? I don't think so. I know it sounds like something I should have absolutely done, but like I said, it wasn't a shock. She knew it was a grave situation and at ten-years-old, as traumatic as it was it was, something that was fully anticipated from the moment she walked out of the hospital.

I can't really remember the rationale of why I let her leave or let Ellen tell her, but looking back now I can say that they were little girls and I was doing everything I could to simultaneously include them and protect them. Trust me, it's a very tight rope to walk.

Between the events that had just transpired, being smack dab in the middle of winter and in the darkest part of the middle of the night, the car ride home felt like it took forever. Nobody talked. We didn't turn on the radio. With the exception of the sniffling, it was absolutely silent. As we got home, everybody was completely spent. Jackie went into her room and got ready for bed fairly quickly. Amber was still at my sister's, so I tucked Jackie in and then went downstairs.

As it turned out, some of the people that were at the hospital came over to stay with me. They all came by and we sat around the kitchen, had some drinks, and told stories for hours. It was good for me to laugh and I was glad that they were there. Had I come home alone I don't know that I could have handled it. When I finally did go to bed, it was awkward. Although I felt numb and exhausted, I could sense a different air in the room. I had grown somewhat used to her not being in bed with me, but it felt different than before. It was as if I could feel that she wasn't alive anymore. Out of habit, I lied down on my side of the bed, but my God did I miss her. I reached over and grabbed her pillow, pressing it to my face to catch any remaining whiff of her scent. The reality was too much for me.

I've heard stories about people wondering or obsessing about what was happening with their loved one's body once they had died; they visualize where the body goes, the inside of the morgue…creepy things like that. I don't know why, but I didn't. When I walked out of the hospital that night, I think some sort of switch went off in my brain that saw her body as only a vessel that was no longer her.

You would think I would've slept forever having been so exhausted, but my body was restless, and I woke up after only a few hours. Never before have I woken up with such a feeling of heaviness and sadness pressing down on me. It actually felt like a manhole cover sitting on my chest. I laid there for a few minutes just stirring in the sadness, but then my mind jumped to all the things I had to do, yet had no idea how to. All my preparations for this day were purely mental. I had to buy a burial plot, book and arrange a funeral, and get her obituary to the newspaper. You would have thought I would have at least touched on these things before, but I never did. In part it was because I thought we had more time. The other reason for it was her denial. That goes back to the communication issues we had and my lack of strength to force the issue. Things like this were too morbid for me to take on back then, so I always pushed it off, thinking I would just take care of it when the time came. Well, as I lay there in bed that first morning, the stench in the air told me that the time had come.

It was too much for me then and it is too much for me now. I could feel that she was gone and just burst out into tears. I knew I would never wake up with her again, or ever see her again; I felt thrown into the thrust of her absence, and it overwhelmed me. It was only 7am and I already felt beaten for the day.

It was a process for me to get out of bed that day and for a lot of days after. Even today, mornings are still always the roughest. That first day was the worst. It was all about doing things in steps. I forced myself to get out of bed and into the shower. After the shower I sat on the bed and very easily could have just lied back down and started bawling again. I had to push myself to get dressed and go downstairs.

As I was moving around in the kitchen people were starting to wake up, and you could tell they were waking up with me on their minds.

Mark spent the night on the couch and was already up planning a grocery run. My buddy Carl called to check on me. My sister Robyn called to let me know she was on her way over and was going to go through some pictures with the girls to make a nice photo collage. I was amazed at the outpouring of support but at the same time, not at all surprised. I just shuffled through it because my mind was filled with the desolate anticipation of going to the funeral home.

As I mentioned, Mom and I spoke the night before at the hospital before Gina passed and made some plans. When she did go, Mom called the funeral home and arranged a meeting for 8am.

I let Jackie sleep in. I figured it would be better to let her get her rest while I went and took care of the details. Sandy and Charlie spent the night and told me they would stay with Jackie while I went and made the funeral arrangements. Amber was still sleeping at my sister Ellen's house.

Walking out of the house, I remember hearing Mark go over the list of things he had to get from the store. My sister Robyn had arrived by then and was helping him with the list, as everyone knew people would be coming in and out and an Irish wake would materialize. Less than eight hours after Gina died, people were jumping onboard to help fill her role. It didn't make me feel much better, but it was nice knowing I had so many people around me to help because already it was too much for me to handle.

45

DEATH SHOPPING

IT FELT STRANGE PULLING the car out of the driveway. It was very awkward and very unnatural. Normally when I get in the car, the first thing I do is tune the radio to either The Score (a local sports radio station) or a news station. Today I didn't reach for the radio. I rode in silence and about halfway to the funeral home I started crying again. It was that whole wave thing where the tears just come rushing up on you and you can't stop them. So there I was, stuck in morning traffic, crying, and thinking about how bizarre it was for me to be forty years old and driving to make my wife's funeral arrangements.

Having grown up in the area I knew where the funeral home was and while it wasn't far, it was far enough away to give me time to think. I was still obsessing about that last comment Gina made to me. Already that statement was haunting me and there was no way I would ever know what she meant by that.

Turning into the funeral home parking lot, I started to get light headed. I had been here before for other people's services but never in a million years did I ever entertain the notion that I would be here for my wife. I parked next to my mom's car and walked in, not knowing what to expect. My mom, bless her heart, had gotten there early and was waiting for me in the office. I joined them and right from the moment the funeral director shook my hand, it felt like I was being pulled into a business deal. Now to be fair, this is his business. He does this with hundreds of families a year and I'm sure they all feel just as much grief and naivety as I felt. I'm not saying the guy was being insincere, but everything just felt so cookie-cutter.

As soon as I sat down, we started talking about the timing of the wake and funeral. It was Friday, so we decided to do a one-day wake on Sunday and a funeral on Monday. That would give them time to get the obituary written and distributed. I didn't realize that they actually write the obituary for you. (You can write it yourself if you want, but they have a template they follow that most people use.) Then it was on to selecting a casket. I had never even thought to play this part out in my head so it caught me a little off guard. Going down those stairs and into that showroom was probably one of the creepiest feelings I've ever had.

If I can offer a bit of advice here it's this…take somebody with you to do this. There are a number of reasons why I say that and the creepy factor is only one of them. When you walk into that showroom, it's like walking into a car lot, only you have to make a decision within fifteen minutes and you have no idea about anything. All you know is that you are so grief-stricken and freaked out, you can't think clearly. Luckily, I had my mom there with me, and I suggest that you bring someone with you too.

In all fairness to the funeral director, this is their business, so they want to sell you the most expensive casket they can. He started pointing out different caskets and to be honest, they all started to run together to me. Your brain starts to work so fast and process so much that it literally goes into overload. What represents her the best? Does she really need all the ornate 'extras' that drive the price sky high? But this is the last thing I'll ever buy for her, shouldn't I not pay attention to price? You start to dismiss the financial factor and that's where they get you. I don't want to sound like a curmudgeon but it's the truth. You start to shop with your heart and at that moment, there is no limit to what you will do. Do yourself a favor, take someone with you.

Once we selected a casket, we went back upstairs to the office where he pulled out a contract, and if I didn't know any better, I would have thought I was buying a car. He went through it line by line, filling in the information off his notes. Name, dates, casket model, etc. Once he had it all plugged in he printed it out, I signed it, and that was that. One thing I learned was that funerals are not only expensive, (ours totaled out at $18k and I stayed pretty much middle of the road with all of my choices), but they entail a long and intricate process. I had to put down a deposit, but the balance wasn't due for weeks later. They give you time to get through the funeral process and then deal with the insurance companies to collect on any policies before you have to settle up on the balance.

The next thing on the checklist was figuring out what flowers we wanted for the casket. As luck would have it, there was a florist next door (location, location, location - right?) so we walked over there. As creepy as it was walking into the casket showroom, walking into the florist was such a welcome experience. Having the scent of all of those flowers wash over my face was such a jolt from the room I had just left.

Right then, the tears ambushed me and there was nothing I could do to stop them. Like I said earlier, it comes in waves, like a sudden tsunami, and there is no way to hold them back. For the first year, it happened often and without warning. Sometimes it's triggered by something that reminds me of her, and other times, it just happens out of the blue. As time goes on the episodes start to space themselves out more but let me tell you, when they hit you…they hit you.

The initial meeting with the florist was reminiscent of that with the funeral director. It's not that she wasn't being sincere when she offered her condolences, but it's a business, so once they get past that formality their job is to sell you. They show you the most elaborate and expensive options first and then work down from there. I thank God I had my mom with me to step in with rational thinking. She kept things under control.

So there it was. The entire process took about ninety minutes and with that I was back in my car and on my way home. I replayed the whole experience in my head all the way home and cried the entire time. My feelings of loneliness were escalating to new and unexplored levels. Increasingly, I got to know loneliness in a deeper and more intimate way and that's just normal. Especially now, you start to slip into this whole self-pity frame of mind. She's not there to focus on anymore so you start to focus on the hole that's left there…and the hole that's now left in you.

46

ETERNAL DECISIONS

COMING OVER THE HILL, I saw cars. A lot of them. You could tell from down the street that the house was buzzing. I parked and came in through the garage and there were people everywhere. I could see everybody looking at me when I walked in and you could see the sadness in their eyes; it was sadness for Gina, sadness for me, sadness for the girls. It was all right there, staring at me.

I immediately went to find the girls but they were occupied with a lot of neighborhood kids who had come over to play. I'm sure this was their parents' idea, but nonetheless, it was nice. People were coming in and going out at almost the same rate. There were huge spreads of food. You name it and it was there. Mark came back and brought the booze with him and Carl brought a huge deli platter. I sat down and immediately, the stories started flowing. I'm not sure if that was the right way to do it, hanging out with so many people only hours after my wife had died, but it was the best thing for me and for the girls. I felt numb but relieved that there were no tears there, just a lot of laughs. I was enjoying the company and the distraction. Besides, it kept the time moving along, which is not always easy to do.

Gina hadn't discussed much when it came to her funeral arrangements but she did make that known to me that she loved Windridge Cemetery. I had called them when I got back from the funeral home and set up an afternoon appointment to go to the cemetery and pick out a plot. That was weighing on my mind, but even with that, there was something about the camaraderie around me that allowed me to keep checking the clock, yet still come right back into the conversation. By the time I had to leave, Jackson had arrived so he went with me to the cemetery. My buddies Carl and Mark came too. Before we left I went and told the girls where I was going and they didn't seem too interested in going with. All Amber said to me was 'Get Mom a pretty spot.'

Mark drove, so we all piled in his car. The cemetery was only ten minutes away and I know this is going to sound crazy, but it was actually a fun drive. Mark kept us all laughing; even Jackson was laughing and joking. Hard to believe, but it was the best I had seen him. I was laughing too, and I don't know if it was because I was genuinely amused, or just relieved that I didn't have to be doing this alone.

We had an appointment so they were expecting me when I walked in. I don't know that they were expecting four guys to walk in, but I'm sure in their line of business they see a lot of different things. I was glad the guys came with me because once I saw the suited director, all that laughter and any good vibes went right out the window. Immediately it was like being back in the funeral home. He offered his sincere, but canned condolences and then went right into the business of selling me something for my wife's burial. Again, it was like buying a car. We talked a little bit about Gina, he asked me to describe her to him, and then said he had some plots he thought might be a good fit.

Jackson and I got into a car with him, Carl and Mark stayed back, and we rode out through the grounds to look at what piece of property he thought would 'represent' Gina. We got out of the car and walked up to a few plots. That was weird. I was looking at these areas and wondering how they could possibly represent her. Mind you, it was February in Chicago, so all I was really looking at was snow-covered ground. I did notice by glancing at the surrounding headstones, that there were a lot of younger people buried in one certain area. It was on a sloped part of the ground with a waterfall just over to the side, with a gazebo just down from the plot he was showing me. That was what really sold me. The waterfall was nice and I knew the girls would love it, but Gina loved gazebos. I was sold. This was where she would be.

It took all of an hour to drive there, see it, and make all the decisions. What took longer was writing out the actual contract. Like I said, it's a business, so he took that opportunity to upsell me into buying my plot as well. I didn't care though. In fact, it was probably for the best because had I not bought it and someone else ended up next to her, I'm sure I would have felt uneasy. Again, they only required a deposit and allowed you to finance the balance. I just paid it all off when the life insurance money came in. There was no sense in having that bill show up at the house each month. I was already going to be reminded in a million different ways every day that she was dead. No sense in having to get a bill for it too.

While the guy was writing the contract out, my buddies were keeping the mood light by cracking stupid jokes and making me laugh. I'm sure it was probably more appropriate to be crying and grieving, but I was so cried out at that point that the mindless chatter and laughing was good for me. Besides, this didn't feel like I thought it would. I guess I thought that handling arrangements at the cemetery would kick me harder than anything, but in reality it was the easier part of the arrangements. Maybe that's because I was all cried out from the funeral home and the florist earlier that day, but this felt like what it was—a real estate purchase.

By the time we got home, it was roughly 5pm and there were still a lot of people and a lot of kids around. To be honest, there was a full-blown Irish wake in progress. Cocktails were flowing, food was being served, and everyone was just hanging out swapping Gina stories. Everyone was amazingly generous and uplifting; I really don't know if I could have gotten through the day any other way.

Not long into my first drink, Dr. Smith called. I took the phone and excused myself to another room. He asked how I was and told me that he was sorry for my loss. Unfortunately for him, he caught me at a strong moment. As soon as he stopped talking, I laid into him, exclaiming exactly how disappointed I was in him. I told him how bad Gina wanted him to be there, but because of his stupid-ass policy, he took the ride with us but wasn't there at the end. I could hear the guilt in his sigh. There wasn't much more to it. He said his piece and I said mine, and we hung up the phone.

I was exhausted but I didn't feel it. I was cruising on fumes at this point but the phone call gave me a jolt of adrenaline. I went back and rejoined the group. I sat down and Mark handed me a Makers Mark and water. At first I flinched about the kids seeing me like this, but I figured I never hid it from them before so why worry about it now. I had a few and got a little buzzed. About two or three hours later, I was feeling better than I probably should have, and decided to pull out the Christmas video…the one we put together for Gina that kind of chronicled our life. I wanted everyone to see it and to see her story.

Everyone grabbed their drinks and huddled around the TV in the living room, the same place where I watched it just a month and a half ago with Gina. It was eighteen minutes long and that did the trick. Not only did it bring the laughter to a screeching halt, it brought out all the grief and tears not only in me, but in everyone else in the room.

That was the moment for me. That right there was my first really uncontrollable cry. I'm sure the booze helped it along but regardless, I was a mess. The girls had nestled into each of my arms and they were right there, crying along side me. Jackson left not long after we got home from the cemetery, so he wasn't there. It was a good cry, for all of us. It also seemed like a good place to end the evening for a lot of folks. At this point it was 11pm and we were all starting to hit that wall. My buddy Mark stayed over again, but everyone else seemed to filter out to their own homes. After everyone left, I took the girls upstairs and tucked them into bed. It was tough, doing that alone again. It's not that I hadn't done it. Hell, I had done it plenty of times before, but now my own brain was playing games with me, reminding me that this was how it would be for the rest of our lives.

The next morning I woke up with a mixture of that empty, lonely feeling and a hangover. All the plans for the funeral were made so there wasn't anywhere I really needed to be, and that was the hardest part. I imagine that's the case for every man. Once you get through the robot motions, you have to fill the time and deal with your own thoughts and feelings, but you have no idea how. To be honest, I kind of liked the forced attentiveness making the arrangements provided. With nothing to get done, I just gave into my sadness and shuffled through the day.

There actually were two things for me to do, but I was dreading them. I had to write a eulogy and I had to pick out an outfit for Gina to be laid out in. The girls and my neighbor Holly helped me pick out an outfit and let me tell you, that was tough. You try not to think about it, but deep down you know that not only is this the last thing people are ever going to see her in, it's what she'll be wearing for eternity. In some ways too, it was the last thing I would ever do for her. I think that was the part that really hit me the most.

On top of everything else, the minute I opened the closet doors, her scent wafted over me. The girls went at it, bringing out all these different dresses for me to see and trying on her jewelry, but each dress they brought out carried with it a different memory. This was tough for me. Despite their understanding of the situation, in their minds they were just picking out a dress for Mommy to wear. For me, I was just trying to get myself through it. The girls seemed so okay with it I found myself becoming a little selfish, just worrying about my own pain. I must have said something because they were very protective of Gina's things and more than once were very adamant about me not getting rid of anything.

Initially, I had a favorite party dress she used to wear. It was always my favorite dress on her. She and I both loved it because it showed off her curves and a hint of cleavage. I wanted that one but (thankfully) Holly talked me into something a little more conservative. The funeral home had given me instructions on what to bring and thank God they did because I would have never thought of half of it- a dress, underwear, nylons, jewelry, and believe it or not – no shoes.

Once we were done, it took me about an hour or so to pull myself back together. After I did, I loaded the clothes into the car to take to the funeral home. It was nice opening the door and letting that cold, fresh air hit me in the face. The drive itself was one of the saddest I've ever taken. I couldn't get it out of my mind what those hanging clothes in the back seat represented. It was a quick ride and while I was still focused on the outfit in the back, as I turned into the parking lot another sick thought crossed my mind – I'm here for my wife. I know by now I have had more than ample time to grasp that, but you don't really comprehend it until it hauls back and smacks you.

I went in and dropped off the clothes and that's really what it was: a drop off. It didn't take more than ten minutes. He gave me some last minute instructions about the services and told me to start thinking about pallbearers. I knew already who they were going to be; I asked my buddies as well as my two brother-in-laws to play those roles. I know some people really spend time measuring who meant what to their wife, but for me, I just went with whom I was leaning on. These were my friends and she loved them too. Jackson was a pallbearer as well and I know deep down she would have been fine with my decisions.

As I was leaving, strangely enough the eulogy started writing itself in my head. Amidst the eerily quiet setting of the funeral home in the daylight, all of these emotions and thoughts started taking shape in my head. When I got home, I said hello to Holly and the girls, and went straight to my office to work on it. I didn't even bother with the computer, I just started writing it down on a legal pad. I'm not a writer, but I imagine that's how songwriters or poets act when something comes to them. I sat in that office for hours. There was so much to say and my thoughts were completely scattered. I wanted it to be real but succinct and eloquent. I didn't want it to be some hodge-podge gathering of thoughts. Once it was done, I went and got Amber. Remember I'm a salesman, not an office guy, so my typing skills are less than stellar and my handwriting is even worse. I asked her if she would type up a speech that Daddy had to give about Mommy. She nodded her little head up and down so we sat down at the computer and we did it together. For her, she felt proud to be doing such an important job, but for me, I think I could mark that moment as the beginning of my new 'mother' role.

Jackson was still off doing his own thing and I thought it best to let him work through it on his own. I gathered up the girls and we headed out for some food, just the three of us. We went to a place called Village Squire, which was a restaurant that Gina used to love. We used to go there a lot as a family. To be honest, I don't know if it was a conscious decision or not, but as we sat there the girls and I really came together in a way that I didn't know was possible. Of course we had many intimate moments during this whole ordeal, but with all of the preparations behind us now, it seemed like we really gelled. To use a sports analogy, if I had to pick a moment when we really came together as a team – that would be it. There was a lot of Mom talk and a lot of talk about the upcoming funeral. By the time we got home all of us were exhausted. I put the girls in bed and there were a lot of hugs, but oddly no tears.

I went to my room and lay down in the bed and had another one of those first time moments. This was the first time that I was really alone at night. Nobody in bed with me, nobody downstairs, nothing…and I lost it. It was another one of those uncontrollable cries, and it was all I could do to not let the girls hear me. When I was done, I laid there for what felt like hours. It was eerily lonely and really strange lying in that bed alone. As drained and cried out as I was, I couldn't fall asleep. I took a Tylenol PM and that did the trick. I slept so hard I don't even think I dreamed.

Between the physical exhaustion and the Tylenol, I slept much later than normal. I didn't wake up until 9:30am, and even then, I would have continued sleeping if the phone hadn't rung. The girls woke up on their own at about the same time so we all went down and had cereal together. That morning was tough for me. I just sat there, watching the girls eat their cereal in pajamas, and I wondered: will I ever get used to this? Can I do this? Can I be everything these girls are going to need me to be? I mean, I had always been an involved Dad, but this was going to be totally different.

My neighbor Holly came over a few hours later to help get the girls ready. I had to literally push myself to get into the shower. Between being so sad and feeling so overwhelmed by the life that loomed ahead of me, all I really wanted to do was crawl back into bed. But I couldn't.

Today was the day.

I showered, got dressed, and headed downstairs. As I came down the stairs there was a weird sense of anticipation that had crept into the pit of my stomach. I know this sounds awkward, but it felt similar as to when I'm getting ready for a big sales pitch. There was going to be a huge group I had to entertain, the meet and greet, the speech, the show. Don't mistake adrenaline for excitement, but I was very adrenalized for the day.

The minute I laid eyes on the girls, I almost welled up again. They looked so cute and I couldn't help but think, "…these little girls don't have a Mommy anymore."

Fear crept up on me as we loaded into the car. I knew I was going to see my wife lying there, dead, in a casket. Even though there were no surprises waiting for me since I had made all of the arrangements, I was scared to death of what lay in store for me. We had to be at the funeral home by 2pm for family time. The wake was scheduled to open to the public at 3pm. The girls were surprisingly strong on the ride over. They asked a lot of questions and I tried to prepare them as much as I could. I told them Mommy would be wearing the dress they picked out…things like that. I felt alone but strong with the kids as we drove down to the funeral home. We pulled up to the funeral home and there were still no tears yet. Not from me and not from the girls. I couldn't believe though as I put the car in park that it was our 'turn' at this funeral home. That I was going to be the husband at the front of the room shaking hands and sitting on that front couch.

I made it a point to be focused on the girls as we climbed out of the car. I'm not entirely sure if that was due to my parental instinct, or in order to avoid my own thoughts and fears. Either way, you could see in their eyes they were just as hesitant to get this day going as I was. Thankfully, my folks were already there and they comforted us out in the parking lot. As we walked into the funeral home together I could sense the anticipation building inside me. I was scared to see what she looked like. After all, this was a woman that I had seen practically every day for the last seventeen years. The last thing I wanted was for them to do some sort of butcher job on her makeup and have her be unrecognizable. I'd seen that at funerals before, where the makeup artist does what she can but the deceased ends up looking like a poorly made wax figure.

We waited outside the viewing room for everyone to get there. They offered me the chance to go in first but I wanted to wait. I'm sure it looked like I was being polite but in reality, I didn't want to do that on my own. Once everyone did arrive, I went in first with the both girls holding my hands, and Jackson. Opening that door was something else. It was like stepping into another world. The still of the air really takes you over. I could see her the moment we walked in and my heart just dropped. The tears came immediately, but I was able to keep it together long enough for us to walk up to the casket. Once we got there and she really came into view, we simultaneously broke down and just lost it.

This was the first time any of us had seen her since the hospital room when she passed away. Even with all of the preparations and visiting gravesites, picking out caskets, etc; this was when reality kicked me in the balls. This was literally the face of death I had been so scared of. In an instant, all of those 'movie' memories went through my head. It was rough. That moment took me down like I've never been taken down before and will never be taken down again. I'd like to say I held the girls and Jackson and we all cried together but to be honest I don't know if I was holding them or if they were holding me. We were just a mess of arms and tears as we all cried together.

My folks and my sisters had come in behind us. After giving us a minute or two, my mom came up and put her hand on my shoulder. I have to tell you, that felt so good. I'm no mama's boy by any stretch. In fact, I'm always the guy playing Mr. Fix It for everyone else, but it felt good that someone had my back. My mom took on the role of 'watchdog' from that point on. She kept a close eye on the kids and a close eye on me. I can't even begin to tell you how thankful I am to have had her by my side. I realize not everyone has that kind of relationship with their parents, but if I have one piece of advice on how to get through these few days, it's have someone there that can play that role.

I'll tell you, that hour is a weird hour but I'm glad they do it that way. It took me thirty minutes or so before I could really pull it all back together and get comfortable with my surroundings, to ease into the idea that Gina's body was laying up there. As it turned out, my folks and my sisters were the only ones that showed up for the family hour. Her family came later and while it surprised me, it didn't bother me one bit. Not only did I enjoy the intimacy of just me, my girls, Jackson and my immediate family at this point, I needed it. I had very little communication with Gina's family and given our tumultuous relationship, that was fine with me.

By the time the doors opened to the public, I was ready for some new people. Overall the day went by kind of fast. The wake was slated from 3pm until 9pm, and it was a whirlwind of family, friends, business associates, and even some old friends and college buddies I had lost touch with. Even my insurance guy showed up.

Things got a little weird because her family showed up late. We were still kind of estranged because they held a lot of anger towards me, but I didn't really care. I figured this wasn't about them or me and my focus was elsewhere at this point. Even still, they were cold and distant to me and the kids. I knew they didn't like me but I figured of all days, they could put it aside today. Apparently I was wrong, but that didn't bother me. What did chap my ass however was the way they acted at the front of the room. After all these years of them being distant to Gina, now all of a sudden they perch themselves in the front of the room and put on this show as if they were such a close family and were all heartbroken over this. Bullshit! I was already emotionally charged, and that fired me up more than anything. My mom and sisters talked me down as I barked beneath my breath.

I stayed in front of the room as the 'greeter' or 'mourning husband' most of the day. From time to time I would check in on the kids, but like I said, my mom had that under control so that allowed me to kind of stay by Gina and talk with everyone that came. As the day progressed, it seemed to get easier for all of us. The kids got more and more accustomed to the day and played with their cousins. I was in a sort of autopilot mode greeting everyone and thanking them for coming. I was still having a hard time looking at Gina, so I positioned myself in a way where I was pretty much focused straight ahead, looking more towards the line of people as opposed to Gina.

We had an unbelievable assortment of food at the wake; everyone must have felt like they had to bring a dish, from deli trays to plates of cookies. I had stayed up by Gina's casket for so long that at some point during the evening someone brought me a sandwich.

As the end of the evening neared, I kind of took it as the end. I had come to feel a certain solace and comfort because of all the support. I felt just as broken as I did last night but for the moment I didn't feel alone. I had the girls, my family, and this tremendous outpouring of support from my friends. For those of you who ever have a friend in this situation, do them a favor and go to the wake. I can't even begin to tell you how much of a difference it makes for the guy (or gal) standing up there shaking hands. The love and support they feel is immeasurable.

The night ended pretty uneventfully. We did a little prayer as a group and then the funeral director closed the room so the kids and I could say our private goodbye. We went as a family up in front of Gina and said goodbye. The tears came a bit harder once again, but not like earlier. I don't know if that's because we were exhausted from the day or if it was because we were so much more acclimated to where we were. Once we were done, we left through the door closest to the casket. I don't know that we could have walked out the back of the room. We probably would have all kept looking back and I didn't want to be doing that. At this point I tried to be the bigger man and took the kids over to Gina's family who were waiting just outside the doors. We said goodbye to them and let them have their alone time with her.

My folks waited for us and as we left, we all thought it would be a good idea to get a bite to eat and me a cocktail. It wasn't that anyone was hungry, but I needed to decompress a bit and kind of come down from the day. We didn't stay long, maybe an hour or so, but this was a much better transition for both the kids and I as opposed to just going straight home. We just kind of hung out talking about the day and what was on tap for tomorrow.

By the time we left all of us were ready to fall asleep, knowing we had a big day ahead of us. The car ride home was quiet. The kids dozed off and I was all talked out. I just kind of breathed in the briskness of the winter air. It was calming. As soon as we got home I went to get ready for bed and so did the girls. I was surprised at how independent they were through these couple of days. They got their PJ's on and brushed their teeth. By the time I came down the hall they were waiting for me to tuck them in. We did our kiss ritual: I kissed them goodnight and then turned out the light. Jackson was staying with us and was trying to be helpful. He was still very far to the right with his faith and angry with me, but that night he was okay. We said goodnight, I told him I loved him and then I went to my room to get ready for bed.

When I opened the closet to put my clothes away, her scent hit me again. It was hard to be in the room that night, and I would come to learn that feeling would remain for some time. A mixture of sadness and fatigue came over me where I really wanted to cry and felt like I had to, but I didn't even have the energy to break down.

I lied in bed and started thinking about the funeral and to be honest, I was almost looking forward to it. Not that I wanted to put Gina in the ground, but I was so tired of everything this cancer had done to her, me, our family and our lives that I was ready to leave it all behind. What scared me was that after tomorrow, the most final act of it all, I was really going to be on my own with the kids. I know how funerals go. Everybody flocks when there's a death, and throughout the wake and funeral you can't turn around without someone there who wants to help. But once you put the body in the ground, everyone resumes their own lives, just as before. I knew full well that was going to happen with me too, so the impending knowledge that this whole group of people would be fading was a bit unsettling to me. Not that I felt like I needed the throngs of people around, but I was nervous to really be there on my own.

Getting back to the moment, I worried about the girls too. I was worried how they were going to be at the funeral. Not only were there the normal aspects of the funeral, I had decided to show the video that we made for her for Christmas after the eulogy. I thought Gina deserved it, but I was worried about the girls seeing it in that setting. In the midst of all my thinking, somewhere along the line my body just shut itself off and I fell into one of the hardest sleeps I have ever had.

47

NOW I LAY ME DOWN TO SLEEP

I WOKE UP AT 7:30am feeling just as exhausted as I had when I fell asleep. Mornings are always hard for me but this one was especially tough. I really had to push myself to get out of bed. I laid there thinking for a minute, and one of the worst thoughts to wake up to is the realization that it's the final day you will ever lay eyes on your wife. The idea sent a shudder rippling through my body.

Even though the funeral home wasn't too far, the fact that we had to be there by 8:30am meant I already overslept. I hurried down the hall to wake the girls. Just as I started to get them ready, my neighbors Jim and Holly came over with that very task in mind and that was a lifesaver. Holly tended to the girls while I got ready. We all had a quick breakfast and were out the door.

The car ride to the funeral home was a lot like the one the day before: very quiet and very solemn. There were no tears yet, but there was an uneasy feeling that hung in the air. I was wrestling with my own feelings and more scared to go today than I had been to go to the wake. Jackson drove by himself so it was only me and the girls in the car. They zapped me with a few questions, asking whether we'd get to see her again and if we'd get to see her go into the ground? It broke my heart to hear these little girls ask these questions. They should have had their whole lives ahead of them with their mother. They should've been riding with their Mommy to some Girl Scout meeting or gymnastics class, but instead they were riding with their Dad to Mommy's funeral.

I looked in the rear view mirror at them at one point when I was answering their questions, and that vision will stay with me forever. Even now, as the girls are well into their late teens and early twenties, I wonder if I am filling that void for them.

When we walked into the funeral home, it seemed like everyone got there before us. My folks, my sisters, and my cousins were all there with their families waiting for us. Her family was there too, which was very tough. The plan was for us to have a private, final viewing before the doors opened for the public. I held the girls tight to me as the anxiety and butterflies went into overdrive. I knew this was it. The funeral director opened the doors for us and just like yesterday, the tears started immediately as we walked up to Gina. The girls were hugging me as they talked to her. They reached out to touch her so I did with them.

I hadn't touched her yesterday, so this was the first time I had touched her since she died. When I touched her it was weird. She felt so different. I don't know what I was expecting but it didn't feel like her. Her hand was cold and rigid. It was a surreal experience and I thought right then, "…this is just a body. This isn't my wife."

Our time in there was short as the funeral was scheduled to start shortly, so we took our seats upfront as the people started coming in. This was a pretty quick event. The service was short. At one point I was paying attention, but with my arms around the girls I was staring at Gina and zoned out. I wanted to look at her as long as I could because I knew in an hour or so I would never be able to lay eyes on her again.

As the service ended, everyone paraded past her casket to say their final goodbye. Once the final person had gone by it was just us. We stood up and immediately the pit in my stomach sunk my knees. I was fully aware that this was it, this was the last sight of her and the girls knew it too. You could feel it in their sobbing. I held them tight as we walked up to Gina in part to comfort them and in part to comfort me. We all cried and embraced. My heart was breaking right there. It was breaking for Gina; the girls, Jackson, and for me. This went on for about five minutes but it felt like forever. None of us wanted to walk away. Eventually I had to pull the girls back and told them to say goodbye to Mommy. The girls put a few things in the casket that they wanted Mommy to have and we turned to leave.

As we left, I had this permeating feeling through all the tears that we were leaving something behind. We walked out of that room as we are now, with Gina behind us. We left that room strong, but broken.

The casket remained open when we left and I'm glad it was. I don't know that I would have been able to handle watching them close it on her. They didn't close it until after we were out of the room and had closed the doors behind us. Like every other step of this process, my folks and sisters were waiting for us. The girls were both crying with one on each side of me kind of resting their heads on my hips. My mom came right up to us and just held us. The only other people there were the pallbearers, and they were just standing there trying to not make eye contact with me. I scanned each of them and you could see they all had the same sad look on their faces and the same tear in the corner of their eyes.

It wasn't too long before they reopened the doors for the pallbearers to carry Gina to the hearse. I took the girls and Jackson and we let the casket lead us. The kids stared at their mom while I made it a point to look everywhere except the casket. As we came through the doorway and entered outside, I could see into the first few cars and you could see it in their eyes. Not one of them was looking at the casket, they were looking at the girls. I could almost hear them through their windshields saying to their husbands and wives how sad it was for those little girls to have to grow up without a Mommy. Honest to God, it was as if I was watching a movie. As we got to the hearse I still didn't watch as they loaded Gina in. I watched other people watch, but I didn't look myself. I just kept my arms around the girls and waited for someone to tell us to get into the limo.

From there it was on to the church for a memorial service. I selected this particular church because Gina and I had gone here together before. I liked it for the sentimental attachment, but also because it was Christian without being as intense as her Christian Fellowship church. Even though I selected the church, I let Jackson handle the 'booking' of the pastor because he and his mom had been so involved in their church. As it would turn out, we ended up with an associate pastor and not a pastor who knew Gina. As soon as the pastor started speaking, I wished that he had actually known her. He seemed so damn generic in what he said. At this point there was no changing it and besides, I didn't want to hurt Jackson's feelings or offend him in any way.

This would have been uneventful if not for two things. First and foremost, I wanted to play the video that we gave Gina for Christmas at this last stop. As it turns out they weren't set up to accommodate this; however, I would've liked to see them make a little more of an effort. After all, this wasn't some rinky-dinky establishment. It's a mega church with large-scale production capabilities. It might not have been a huge deal to many people to have this request denied, but I'm a bit of a fireball anyhow…not to mention I was short on temper and full of emotions that day. Never a good mix.

This was also where my eulogy for her was to be delivered. I chose to do it here because it would be based around a spiritual service as opposed to a 'death-house' of a funeral home, and Gina would have preferred that, being as she was very much in faith. When it came time for the eulogy, my brother-in-law stepped forward. I asked him to read it because I knew I wouldn't be able to get through it; it was too much for me. It was hard enough to write. As he started, it became more than obvious I was correct – I never would have been able to read it. He didn't get through the first sentence and everything I worried about in being the guy on display, people looking at me, etc, went out the window because I lost it. The girls, Jackson, me…we all lost it. After all he wasn't just reading a speech, he KNEW Gina. They were family. He did a better job than I could have ever dreamed of doing.

Next was a quiet ride to the cemetery. I kept rubbing the girls' shoulders but mostly I was trying to compose myself. As hard as it was seeing her in that casket, watching them put her in the ground was something that I wasn't ready for. Here I was, the guardian of these three kids, worrying whether I would be able to hold it together myself, much less hold them together.

When we arrived at the cemetery, I held the kids back as they unloaded Gina from the hearse. I know they had plenty of unpleasant pictures burned into their minds already, but I didn't think it would be a good visual for them to see their mother's casket pulled out of a hearse as if it were a desk set from IKEA. So we sat in the limo as the people emerged from their cars. I noticed a few people who didn't come to the wake but made it to the funeral and that made me smile. It's always nice when people care like that, especially when it's that order. A lot of people make an appearance at a wake because that's easy. It's after work, so you can swing by on your way home. A quick fifteen-minute appearance and you're done. But for them to take off work and dedicate their morning to something like this, that really says something not only about the people, but about what Gina (or we) meant to them.

I was hesitant to get out of the car. I never did enjoy the spotlight, so being on display those few days felt a little awkward for me. The night before was different because it was solely about her, but the cemetery is where people tend to focus on the loved one left behind. Think about it, in any movie from "Old School" to the end of "We Are Marshall," who does the gravesite or cemetery chapel scene focus on? The grieving ones left behind. It's no different in real life. I knew full well that everyone would occasionally glance at the casket, but they continually turned their focus to me and the kids.

We finally got out of the car and moved on to the gravesite for the final send off. I had planned on a graveside prayer from the pastor and then my fraternity brothers were going to do a fraternity send off to her. They asked me at the wake about doing this and I agreed. After all, Gina knew and loved these guys and I thought it would be nice. Granted they were my college frat buddies, but they meant more than that to both of us. We had grown to be great friends and very much in each other's lives ever since then, so it wasn't like some "Animal House" reunion or anything like that. I realize it was a bit unorthodox but I wasn't worried about that. Odd, considering I was so worried about being a focal point throughout this process, but I didn't care. I thought it was a nice parting gesture from my guys and it was something that I think would have made Gina smile.

I found out later some people kind of spooked as they pulled up to the grave. There was a gazebo pretty close to Gina's gravesite and a lot of people thought that might have been some sort of vision she had. You see, Gina hired a woman to paint a mural in our house and her painting included a gazebo.

As we stood huddled around the grave, that's when I found out Jackson had told the pastor he wasn't needed for this part. To say I was mortified is an understatement. No pastor at the gravesite? There everyone was, standing in the freezing Chicago weather, and all they (and Gina) were going to get was a fraternity brother send off? Not only that, there were no chairs for anyone to sit on. I was so embarrassed that I couldn't even cry. The service was quick and that was that. We didn't have her lowered into the ground in front of everyone, but in this instance it wasn't an option. This particular cemetery doesn't do that when the public is there. I don't know that I would have done it anyhow.

After we made the lunch announcement, everyone dispersed pretty quickly. Like I said, it was pretty damn cold. Even the girls were ready to head for the hills, and my frozen ass was okay with that. After all, I figured we could always come back.

We held the luncheon at the same place we had Jackson's high school graduation party a few years earlier, and it was only five minutes away. It was a small gathering; maybe fifty people showed up and the bulk of them were immediate family. I always thought people fell into two groups when it came to a funeral luncheon: they were either close family and friends or they felt awkward about hanging around and eating for free. At this point, it didn't really matter to me. I was glad for the people who came. My mind was a mixed bag of thoughts and feelings between being relieved that everything was over and scared of what the future held.

Between my folks and Nona, our housekeeper and nanny, I knew I could relax a little. The girls were better hanging out with their cousins. I think being around kids their own age really helped them shake things loose a little bit. They were able to bop around a bit and let go of the heavy load that had been on top of them for the last few days. We stayed a few hours and that really helped me too. I was able to sit back and finally take a deep breath. I didn't have to be on. I didn't have to make the rounds. I was able to sit down at a table and breathe. Everyone found their way to me to say thanks and offer their condolences one last time. When it was time to go my folks walked us to the car and we said goodbye there. As we loaded into the car and pulled out of the parking lot, I actually smiled. I smiled because as scared as I was about the uncertainty of what lay ahead for us as a family, I knew this was the last time we would ever have to drive away from all of this.

4 8

THE FIRST DAY OF THE REST OF OUR LIVES

WE WERE ALL PRETTY exhausted when we got home. We changed into comfortable clothes and just hung out in the house for the rest of the day. I sat down on the couch and mindlessly stared at the TV. The girls and Jackson each headed up to their rooms. We had a light dinner and were all in bed by 9pm.

The next day was Tuesday, the first day of our new normal routine of life. I thought it was pretty important the girls got back in the swing of things for a few reasons. First and foremost, I wanted to get their minds off everything, but also, I wanted to get that one last pity day out of the way. That first day that anyone returns to work or school after being through an ordeal like this prompts a thousand new condolences. I wanted them to be able to put that behind them pretty quickly.

I got up to wake them for school but they were already awake. I helped the girls get ready and that was a strange moment for me. This had always been Gina's job and now, it was mine. It was very strange and overwhelming helping them pick out clothes, brush their hair, feed them breakfast, and then drive them to school. I almost got emotional a few times along the drive, but I suppressed it. I walked into school with them to clear up any notes that they might need. It wasn't as if the school didn't know, but I just felt like it was something I should do. The girls walked into the principal's office with me, but they were quickly dispatched to their classes so I could talk to the principal. Standing there watching them walk away with their little backpacks really did a number on me. I didn't lose it, but the tears definitely started to well up in my eyes.

Everyone at the school was great. They had already made arrangements for the girls to see counselors whenever they wanted. The rest of the administration was very supportive as well and that helped both them and me tremendously. If you ever have to go through this, go talk to the principal to see if you can set something like that up.

Driving home I knew I was going to need to figure this all out. Luckily, we already had Nona in the mix, and the kids were comfortable with her. I don't know that I wanted another new thing coming into their lives at this point. There was enough change to deal with already. A new woman might have been too much.

School started at 8:45am and I was taking the week off from work, so it was about 9am when I returned to the empty house. It possessed an odd silence, and all I could do was stand in the kitchen and kind of look around, trying to decide what to do first. My mom called to check in and gave me some good advice – don't sink in this. She knew these first few days were going to be hard and foreign to me and as a concerned parent and friend, she didn't want me to crumble beneath the silence of it all. She was right. There were things I had to get done and things I needed the kids to get done. Getting them back into school was the first thing and that went pretty well. In fact, they were actually looking forward to going back to school and being with their friends again.

As for me, I ended up spending most of that morning going through sympathy cards and the visitor book from the wake. It was an odd and lonely process as I wrote out the thank you cards and popped them in the mail. I wanted that off my list as soon as I could. It would have been rude to let too much time pass and that was a task I didn't want sitting on my head. If you have to do this, give yourself some time because it takes a few hours to do them if you want to write more than just 'thanks' in there. I felt like everyone deserved a nice little note. After all, they took the time to come out for us, the least I could do was send them a nice note acknowledging their kindness. Reading them really made me feel good again. If I felt at all alone against the world going into that task, I sure didn't when I was done. It brought me a sense of peace. I didn't even cry while I was doing this. It was oddly therapeutic.

After I got those done, I wanted to get the bills knocked out too. That was another thing I never had to handle before. As the days and months wore on, I would find myself habitually looking for something like a bill folder, or a pot-holder, and saying aloud "Gina, where is the…" whatever I was looking for. It's not that I forgot; how the hell do you forget that your wife died? But it was a habit and each time I did it, I caught myself and wondered if I was losing my mind.

I've heard stories from other people too who have gotten this surprise, but usually it was with their mothers or grandmothers after they had passed away. I mentioned before that Gina and I sat down and she showed me then that she had a bit of a soft spot for home shopping because I owed $5,000 worth of balances to both the Home Shopping Network and to QVC. In looking back through the invoices, it was mostly jewelry and mostly towards the end of her days. When I went looking, I found all of the jewelry upstairs in our bedroom, almost all of it still in its packaging. I figure she was probably planning on giving them as gifts to the girls and some of her friends, but she just ran out of time.

Sitting in our bedroom with all of this ungifted jewelry, I lost it again. Here it was, only February, and this was already hands down the worst year of my life, and from where I was standing it only looked like it was going to get worse and bleaker. It wasn't just her death; it was the whole upheaval of our lives. I know it might sound selfish that I was crying about my life's upheaval when my wife literally lost hers, but I was so overwhelmed.

Going through some paperwork I found a gift certificate for a massage Gina had bought for me. I thought about it for a minute and that seemed like the best time to go get it. It struck me that not only was that something I could really use, it was something she had given me. This massage was something she wanted me to have. I'm a believer in signs and for some reason this struck me as her reaching back and trying to make me feel a little better after all we had just gone through. Crazy, I know, but when you let it, the mind can take you to some pretty believable places.

I called and set up an appointment that afternoon and when I got there, I was torn. I sat in my car just looking at the certificate. Gina had written a note inside to me and I was going to have to give that up; I was getting this massage not just because I needed one, but because *she* gave it to me. I didn't want this gift from her lying around unused. She bought it for me because she wanted me to have it. I missed her and this was a way to bring all of those things to a close, if even for a little bit. It was almost my way of honoring her with some alone 'us' time after everyone had gone back to their lives.

Handing it over was difficult. I kind of sideswiped the lady at the counter by mentioning Gina and her death, but I had a hard time letting go of the certificate. It felt really strange to hear myself tell her that too because this was really the first 'stranger' I had to explain my situation to. She politely offered her condolences and to be honest, the sympathy felt good. It felt good because the conversation and sympathy from this woman kept Gina from slipping into the past. As much as I've been saying how much I wanted to leave all of this behind us and move on, in reality I was torn by wanting to keep her current too.

That was the first moment that I began to feel like people were treating me differently; whether or not it was only in my head, I felt that they were treating me with pity and kid gloves. It seemed to happen often, whether it was the lady at the spa or my buddies after we played basketball. Even stranger, it was okay with me. There was a comfort in it. I know that sounds sad and it's hard for me to say because I'm not the kind of guy who ever wanted anybody's pity or help. I've always taken pride in being the guy who lowers his shoulder and gets the job done. But in the midst of that intense, lonely feeling that I was in, I welcomed it.

As I lay on the table, I closed my eyes and imagined it was Gina's hands rubbing my back and shoulders. I know this sounds crazy, but I let myself go and enjoy the last time that she would in any way wrap her arms around me. When I left the spa, I wondered if I could ever feel that way again, or if I would ever be able to meet anyone again. Not that I was looking to meet anyone or anything, that was the furthest thing from my mind, but I wondered if that intimate and emotional part of my life was over. In that moment, I couldn't see it ever coming back.

The girls got home around 3pm that afternoon and were anxious to tell me about their day, which was a first for me. Usually by the time I got home from work they had already bombarded their mother with their stories and notes from the day and I would get the cliff note version of whatever was exceptionally cool. As I listened to them tell me about how so-and-so did this or that, I smiled but inside my heart was breaking. I was glad to hear it all but I was sad that I was doing it in place of Gina.

Dinner felt awkward. When I set the table, I hesitated for a moment before I set out the plates. Normally we would eat at the dinner table and we each had our own chair that we usually sat in. I wasn't ready to do that with Gina's chair being empty so I set us up at the breakfast island in the kitchen. It was almost as if we were flying in the 'missing man' formation or something. It would take us awhile to get back to eating at the dinner table. I don't even know why exactly. It's not like it's this looming castle-like dining room set or anything. We just didn't do it.

That whole week I didn't do much in the way of cooking. We either ate out or we ate at my mother's. Plus, we would pick a lot because there was food everywhere! The neighbor ladies came by often with casseroles and crock pots full of food. I had so many dishes I couldn't remember whose Corningwear was whose. They would pop in late in the afternoon or early in the evening, ring the doorbell, and boom— there's another woman with a pot full of food. It was nice, but to be honest, it began to irritate me. Not the food—the food was fantastic— and I don't mean to sound ungrateful. But I couldn't just open the door and grab the dish. The talking that went with each delivery was incessant and could go on for half an hour. That's what drove me bonkers. The talking got to be too much because it was the same conversation all over again with each different woman. I never got a minute to sit down by myself and breathe. I just wanted to sleep or be alone for an hour to decompress. I know everyone meant well, but it was just too much.

On the other hand, the phone had stopped ringing. A week before it was ringing off the hook, but it quickly dwindled down to calls from just my mother and sisters, (albeit they called fifteen times a day). I understood, and while I admit that many times I saw the caller ID and answered it with a roll of the eyes, I knew they were calling to check on us because they loved us and were worried about me falling into a drunken mess. To be honest, I'm pretty proud of the fact that I kept myself out of the bottle the way I did. It was more than I had expected from myself.

Bedtime that night was a different story. As easy as it was throughout the evening, bedtime was a different animal. Once I got them tucked in and we did our routine (eyes, nose, ears, head butt) Jackie stopped me before I got to the door. She asked if she could tell me something, so naturally I said 'sure.' What followed was a lot of deep, emotional sentiments that shocked me to hear coming from such a little girl. She got very deep, telling me that Mommy was in her heart and that she knows that she's still here. On the other hand, Amber seemed to toughen up and tried to soldier through it.

Jackson was just cold to me. I know a lot of it can be contributed to the combination of feelings of loss and abandonment with an adolescent psyche, but he was really pissed off at me. That's why I don't mention him much in all of this. A lot of times, he just wasn't around. Between working over night and acting so distant with me and the girls, he was very invisible and hardly around.

49

TRYING TO FIND A FOOTING

THAT INITIAL WEEK I got us all in to see a counselor. The hospice facility that I had talked with in the hospital offered grief counseling. I think it was Thursday night that we went, and as it turned out, that would be the only family counseling session we did together. Jackie was already going on her own, and I know it seems crazy, but Amber didn't seem to need it.

I know I should have kept Amber in longer, probably the same eight-to-ten weeks I kept Jackie in, but in all honesty, I seriously thought she was handling it okay on her own. She seemed to be very well adjusted.

It was a mistake. I didn't know it at the time but she was harboring a lot of pent up emotions. Even all these years later, she harbors a lot of anger and I blame myself for that. Her anger isn't necessarily directed at any one person in particular; she just seems to carry a lot of it in general. One thing I noticed as she grew up was that she gravitated to hanging out at friends' or boyfriends' houses where there were both parents. It wasn't anything overtly conspicuous, but I don't think it was necessarily a coincidence either. She craves that and that's something that I can't give her.

I figured this out months later when I did end up in a solid relationship with a woman named Denise. I could tell because that was the time when she grew more comfortable in our house and stayed home much more often. I missed it early on and I kick myself for that to this day, but it's always the tough one who really is the one who's hurting the most. In retrospect, I should have realized her tough exterior was making deeper scars.

Jackson went with us to the family session, but he dove into his faith to work through things and that was okay with me. Lord knows (no pun intended) that I don't like the people he's surrounded with at his church, but it's where he and his mother felt comfortable and that's what faith is all about. I am a spiritual person and I do have faith, but they just seemed very extreme and cultish to me. I let it go though because any pushback from me would have only caused a bigger rift and driven him further away from me and the girls.

As for me, I only did the one family session of counseling and didn't go back to counseling at all until many years later. There were a lot of reasons for my initial decision not to continue with it. I talked to friends, I felt like I was doing okay, it restricted my schedule, and to be honest, I felt like I was too tough for counseling. I'm a grab-life-by-the-balls kind of guy and my vision of counseling was to help harbor the young and the weak. I was wrong, very wrong, but it would take me a lot of years to not only succumb to going but to realize how much better off I would have been had I gone earlier.

The rest of that week I spent organizing finances and insurance, as well as having a lot of heart to heart talks with the girls. Sometimes they would come to me with things, and other times I would initiate a conversation that would turn deep. I don't think the girls looked at it the way I did, but I was trying very hard to feel comfortable as a threesome and it wasn't coming easy. I felt a lot of pressure to fill Gina's role and to be honest, I was trying too damn hard. I obsessed about keeping everything the way she did and making sure no balls hit the ground. It was excruciatingly difficult and to be honest, not necessary. If I had to do it over again, I'd try to relax a bit more and not sweat the small stuff the way I did.

By the end of the week, I was consumed with thoughts about Gina's possessions. She had so much stuff and it was all over every room. She had jewelry and accessories all over our bedroom dresser. Her knick-knacks were all over the family room. We had pictures everywhere. She owned our closet and regardless of how good or bad a day I was having, every time I would open the door it felt as though her ghost was reaching out and punching me in the heart. The scent of her washed over me every damn time. Even our laundry detergent smelled like her. I couldn't bring myself to move any of her things so I just lived around it. I even left her toothbrush in the bathroom.

I didn't do any redecorating for about a year and left all of her personal items like her toothbrush where it was for about six weeks. Even something as simple as throwing away a toothbrush, which is something we all do many times a year, was difficult for me. It was the same with her clothes. I avoided it for about six weeks but eventually I had to get rid of them, for the sake of my own mental health. I kept some of the important things like her wedding dress and certain items the girls would want, but everything else had to go. I thought the best way to go about it was to invite a few of her friends and Nona to go through her clothes to see what they would like. She had a beautiful wardrobe so there was no reason it shouldn't be worn, and there was no one better to wear them than people who loved her.

On the other hand, it took me about ten years to clean out her bathroom drawer with her lotions and foot massager. It got easier as time went by to ignore those things and I'm sure any therapist will tell you that's way too long to hang on.

That weekend things almost felt normal again. Not that I didn't notice the big gaping hole in our lives, but when Gina was alive weekends were always my time with the kids. That Saturday was kind of back to normal in a sense for the girls too. They were coming off a week of school, with no trips between home and the hospital, and no commotion or throngs of people in the house. I tried to treat it as a normal weekend for them as much as me because Lord knew I could use one. I took the girls to the YMCA to swim and that was awesome. That might have been one of the best decisions I made in this whole aftermath. The kids just let loose, splashing around and jumping into the pool, and I loved watching them have such a good time. I got my usual whimsical feeling about being a solo parent, but I tried to push that feeling aside and just enjoy the girls. After we splashed around awhile we went and had lunch. It was awesome just laughing with the kids. No real Mommy talk, no death circling above our heads. It just felt great.

By Sunday, I was ready to go back to work. That was also the day Nona, our housekeeper, was moving in. Now I understand not everyone that goes through this has the means to have a live-in housekeeper/nanny, but I was lucky enough that we had both the space and the finances to afford something like this. Besides, like I said, we knew her and she was someone I could trust to be with my girls.

The girls were looking forward to Nona moving in. Like I said before, they already knew, liked, and trusted her so it made the transition easy. When we picked her up at the train station, the girls greeted her with a huge hug. That really put me at ease because even though we had discussed it and all, kids are fickle and they can change their mind about what they like at any moment.

The honeymoon lasted for about two months.

5 0

IN AND OUT

AS TIME WENT ON, Amber got frustrated with Nona. Some of it was Amber defending her turf to a degree, and subconsciously she tried to take over some of the role of Gina. It wasn't just with Nona though. She fought off any woman that came around. Nona's stint in the house didn't last long, maybe two or three months, and then it was easier for everyone for her to have her own place. She understood why Amber was acting the way she was, and she didn't want to abandon us, but she needed her own space too. She ended up getting a little place in the city and commuted back and forth via train. She was at the house when the girls got home from school, she prepared supper, and then she'd wrap things up and leave around 8pm.

Truth be told, it was weird for me when she was living there too. It felt like I was disrespecting Gina by having a woman living in the house and doing a lot of the things for both me and the girls that she used to do. But that was like the devil on my left shoulder talking. The big picture was that having Nona there really allowed me to refocus and get my head back in order and our life back on track. Having her there meant I could do what I needed to and not have to rush home from work every day or waste our weekends together grocery shopping instead of bonding over something fun. I also didn't need to spend my time worrying about dinner and rides home from school. Nona could handle those duties, and I could be Dad.

We ended up keeping Nona for three years. In reality, we could have gotten away with only two.

5 1

LIFE DOESN'T STOP

I WENT BACK TO work that following Monday, a week to the day after the funeral. Believe it or not, I couldn't wait to get back to work. I was looking forward to it so much that I got into the office at 7am that morning. Now that I had the kids back in their normal routine, I was anxious to return to my own.

For the most part, everyone made a nice comment about being glad to see me back, but outside of that, it pretty much went back to business as usual. I was glad, because I was worried that some people might draw out the pity party. I was happy to see life just kind of move on and not be so focused on death.

At home, I was still trying to get my find my footing. Some days were better than others but I still felt unsure of myself a lot of times. It was probably similar to how a quarterback feels when he goes from running the show in college to taking over a pro team. You know you have the abilities but the game moves so much faster. That's how it was in our house, and I was now the guy under center.

The thing is, even without Gina's death, this calendar year was going to be a tsunami of changes in our house. Jackson was going off to college in the fall so there were a ton of things that went with that. In addition to his aviation school, there was documentation to be taken care of, tuition applications and requirements, housing, and other things that Gina would have handled. The girls had their own things going on as well with PTO, homework, and sports schedules.

I quickly learned that life doesn't stop just because someone else's does.

Running a household (with kids no less) takes a great amount of energy. If you ever hear women say they have a full time job as a stay-at-home mom, don't scoff at it. They're right. It takes a lot of energy, so much that I often found myself holding back energy at work to conserve it for home. I could feel myself pursuing sales less intensely than I needed to. Whether it meant taking care of existing clients or trying to build new ones, my effort diminished due to concerns over the house

Luckily, I recognized this pretty early on and addressed it. I found the best way to deal with it all was to prioritize. I lit up the PTO right away. Rather than deal with their seasonal efforts of popcorn sales, holiday wrapping paper sales, or any other time sucking effort, I just cut a check. I told them this was my one donation for the year and asked them not to bother me with anything else fundraising related. I'm sure I didn't make any friends that way but we both got what we needed out of it. Boom. Done. More time to move on to other things.

Birthdays and sports schedules were different and something I never had to worry about before. Gina handled the sports schedules and would just let me know a day or two in advance if the kids had any sort of game. If I had something coming up or a guys weekend of golf or something, I would check with her to see if there was anything I needed to be aware of. Birthdays were never even on my radar. Gina just took care of any gifts or cards and signed my name. I would find out at dinner what we gave to whom and if I needed to make a phone call to say Happy Birthday to someone. Not anymore. Now I was going to have to keep track of it all. It wasn't difficult, just time consuming.

Depression had kind of taken hold of me throughout the winter; it is the season that, besides its chill, represents the passing of things in nature. On top of all of that, I was raised Catholic and Lent had started on February 13th. I was obviously battling depression at this point, and its known fact that alcohol is a depressant, so I picked Lent as an opportunity to kind of get myself back on track. I gave up drinking for Lent.

As the weeks and months went on, I found a little bit of a groove, but for the most part this was one winter I had to trudge through in every sense of the word. Nothing was making me happy. Sports have always been a release for me, whether that means watching or playing, but they seemed to fall by the way side. I really spent each day just trying to get through it so I could go to bed. The girls had bounced back seemingly nicely. They were fully involved in everything at school, they were playing with their friends and Nona was helping to steer their ship. In fact, she was very attentive to them so I didn't have to be as much. Not that I was absent, but it enabled me to crawl inside myself more than most people could and probably more than I should've been allowed.

As the calendar turned to March, my family talked me into scooping the kids up and heading to Florida for Spring Break. This winter had been harsh, and with the added stress of what we'd been through, they figured we could use a bit of warm weather and sunshine. The girls were elated when I told them and immediately began jumping up and down. I felt relieved; just to see them experience normal, childlike jubilation made me feel like we were going to be okay.

Packing for the trip was a huge learning experience, and one of the things I learned was that packing is a pain in the ass. Any other time we traveled, as you might imagine, it was Gina who would handle everything: tickets, accommodations, packing, etc. My job was to work until it was time to go and then be ready when she told me to be. Now I was the one packing the bags not only for myself, but for the girls. Plus I had to make arrangements for the mail, cats, and all sorts of other little odds and ends I never would have even considered just six months prior. I was crabby for the most part but only because I was so overwhelmed by this. It's amazing that I can handle multi-million dollars worth of business and keep everything flowing smoothly, but packing for a trip with two little girls was almost more than I could handle.

I also had stepped away from all of my stress relievers in my life. In addition to not drinking for Lent, I normally played basketball after work a few times a week. I wasn't in a structured league but once or twice a week, a group of us guys would get together and play ball. Once Gina passed, I quit going because I obviously had more on my plate at home. Now that a month or so had passed, I found myself really wanting to get back to playing. I don't know if it was because the NCAA March Madness tournament was going on and basketball was everywhere you looked, or if it was because I truly missed the game. It was probably a combination of both. After all, I was starting to raise my head above water now and I needed something to sustain me.

I tried but going back to the old Y but it was too much for me. For whatever reason, it reminded me of Gina. I don't know why, but something about that place just screamed Gina to me and it was too much. So I went and found a new gym not too far from the house where some guys played and ingratiated myself into that group. My jump shot might have abandoned me but it felt really good to get out there running around and sweating again.

We had a lot of family things coming up. The Florida Spring Break trip was set for March and then we had two trips in April. We were going to Arizona to send Jackson to aviation school and I also had a wedding in Vegas on the books.

When Spring Break finally came around, I don't know if anyone was happier for it to arrive than I was. I needed to get out of the cold and out of the house. It wasn't just me and the kids going, it was an all encompassing family thing. The only person not going was Jackson as he was still in college and had class. Chalk it up to bad timing, but his birthday fell during the time we were gone. In a combination of us being gone and everyone still being in a funk, his first birthday without his mom kind of just came and went. I bought him a gift and a card, but there was no real fanfare or celebration.

There were so many kids and luggage that it was actually easier to drive. I was looking forward to the ride down anyhow. I had a van so I loaded it up with my girls, my sister Ellen, and her kids as well.

Once it got warm enough to drive with the windows down and the air blowing through the car, it became an enjoyable ride. I think people underestimate how soothing a good windows down, warm weather drive can be, especially the first one on the other end of a long, cold winter. The kids entertained themselves in the backseat with DVDs and games so that let me and my sister enjoy each other's company with the radio up front. It was a nice drive and felt good to be rolling along with the kids in the back. I don't think it was intentional but we didn't even talk about Gina. We talked a lot about where I was with things at home, and I asked her a load of domestic questions. It was nice. I learned a lot.

We drove all day until we hit Atlanta. I'm not twenty-two years old anymore so I wasn't even planning on attempting the straight-through drive. We pulled in and got some dinner, checked into a hotel for the night and then continued on to Florida in the morning. I shared a room with my girls and Ellen stayed in one with her kids. That was kind of fun for me, building that memory with the girls. They loved being in a hotel even if it was just a check-in-and-go-to-bed kind of thing. They laughed and giggled as they got changed into their pajamas and hopped up on the bed they were going to share. I couldn't help but smile as I brushed my teeth. Looking at them, I remember thinking that I had everything handled. They were laughing and carrying on like normal kids, and I remember thinking, "They're good. I've got this."

The next morning we loaded back up in the van and headed for my folk's house in Kissimmee, FL. We'd been there a number of times before for family vacations. I was doing fine until we hit the exit from the highway that takes us into town. Out of nowhere, that 'broken' feeling came over me again. We had come here often as a family and we had taken this same turn so many times before. The closer we got to the house, the more the anxiety built up inside me. I was almost scared to pull into the driveway.

Now I'm not the kind of guy to notice signs and intervention and all that stuff, but more and more, I was noticing strange things. As we walked into the house, the song "Sail Away With Me" by David Gray started coursing through the speakers. That was the last straw- I lost it. That was one of Gina's favorite songs and here it was, seemingly waiting for me as I walked in the door. It hit me like a ton of bricks and floored me for at least ten minutes. Everyone huddled around me and tried to hug it out of me but I couldn't stop. It was another one of those uncontrollable cries that just takes over.

When I was done, I can't even begin to tell you how much better I felt. It felt like a cork had popped and let all the pressure out. I didn't realize it, but I needed that. The rest of the trip was easier because of it. We did all the normal things you do as a family with kids that age: played in the pool, visited the water parks, etc. Mom cooked every day, which allowed us to eat in the sunshine and splash around in the pool. I noticed myself missing Gina being there, but for the most part I felt okay. I actually started to feel a little bit more repaired. I know that sounds crazy, seeing as I was a blubbering mess a few days ago, but it was probably here where I started to become a pendulum unto myself. One day I felt broken and overwhelmed and the next I felt repaired and okay.

It helped me a lot to see the kids playing around in the sunshine, acting their age again. I also had the chance to really talk to my sister. Sitting under the sun, feeling the warmth on my body, watching the kids at ease; I felt like I might have finally won that first round of depression and grief.

5 2

A LOT OF WRONG IN A LITTLE TIME

THE VERY NEXT MONTH I was taking Jackson to Arizona to enroll him in an aviation school. It was a quick turnaround, but I was looking forward to it for us. He and I hadn't been very close in awhile so I thought this might be a nice springboard for us to put things back together. The girls were going to stay home and between Nona and my family, they were going to be well taken care of.

The trip was only four days and we had a good time. We got to the school and got him squared away with his registration, housing, etc. After we did all of that, we went to stay with a buddy of mine in Fountain Hills. We spent that weekend hanging out at the pool, eating, and laughing. It was a nice bonding experience, and it was very much what we needed to start bringing us back together.

We got back home and once again, I had a short turnaround before my next trip. I will say this, I don't like traveling when I'm in a normal state of mind, much less two months after I lost my wife. Even still, the final trip of the three was mine and mine alone. I didn't have any family with me. This was the Vegas weekend and only my buddy Mark was going with me. The couple who was getting married invited me to get me out, but that turned out to be a bad idea. Normally anyone in their right mind is excited about a weekend trip to Vegas. Especially when you're leaving a cold and rainy Chicago. What I didn't think about before hand was how very self-conscious I would feel walking into this wedding alone. I wasn't anticipating anyone's sympathy or anything like that, it just felt weird not having Gina by my side. I couldn't even begin to remember the last time I was at a function without her on my arm.

Watching them get married really affected me. I don't know why, but I never considered the fact that watching something like that would take me back so hard. It really did though. Even though I was watching them, all I could see was the wife I no longer had. I watched as the vows progressed and when I heard the words "til death do us part" my heart sank. It was as if Mike Tyson himself had walked into the room and landed a right hook smack dab in the middle of my chest. My eyes welled up with tears but it wasn't for the bride and groom. It was for what was missing in the seat next to me. That was about all I could handle. From that point, on Vegas became a drink-fest for me. I drank to forget. I drank to smile. I drank to drown. I drank it all down.

After awhile, a buddy of mine and I left the reception and went out in search of trouble. We found some craps tables and really went to town. The drinks were flowing, the dice were rolling and as it turned out, I had a nice little run.

Eventually we walked away from the table, no longer fulfilled by the rush, and looked for some other form of excitement. We found some ladies who were looking for company so we entertained them for awhile. By this point, I was schnockered, and really feeling lonely. Not to mention that it had been a long time since I'd felt the touch of a woman. I didn't even care that they were prostitutes. We were in Vegas, I was drunk, and I was looking for fun. We ended up taking them back to the rooms but that's pretty much where it ended for me. In hindsight, it's probably the best thing that could have happened to me because I was nowhere near ready to be with a woman. Thanks to Ketel One, I didn't have to worry about that anyhow.

It was a quick trip and before I knew it I was back home. Immersed in reality, I took a left turn when I should have settled back in. For some time after that I took over the responsibilities I had to but I wasn't quite the father I had been before I left. I don't know why but I found myself becoming more and more obsessed with my own omissions. In a sense, I went back to being what I was before Gina died. I was the provider. I got my tasks done, brought the money in, and then put the rest on Nona, much like I did with Gina. I started staying out late. I missed tons of dinners. A lot of times I wasn't even home in time to put the kids to bed. I hate to admit it, but I fell into such a self-pitying episode that if the girls couldn't buy it or get what they needed from Nona, they were essentially on their own. Even sadder, they knew I wasn't home and when they remind me of that now, it hurts. I should have been there more, but Vegas seemed to put me in this very selfish place. I was mad. I was frustrated. I was sad. Work wasn't going very well at that point either, which contributed to my cause.

When I was home, I still felt uneasy under center. The house felt very cold and empty to me. It was still all her. Her decorations. Her arrangements. I was trying to figure out how Gina did what she did, but that whole thing felt like it was all was just in effort to fill a void. It felt like someone had carved the heart out of it and we were living in its shell.

In every way you can imagine, just a few months after we buried her I was making every wrong move and choice you could possibly make.

5 3

THE TRAFFIC GOES AWAY

WE STILL LIVE IN the house and to this day, we notice the missing element of Gina. In the months following Gina's death, my family kept checking in on us but they gradually stepped back. Everyone but my mother—she stayed on my ass. To be quite honest, in a weird way she probably drove me to do my own thing more than anyone. I reacted like a teenager, but she made me so defiant that I began to stand on my two feet again.

If I was smart, I would have embraced her help. I might have told her to phrase things differently or back off a bit as she was driving me crazy, but I would have embraced it.

It did bother me that the visitors stopped coming, even my mom. That pissed me off and I resented the fact that nobody would pop in on us. I know that sounds ironic but I think it's got more to do with the girls than me. They didn't give me any reason to think that, so it's quite possible that I was just projecting my own insecurities onto them, but I think subconsciously the girls felt abandoned. I know I did. The girls were rebounding from what might be the hardest thing they will ever go through in their life, and they were doing it with the help of each other and Nona. I won't even give myself any credit because at that point, I was too busy being a selfish ass. During this period, however, my girls grew very tight with each other. Not just as sisters, but on all levels. They became true friends and really learned how to lean on each other, which I'm sure will follow them through the rest of their lives. Yes, they grew up in a hurry and they lost a big chunk of their innocence through this, but they have each other's back like you wouldn't believe. God help the person who ever hurts either one of them, because if you take on one, you take on two.

As spring rolled on and summer arrived, I found myself trying not to talk about Gina with the kids. I thought it best if we kept the memories in our head but focused on the future and moving on. That was another huge mistake on my part and I imagine had I been in therapy, I would have realized this. At the time, I thought Jackie was getting what she needed through her counselor, and while Amber didn't talk much about her mom, I took that as her handling it well, when it was really her suppressing it. As for Jackson, he and I couldn't be farther apart by this point. He rode me continually about my lack of faith and my drinking, so I didn't want anything to do with him. I know that's not the right way to approach things but again, I was so self-absorbed at this point that I made all the wrong decisions.

I should point out that it's not that I wouldn't talk about Gina to the girls. If they wanted to talk about her I would, I just never pushed the conversation along. I would answer their questions and then change the subject. It would take me years to realize that by me ignoring this, it was putting a communicative wall up between us. It was driving a wedge. It was ironic; I, the excessive communicator, was doing exactly to my girls what I always bitched about Gina doing to me.

I think the main problem was while I was trying to get used to my new role of being the clearinghouse for everything, I wasn't. I had a hard time connecting with the fact that I wasn't just the fun Dad anymore who got to enjoy my family. Now I had increased roles and responsibilities and had to be the one who ran everything. I had to be the guy who juggled the finances, got everyone to and from and attended all their games, handed out the groundings, delivered the hugs, ensured dinners were taken care of, lunch money was had, holiday decorations were hung, and a million other things on top of these.

The funeral home had given me some pamphlets on grief and so did the hospice people. They must have put me on some sort of mailing list because I repeatedly got a lot of very helpful information in newsletters and things of the sort. I didn't buy any books or anything, which I really wish I would have. To be honest, that's the main reason for this book now. After all, it's easier to spot a dick in the room when that dick isn't you.

Even to this point, the girls would often come sleep in my bed. Part of it was because they felt bad for me to be alone (I know because they would tell me), but I think the other part of it was that they really just wanted to sleep in their mommy's bed. That comforted them. We would lay in there and talk about Mommy and the tears would always flow, from both them and me. I worried sometimes maybe we should be moving past this, but I always let it go. They were adjusting well in school and their grades were good. I thought those were the telltale signs of whether or not they were doing okay, so I figured this was probably a good thing for them to adjust. To be completely honest, I liked having the girls there at night. It really sucked sleeping alone. Having not gone to counseling or anything, there were a lot of times where I would go in that room or lie in that bed and the tears would just come running. Having the girls in there helped soothe that for me.

5 4

BEWARE OF PREDATORS

I DON'T KNOW IF it was the onslaught of trips but spring went by pretty quick. When we were all home and our luggage was put away, we had one more 'day' trip scheduled to take. We had a family tradition of going to Six Flags Great America every spring and when I say we, I mean me and the girls. Even before Gina had gotten sick or died, that was always OUR day together. I always called it Daddy/Daughter Ditch Day, and we had been doing it for years. That particular year, it was a nice day out, and again, walking through there with the girls bouncing from ride to ride, I felt like I had it under control again.

Before you knew it, summer was here and school was getting out. That was going to be a completely different animal and one that scared the holy hell out of me. It was one thing for the kids to be out of school for a week. I took the time off work and we all hung out together. But it wasn't as if I could take off the entire summer. This was going to be a bit more of a challenge for me with the kids not having any sort of structured days to adhere to. Not to mention I was going to have to make sure that they continued with their sports, and that they got to all their practices and games. Plus I was going to have to watch for the announcements for fall soccer sign-ups, winter basketball sign-ups, etc.

This was also going to be the first time I had to deal with somebody trying to take advantage of me and play on my state of mind. Back in the spring when I went to Arizona with Jackson for his school, it was a quick trip so I had some people who were very close to me house sit and watch the girls. I didn't think much of it but when I got back late Sunday I found out that Amber's whole closet had collapsed. She had so many clothes and crap that the racks couldn't hang anymore and finally came crashing down. The first thing that came to my mind was that Gina would have laughed at that. I called for some closet company to come and give me an estimate about installing built-in closet organizers.

That's the only way I would have probably ever noticed. Amber's closet collapse made me take a look inside mine when I was changing just to see how sturdy mine was. I noticed that belongings in my closet had shifted. It was as if someone had been nosing around and moved some items. I don't know what made me do it, but I looked where I had hidden some of Gina's jewelry when we cleaned out her things back in March.

It was gone.

Without naming names, there were only four people plus me who had known about this jewelry so they instantly came to mind. It was bolstered by the recollection of me hearing someone go on and on about it after she had passed away. I never said anything to her about it but I did ask Amber if the people who were house sitting went into my bedroom while I was out of town. It's hard to pin somebody stealing something on the word of a ten-year-old, but Amber swore up and down that she overheard them one night.

It's odd because when I was working out all the insurance details after Gina had passed, my agent had warned me to watch out for predators. Not creditors but actual predators—people that would steal from me. I will say this, I don't know who stole the jewelry. It could have been any one of the people who knew it was there, it could have been someone they knew. It could have been the cleaning people for all I know. It just sucked that it forced me back into feeling as if the world was stacked against me all over again. Instantly I went from feeling like I had a handle on things to feeling overwhelmed again.

Here we were at the start of the summer and I already seemed to be flailing against the rails. This was a totally different animal than when Gina had first died. Sure, I still had Nona to help me hold down the fort (thank God or I really would have lost it), but as I would find out, this entire first year was going to be a huge learning curve for me.

On the advice of my sister, I signed the girls up for Day Camp with the park district in our hometown. I wasn't crazy about the idea, but it was going to be good for everyone involved. I felt a certain amount of guilt about putting them in there. They had been in camps before, but I already felt bad about having Nona kind of 'fill in' as their "Day Mom" until I could get home. In the summertime, Nona assumed all of the duties Gina would have done before. She took them shopping, took them to the pool, and gave them rides to the places they needed to go. I tried to take more days off to spend with them but it wasn't easy to do. It's not that I couldn't get the time; work was more than happy to let me do whatever I needed to do to get things acclimated, but as a salesman you have to sell, and you can't sell while you're splashing around the pool with your kids. My job entails meetings, long drives, client entertaining, etc. It wasn't as if I had a job that I could just hand off to someone else to cover for me. Not if I wanted the commission anyway.

The time I did take off I did everything I could to spend with the girls. We went boating on the lake with friends, we hung out at the pool, I cooked on the grill, and we went out for ice cream. I felt good when I was with the girls, but otherwise, I felt lonely. Not only did I miss having Gina around, I missed the physical elements of our relationship too. It felt like it had been forever since I had kissed a woman or felt an arm around me.

I had gotten away from the bar scene for some time, but I started going back for a drink and some non-death-related adult conversation. Nona was a good sport and would often stay late for me so I could go by after work for a few drinks. I didn't go often at first. It started off as once a week. Before long though, I was going by closer to three times a week.

That's where it started to go bad.

55

IT'S EASY TO LOSE YOUR GRIP

IT'S PRETTY EASY TO see when you have a clear head that there's nothing good to be found in a bar. The people you see sitting on the barstools every day, as much as you get to know them, aren't truly your friends. You think they are though. After all, they laugh at your jokes, cheer when you walk in the room, and make you feel loved.

I'll cut to the chase and tell you that if you can avoid falling into this, then do so. I might be more adventurous than most, but it doesn't matter if we're talking about drinking, partying, or women, the only thing these 'friends' lead to is falling away from being the person you need to be. I'm not saying you shouldn't find time for yourself or that you should avoid bars. It's when you become a regular that it becomes a slippery slope that you quickly slide down. There were a lot of times I asked Nona to stay until 9pm or so, but I didn't even bother coming home until midnight or 2am. Jackson slept until 11pm because he didn't start work until 2am so it didn't matter much to him, but the girls, they were little.

But the partying caused me to forget. It may have been liquor laughter, but it was laughter and I craved that. I felt like I needed to get away from it all and little by little, I started to look forward to my nights out. At my worst point, my days became nothing more than a lead in to my nights. It didn't matter that it was a Tuesday or that the girls were home. I convinced myself that they were fine with Nona; they were taken care of.

I was as lost as a man can get. I had absolutely no faith. I felt no love. In fact, I was more pissed than anything. Pissed at life, pissed at death, pissed at Gina's church for the people at the funeral. I was a really lost soul.

Even though I was partying, I wasn't promiscuous. Even with the loneliness there was no woman involved. All I needed was the party to hold me. It was escapism at its worst. I developed into two different people. During the day I was Tommy or Dad. That was the guy that got the order, made the schedule, hit his budgets, and got things done. At night however, I became Tommy the Party Guy, and that was the dude who always had the next round, and would always stay for one more. As if that wasn't bad enough, these 'friends' of mine were really what you would call 'enablers.' They weren't friends; they just helped me run away from all the bad stuff at home: dead wife, broken closets, limping cats, crying girls. So for me, the drinks were now my happy place.

As summer wore on, the 4th of July came creeping around. This is always such a fun holiday in our area because we have this community picnic. It's a very cool thing that literally everyone in our subdivision goes to. There's a parade for the kids, all kinds of rides and games, plus lots of entertainment for the adults too. It's the kind of thing you would see in a movie. We would go every year and it was always a blast.

This year would be no different. I took the kids and we rode in the parade in the convertible (the same car Gina and I took on our Wisconsin trip in back in the fall). It was fun, but it felt strange without Gina with us. I felt comfortable there, but at the same time I felt different, like I was missing an arm or something. That took me by surprise because even before Gina was gone, I had been doing these neighborhood party deals solo with the kids going all the way back to Halloween. Even still, it was something I was having a hard time getting accustomed to and this particular day further proved that to me.

It was nice to get reacquainted with the neighbors though. I hadn't seen a lot of them since the funeral so being able to talk and hang out without that cloud of death hanging over our conversations was nice. Don't get me wrong, everyone made it a point to say something about Gina, but they pretty much glossed over it and got into some sort of normal conversation. When the night finally fell and the fireworks went off, everything slowed down. Everyone hunkered down on blankets with their wives or husband and their kids. That's when I felt the emptiness again. Even though I was there with the kids, I felt like a third wheel with all the couples around. Especially since it was the first year she was gone, I could feel everyone peeking and staring at us. It's almost as if I could feel their whispers saying "…Oh, I feel so sorry for them."

Moments like that only led me to more partying. I didn't want to feel that. I didn't want to feel those stares. I didn't want to be the guy whose wife died or the widower with his motherless girls at the park.

I didn't have that at the bar. I wasn't Tommy with the dead wife. I was just…Tommy.

Later in the month, I took a day off work and took the girls out on the lake. We went tubing, skiing, and had ourselves a little picnic on the water. It was a really nice day and I was having such a great time watching them shriek with laughter and bounce around the water. It felt like a normal summer day but just like everything else that year, it couldn't just be a great day.

As we were driving back, I got a call from my boss informing me that we (I) had just lost a big account. I'm not going to go into specifics about how much income that account represented to me, but let's just say it was five digits. Honest to God, I just couldn't catch a damn break. It was like I was continually getting kicked in the balls at every turn. Was it not enough that my wife died? Was it not enough that I was trying to figure out life as a single, widowed Dad? Was it not enough that my life was already turned upside down? Now not only did I have to figure out how to live, I had to figure out how to replace that income. You might think it's an easy fix as a sales rep. Just go land another account…right? Wrong. Even for good sales reps, accounts that big aren't that easy. They take months or years of nurturing. Remember, I said MY cut of that was five digits. Their expenditure was six. I was already getting scared about my industry anyhow. While I never let on to anyone, I was already watching intently to see if I should be looking for another career path.

More often than I care to admit I found myself sitting outside in the yard after the kids had gone to bed (on the nights I came home) enjoying a stiff drink or three surrounded by the emptiness around me. As you might imagine, throughout the summer Gina came up in conversation with a variety of people. It's odd but even though she was my wife for so many years and I was with her step by step throughout the entire ordeal, continually talking about it was not my strong suit. I never brought it up and if other people did, I didn't dodge it but I would get onto another subject as soon as I could. In my mind I just wanted to get through it. The conversation. The summer. This mindset. I wanted to fight through it all and come out the other end where it was warm and sunny and it didn't hurt anymore, but every time someone brought it up it just tore the scab off the wound again.

Sadly, I did the same thing with the girls by ignoring the elephant in the room. Jackie talked to Nona a lot that summer and I felt oddly okay with that. I think that was due to my own selfishness, because if she was talking to Nona about it, then I didn't have to relive it again myself. Like a huge hypocrite, nearly every night I was sitting outside with my drink I would think about the girls sleeping inside and I would decide I needed to be more expressive about it with the girls. But then I would start breaking it down and eventually I would convince myself they were doing okay with everything so it was best to leave well enough alone. I know I was doing nothing more than skirting the issue. It was selfish and wrong and is a time in my life that I will always regret.

I did send the girls to a YMCA Grief Camp towards the end of the summer. I forget who turned me onto it but it's a weekend camp for kids who lose their parents or anyone else close to them. I brought it up to the girls one night at dinner and told them what it was all about. To my surprise, not only did they buy right into it, they were excited to go. It wasn't a lot of money and they stayed in cabins at a campground. All the kids were separated by age groups so the girls were split up for the whole thing. There was a ton of stuff involved: activities like rafting and swimming, group talks, etc. I was excited not only about helping the girls, but selfishly about gaining myself a 'weekend pass' from all Dad duties.

I dropped them off Saturday morning and picked them up Sunday night. The girls had a blast and responded to it well. Not only did they have a good time, it really let them know that they weren't some freak circumstance. They got to see that even though you wouldn't normally think so, there are a lot of kids in the same situation as they are. Honestly, I would recommend it to anyone.

By this point, I was starting to somewhat settle in. I had a loose grasp on making all of the decisions regarding the kids, I finally figured out where everything was in the house, and I was getting used to sleeping alone. I didn't like any of it, but I had come around to it. I could feel myself starting to transform from my old self into not just Dad, but both Mom and Dad. I could FEEL myself becoming Mr. Mom. But the more I settled into my role, the more overwhelming it became. Not overwhelming in the sense that I couldn't do it, but in the sense that it takes so much out of you to navigate each day that it gets hard to wallow in your own grief because you simply don't have time for it. The nights would get quiet, but a few drinks and some ESPN Sportscenter would usually take care of the 'home alone' feeling. Women have chocolate and soap operas; I have Ketel One and ESPN.

As August snuck in, it was that infamous time that all mothers love (or dread), but I had never had the pleasure of experiencing. Back to school. Now here's an experience you almost can't prepare for. I'm not talking about school, I'm talking about school clothes shopping.

For the first time in my life, I had to load the kids up and take them school clothes shopping. Not only is this the first time I had to do this, I had to do it with a ten year old and a seven year old girl. I had gotten some suggestions from my mom and my sister Robyn on where to go and what to get them, so armed with that information, I loaded the girls up and away we went. It was like "Sex In The City" for grade school kids. Kohl's, JC Penney, the mall, we went everywhere. This didn't fit. That was ugly. It was a nightmare. Not to mention, I shop the way a guy usually shops. I take something off the rack, check the size, look at the price tag and make a decision. Apparently this is not the way girls shop. Amber was easy to appease, but Jackie was difficult when it came to styles. There was an abundance of trying things on and picking things out. What I thought was going to be an hour or so at Kohl's turned into a full day event. Looking back, it really was comical. It wasn't fun like riding bikes, but it was fun. The girls got all sorts of new stuff and I got some really quality time with them.

After the clothes were done I pulled into Target and took a look at their school supply list. Holy shit! I hadn't looked at it before because I figured it was the basic pencils, folders, and paper type of stuff. I could not believe how much they had on these lists! People had to laugh because I'm sure I looked like a moron running around Target looking for everything.

The real crazy part of it all was that once we got everything home, we had to get rid of their old clothes that didn't fit anymore. Talk about a bitch of a job. Again, we had to try everything on and see what did fit and what didn't. Not only were we fighting earlier about what we could buy, now we were fighting about what to throw out. I can't win! I remember at one point thinking how much I would rather be at a baseball game or something than trying on all this shit. I'm pretty sure I cursed Gina again at that point as well.

When school started the next week that wasn't really much of a big deal. I had to manage the dates of when to sign them up for what, when what season started and so on, but that was something I was good at. Time management and organization is my forte. Finally, I was feeling like I got the swing of things. I was still juggling, but at least my juggling had a rhythm to it.

Right about the time that school started back up, Jackie started having some health issues. Nothing crazy, but since Gina's death, she had developed some bowel problems. They would come and go but in the fall they really seemed to flare up. I took her back and forth to the pediatrician until they decided that it was probably just nerves. Let me tell you, you know you've stepped into the full-parent role when you have to keep a diary of your daughter's bowel movements. She's little so I turned it into a game with her. "Dear Dr. Braverman, today I felt like I pooped out a chicken bone."

Other than the tummy thing with Jackie, things were finally going well. The girls and I were settling into this new way of life when out of the blue, Nona threw a wrench into the system by having to leave in September. She wasn't leaving forever, but she had to go back home to Ecuador and wouldn't be back until November. Talk about a kick in the nuts. I just got this thing figured out!

I realize not everyone has a nanny, but imagine if your babysitter who you had come to trust and the kids were comfortable with had to bail. We don't realize how much we depend on them until we don't have a good one…or they have to leave. Now I had to re-figure schedules, responsibilities, etc. It wasn't the end of the world but it was going to be a huge pain in the ass.

The first thing on the agenda was to find someone to be there when the girls got out of school. As luck would have it, a neighbor offered to help out. I didn't know her incredibly well, but well enough. She watched the girls after school until about 7pm. She made dinner for the girls but it was routinely terrible, as was the laundry that she sometimes attempted. Her shortcomings really made me miss Nona, and the girls missed her too. I ended up whacking the neighbor after about a month and hired an eighteen-year-old girl on a recommendation. She was an old friend of Jackson's so I kind of knew her too.

56

DATING AGAIN

BY THIS TIME IT was mid-August and I had begun dating. Time frames are always tricky when it comes to dating after the death of a spouse. It really has more to do with the individual person and how ready they are to accept a new person.

I met a woman named Denise at a local restaurant/bar called Cheers. She was a waitress there for a few years and she had actually known Gina. I recognized her, but I didn't really know her; I didn't even know her name. One night she was sitting next to me at the bar as I was talking to Kendra, a former bartender. It was nothing in depth, just shooting the shit, and Kendra was hitting on me. At least I think she was hitting on me. It could very well have been nothing more than bartender flirting.

Denise however, kept talking to me about Gina. She had a friend named Mandy who just passed away from breast cancer as well. I don't know what it was, but this was one of the first times I didn't mind talking about Gina. I didn't try to skirt the issue. Maybe it was because it was a combination conversation of Mandy and Gina instead of just focusing on Gina and me. What really struck me was that Denise was so thoughtful about it. In my semi-sober mind, I sized the two of them up and saw Kendra as the predator who just wanted a one-night stand, while Denise seemed to want a man to talk to. She wanted *me* to talk to. Like I said, she already knew of me and most of my story before we ever started chatting.

Lord knows I wasn't looking to meet anyone. I'll admit, there was an obvious sexual frustration, but I wasn't looking for anyone just yet, and while I might flirt and joke, I wasn't ready take it beyond that. I was still scared on when and how to be ready to cross that bridge. As we were talking, Denise was rubbing my forearm but not in a sexual come-on kind of way. It was more of a soothing, reassuring thing, but that touch alerted me to something I hadn't felt in forever. It reminded me how much I missed being touched. I didn't turn it into anything it wasn't, but it sure felt good to feel a woman's hand on my skin. So we talked more and drank more. I wasn't overthinking anything; after all we were talking about Gina and that oddly made it more comfortable. We talked about kids, hers and mine, and a lot of other things. As the night went on, it became apparent that we had more than just small talk between us.

I don't know if it was the drinks or the building comfort level lulling me into that place, but eventually I saw the door open and I took it. I asked her back to my house and she accepted. We drove separately and the entire drive I was sweating. I was excited and exhilarated, but I was nervous that it might get physical. I simultaneously wanted to avoid any intimacy and craved it. My God, I felt like a teenager.

We walked in the door and I knew the kids would be asleep. Nona wasn't there, so we had the house to ourselves. I felt uncomfortable being in the house with another woman because of Gina. It wasn't guilt, but it was something. I can't really put a label on it.

I poured us each a drink and we sat on the couch. Sure enough, she leaned in and instinctively I leaned in as well. That kiss was to me what water is to a parched man in the desert. My God, I missed that so much! Even though Gina had only been gone for six months or so, it had basically been a year since I had any sort of physical intimacy, as her decline started back in August a year earlier. I thought for a minute to cut it off but once I started, the physical urge was too strong for me to stop.

It didn't go any further than a make-out session on the couch, but my God. To top it all off, it wasn't as if I was just indulging in my own needs and wants. I was oddly comfortable with her. The fact that she was such a good communicator was refreshing for me. Not to mention I had a few drinks, so I was pretty loose myself.

However, I was nervous that Jackson would see us because he left for work at 1:30am. We still had some time, but I wasn't counting on us lying down on the couch talking and then falling asleep! Thankfully the couch is a pit couch; you have to actually walk up to it to see someone laying there. He must have walked by and not noticed, or at least if he did, to this day he's never said anything.

But as we lay there, reality hit me. I enjoyed her touch and her head on my chest, but that guilty feeling came over me again. What the hell was I doing? This was Gina's house! It was as if I had the angel on one shoulder and the devil on the other. The angel was reminding me that it was my late wife's home, and her kids were just down the hall, while the devil urged me to soak in the moment. I felt bad, yet I loved the touch.

I woke up sometime around 4:30am. I woke her up and she left. I never verbalized anything about the kids or my guilt, but she understood the girls didn't need to wake up to a strange woman in the house. I got her number and walked her to the door. I watched as she drove away and felt guilty that it was so comfortable for me to do that. I almost wished I would have had a harder time giving in.

The next day at work I kept replaying the previous night's events in my head and wondered if it was too soon. I couldn't answer myself because my guilt was mixed with an equal amount of excitement. I called her a few days later and left a voice mail. We saw each other at the bar a few days after that, and she was nice. Pleasant. With my confidence brimming and my issues not sorted but calmed enough that I felt like I could navigate the guilt, I asked her out on a real date.

And she blew me off.

Yep. She blew me off with some bad excuse. While that might be a knee cutter for most guys, being in sales it was something that I was not only used to, but sort of incentivized me. I didn't get discouraged. We kept talking and before we left, I asked her out again and she said no again. As I drove home I replayed it in my head and came to the same conclusion that all overconfident, Type-A guys come to. She was playing hard to get.

It's like a roller coaster getting back into the dating game. One minute you're engulfed in guilt and the next you're flying high with excitement. As I sank into the couch, I felt very much at peace with the week's events. I had come to the conclusion that I wasn't getting out there too soon. As a man, I was moving forward with my life. I still missed Gina but I felt this was okay. It wasn't like I was thinking about marrying this woman or even bringing her in to meet my kids. I was just taking a few steps forward and having some fun. Out of respect to the girls, I made a deal with myself to never discuss this with them. They were never going to be cool with this and I could not blame them.

I kept talking to Denise though. Not just because I felt the thrill of the hunt, but because I genuinely liked her. We would talk on the phone or we would meet at Cheers for drinks. The conversations were great. She was really easy to talk to. We would start out talking about Gina or Mandy, but it always evolved into more current life things. I noticed that every time I talked to her, I felt better. I didn't feel alone. Beyond the occasional heart pangs, I was getting used to missing Gina.

Every so often I would ask her out again, and after about two weeks she agreed to go out with me. I took her out for a day date in early October. It might seem strange to get back in the game so soon after my wife had passed, but I think it felt okay to me because there was no bad ending between me and Gina. There was no bitter divorce. I wasn't soured by her leaving me or cheating on me or anything like that. This just happened, and it felt right.

This is going to sound very Lloyd Dobbler (John Cusack's character from the movie "Say Anything"), but I planned a nice little date. I packed a lunch in a picnic basket with a nice bottle of wine and thought we would take a nice little drive. It was fall and the leaves were so changing so I figured a lunch outside on a gorgeous day would be just the thing. I felt good as I put it all together, but I was nervous pulling up to her house. She was waiting on the porch and the minute I saw her, all my nerves fell away and I felt that rush in my stomach. Looking at her as I pulled into the driveway, I couldn't help but smile. I felt alive again!

The night before, I told the girls that I was going out on a date. I was nervous about telling them but I didn't want to lie to them. I expected them to be resentful or mad. I filtered it into our dinner conversation, and when I did, I felt like I was walking on eggshells. Surprisingly though, the girls were excited for me. Jackie didn't shock me as much because being so young, she didn't understand much about husbands and wives and things like that. Amber really threw me. I could see this whole process had moved her way beyond her years. Jackson wasn't at dinner with us but when I did tell him later on, it added to his already negative impression of me as a prick. In his defense, he and his mom were very close so I can see where he would have had issues with it. To be entirely honest, I didn't think he would be on board anyhow, but I didn't want to leave him out of the loop I kept the girls in, and I didn't want to lie to him either.

The date itself was awesome. Butterflies were raging through me as if I were a teenager. I was excited in the days leading up to it and once I got there it got easier as it wore on. The drive there was a fight inside me with guilt in one corner and nerves in the other. You have to remember, this wasn't just my first date since Gina passed. This was literally my first 'first date' since I dated Gina.

I planned the full day because I was thinking long-term. Again, I haven't dated in forever and when I was dating back in my twenties, there was no such thing as 'casual dating.' You were either dating someone or you weren't. So I planned a day trip to New Glarus, WI oddly enough, because Gina and I had driven through it last year on our Wisconsin getaway weekend. I don't think it was anything subconscious; I honestly just remembered how awesome it looked as Gina and I drove through.

The drive was gorgeous and we had a great time. Unfortunately, I had to fight the ghost of Gina a lot on that date. In my own head, I did a lot of comparing and contrasting Denise to Gina, starting with the drive when I would look over at her in the passenger seat. I even brought her up in conversation a few times, which I know was probably uncomfortable for Denise, but she didn't seem to mind. If she did, she didn't say anything.

There wasn't a lot of physicality on the date. Things got a little cozy and kissy as we enjoyed our picnic, but that was it. I'll be the first to say, every piece of me was screaming for more. Christ, it had been a year since I've had sex at this point. Not since August of the previous year. Before that it was in Houston in September of the year before. Looking back, that might be one of the reasons why I fell so quickly for Denise; because when we did have sex, not only was it amazing, it was with someone that wanted to have sex with me. The last few years with Gina were more methodical than anything. There's a whole different level to sex when you're dating than when you're married. And again, I hadn't dated for so many years that I didn't know how to differentiate between excitement and love.

We spent the day together and got back home around 7pm. I could have spent the evening with her too, but I wanted to be home in time for dinner with the kids. I was trying very hard to maintain that balance at home of "me" time and "Dad" time. As it turned out, Dad time at dinner became very focused on the *me* time I had during my date. The girls asked a million questions about Denise, what we did, where we went, and all sorts of things.

The discussion felt nice and led me to believe that everything was progressing along nicely. When I lied in bed that night and thought about the day, I had a lot of mixed emotions. I missed Gina, but I was excited about Denise. I noticed that she was a very calming influence for me. I even kicked around the idea of introducing her to the kids.

57

WORST. BIRTHDAY. EVER.

IN BETWEEN MY MEETING Denise and actually taking her on a true date, my 41st birthday came. To be totally honest, it really kind of snuck up on me. Between the kids getting back in school, Nona leaving, my juggling schedules, and this whole flirtatious air with Denise, I didn't even pay attention to it until I turned the calendar to that week and saw it there.

Gina used to always make a big deal out of birthdays and mine was no exception. Whether it was a family dinner or a party for the kids, we just woke up and enjoyed the day that she planned out. This being the first one without her, there was nothing on the agenda. What was I going to do, tell everyone my birthday was coming and ask what they would like to do to celebrate me? Amber had a soccer game that day, but aside from that was nothing on the docket. I thought maybe my mom or my sister would plan a little something but they didn't. Jackson bought me a card which I thought was nice, until I opened it and read the lecture he had written inside it. The girls were so young he just told them to write their names inside it so they did.

It was hands down the worst birthday ever. That old 'home alone' feeling came running back up on me and I found myself missing Gina a lot. It's not that I wanted her there to dote on me, it was just one of those days that you always associate fun things with and they were always with and directly because of her. She really took care of us and I really missed her that day. Sure some calls peppered in throughout the day from my family and some friends, but that was it. To be honest, I don't even know what I was expecting. Maybe for my mom or Jackson to have the girls put something together. A goofy tie maybe? A homemade card? I thought someone would have thought enough of me to do something to acknowledge the day but there was nothing. Nobody even made plans for dinner. I'll never forget how alone and taken for granted I felt that day. I wasn't mad at the girls, hell they were ten and seven, but the best acknowledgement I received all day was a shitty card from Jackson

Yeah, it sucked.

It's amazing how powerful the words "Happy Birthday" can be to someone both when you hear them, and when you don't.

58

KIDS...MEET DENISE

AT THE TIME, I felt like introducing Denise to the kids was the best option for me, and when I brought it up with her she was as excited about it as I was. In retrospect, I can see that was me not just thinking of myself but wanting to return to normality so badly that I ran for it too fast. I couldn't differentiate between being excited about Denise because of the woman she was and filling the void that Gina's death had created. I didn't think about it at the time. Like a surfer, I just got up on that wave and rode it. But now that it's all behind me, I realize that I was jumping the gun way too fast. Denise had been divorced for ten years so she was ready for something, but I wasn't and Lord knows the girls weren't.

None of that stopped my dumb ass; I did it anyways. I was encouraged into my decision in part because the girls were so inquisitive in an excited way at dinner. I knew public opinion wouldn't respond favorably, but I didn't care.

I set it up for a Friday night in October. I figured we would all hang out at the house, order pizza, and keep it casual. When I brought it up to the girls, they literally squealed with excitement. Denise drove herself and when she rang the doorbell, the girls shrieked. I looked at them and I could tell I had two different shrieks on my hands. Amber was excited and giddy but Jackie was nervous. I can't remember who opened the door, but I was in the foyer when Denise walked in. My head was burning hot and my chest was pounding with nerves. I wasn't nervous about Denise, I was nervous about the girls. This was a big moment. My attention was focused squarely on the girls as she walked in and they seemed pretty okay.

I met her with an awkward half-hug. I hadn't even thought about what to do at this point until the moment was there, and I felt very aware of those beady little eyes on us. We all walked into the living room and Denise had a seat. I went into the kitchen and Amber came up to me and whispered "she's pretty." Again, looking back I think Amber was looking for that same return to normality that I was. Her comments and reactions seemed to make me more and more comfortable with the decision. Denise was scared that even though the girls liked the idea of meeting her, they would snap into some sort of rejection and guilt once she entered their house. Luckily that wasn't the case.

I ordered the pizzas and made it a joking process to keep it fun. Friday nights were always game nights in the house, so we kept that going. Denise had daughters (they were eighteen, fourteen, and eleven at the time) so she knew how to interact with the girls. She hit it off with Amber right away, but I kept my attention focused on Jackie. She's always been a deeper kind of person, even back then. I knew that she would 'play nice' but I was going to need to bridge the gap between her and Denise.

Denise stayed until about 11pm or so. All in all, the night was a success in the sense that everyone had a good time. Actually, it went a lot better than I thought it would. Nobody got a new mommy or anything, but it was a light-hearted evening and it was nice to hear laughter in the house on game night again. It made me feel good to be upfront with the girls too.

Later when I was in bed is when it started to bother me. Even though everyone had fun and it seemed like a win, doubts started creeping into my head and the tug of war was on. Did I do the right thing or should I have listened to the people that told me that it was okay to keep certain things from them, like the fact that I was dating? I always lived with the mantra that if it's okay with me, it's okay to see. Maybe I should have held off on telling them. I surely should have held off on them meeting her, but I just wanted a normal life again so damn badly.

5 9

FULL SPEED AHEAD

STARTING AT THAT POINT, Denise began to become integrated really fast. More by her pushing than me pulling, but I didn't exactly discourage it either. There were a lot of dinners, ice cream with the girls, etc. I didn't question it because it felt so good. Unfortunately, I didn't think about it much either, and I was letting my own turmoil allow it. I don't blame anyone for my mistakes but me, but I sure as hell wish she would have recognized my issues and sent me packing. I was a victim of my own insecurities and I was making my girls victims as well.

I planned a game night for two weeks after that initial night. Everything started off well, but before we started playing my neighbor Holly stopped over, so I invited her in. Holly was a cool woman, so the more the merrier right? What I didn't know and had lost the ability to spot, was that Denise was an extremely jealous woman.

It turned out to be a huge mistake. About forty-five minutes after Holly walked through the door, a near catfight ensued. For lack of a better word, Denise got extremely bitchy and while she never did anything in particular to attack anyone, it hung an awkward cloud over the entire night. Mind you, this was happening in front of the girls and they were clearly uncomfortable as well and taken aback. They liked Denise, but they knew and really liked Holly. She was our neighbor for God's sake.

Instead of taking control of the situation, I rationalized the craziness as Denise 'fighting for her man' and let it play out. It boiled to a head and Holly (being the adult) felt the uneasy tension and left. That's when the absurdity really started to fly. As Holly was walking down the driveway Denise opened the door and yelled out after her "…leave me and my family alone."

That smacked me across the face. Family? This was only the second time she had spent time with the girls and me together. I should have dealt with it right then, but I didn't. I was like that guy in the movie who you can't believe can't understand what is happening right in front of his face. Like a pansy, I let it slide and just tried to calm her down. Eventually she calmed down and decided she should head home. After she left, Amber came up to me and wanted to talk about it. She asked me in a very grown up, adult-like manner what Denise meant by her 'my family' remark. Before I even started my sentence, she continued saying flat out that Denise needs to know that she's not part of our family.

You have no idea how sad I felt at that moment right there. There I was, the Dad who is supposed to be the protector, keeping life moving forward for everyone, and I was the one inserting this crazy drama into everyone's lives. Yet even with Amber pointing all of this out to me in her own way, I was so desperate for normalcy that I looked the other way.

That's the power of loneliness; sometimes it can take down even the strongest of men. I'm not proud of it and it's definitely a moment that I am incredibly embarrassed of, but at a time when I should have been solely focused on my kids, I was trying to fix myself first. Even then, when it was clear to anyone watching this Lifetime Movie of a scenario, I stayed when I clearly should have at the very least addressed it, if not bailed completely. My feet weren't underneath me and my head was definitely not screwed on straight. I shouldn't have even been in a relationship yet at all.

That said, I wasn't smart enough to know or recognize any of this at the time. In fact, I'm such an idiot it wasn't long after that Denise and I not only glossed over the 'my family' incident, but took our relationship to the next level.

60

FEELING RIGHT, LOOKING WRONG

ONCE WE BREACHED THE first meeting, Denise and I began to hang out quite a bit at the house. The girls still liked her and the more she came over the more their trepidations seemed to subside. One night she was over and the kids were in bed for the night. We started in the living room like normal, watching TV and playing around with each other. Nothing crazy, just some kissing and petting, but while we were in the midst of it thoughts were racing through my head. I wasn't worried that the girls would see us, but I was thinking more and more about sleeping with her.

It was a wrestling match in my mind for all things mental and physical in this relationship. It felt right, but it looked wrong. Not just in my eyes but I'm sure to everyone around me. I felt guilty too; guilty that I liked Denise so much and guilty that I wanted her so bad. What did that say about my love for Gina? Did that mean I didn't love her? What if the tables were turned? How would I feel about her acting the way I was? I know I would want her to move on. Maybe that's because standing inside of that kind of situation, I have a better understanding of it than most people do.

Another thing that made me feel guilty as hell was my thoughts of Gina. There were a lot of times when Denise and I would be getting semi-physical and Gina would jump into my head. Then I would start comparing, having visions, and pretending even. Crazy right? Luckily the comparing and pretending didn't happen too much. They were built so differently that even when my mind did go there, it couldn't stay for long. Denise had thinner lips, they had different body structures; they smelled different, etc. They were two totally different women.

It quickly became apparent that this was going to be the night. Once we passed that inexplicable moment where we both knew it was happening, my mind started to race. Where? We couldn't do it here on the couch and I didn't feel comfortable taking her to the bedroom. Not only were the girls up there but that was still my bedroom with Gina. I wouldn't feel comfortable up there. I decided to take her to the basement. Don't worry, I wasn't some high school kid sneaking down to Dad's workshop for some nookie. The basement was finished and comfortable. And it was the one part of the house that didn't scream Gina.

I sold her on it because the girls were asleep upstairs and I didn't want them to wake up to this. It was true, but that's where I stopped with my explanation of locations. No need to bring Gina into the moment anymore than she already was. We giggled like kids as we went down the stairs. As we fell into the couch my mind began racing again. I was excited as hell but nervousness ran a close second and guilt wasn't far behind. Was I going to be able to perform? Could I please another woman at this point? I hadn't been with anyone other than Gina in decades!

It was everything I could do to push all of those thoughts and anxieties aside. That makes it sound like a chore, but at some point, once you decide to clear the gate a man's normal instinct takes over. The act itself was okay. I found myself initially going where I always went with Gina back when we were good, but Denise let me know in her own ways that she liked different things. She cued; I adjusted.

I think one of the reasons it felt okay in my head to take this step was because I was in a relationship. It wasn't a fly by night sort of thing or a one-night stand with some floozy I picked up in a bar. We were a couple and that helped put my mind at ease. I will say, Gina did cross my mind at one point, but not in the way you might expect. In all the times I had played this out in my mind, I was worried that I would look down and 'see' Gina's face. Or I would close my eyes and 'feel' Gina's body. That wasn't the case, but she did pop into my mind when I realized I was just in the moment and not worrying about causing her pain or worrying about her self-awareness. I was just enjoying myself and not worrying about building her self-esteem at the same time. If anything, Denise might have been worrying about mine.

Once we were finished, we lied there and cuddled. I was still very comfortable with my decision and very much at ease with Denise. She continued rubbing my arms and my chest and while that might seem pretty normal, it had been an unbelievably long time since I had something like that. Even when Gina and I were intimate, between the cancer and us just being married for so many years, we tended to just lie on our own. No touching. No cuddling. No romance after. Laying here with Denise I felt a real connection that I hadn't felt in many, many years, and it wasn't just sex.

Admittedly, I did feel a tinge of guilt. I pushed it out of my mind by reminding myself that she's not just gone, she's really gone. I wasn't cheating on my wife nor was I moving on from a divorce. She was dead. Gone. What entered my mind after the cheating guilt left was the slight feeling that as happy and relaxed as I was, maybe this was too fast. It was, but I longed for everything that was laying there with me. Companionship. Partnership. Love...or what I perceived as love.

She didn't spend the night and after she left, I don't remember looking for any sort of forgiveness. I didn't regret the decision that I made. It was what I wanted and what I needed. Not to mention after one year of celibacy, I had a serious afterglow effect working for me too. That was the only time I watched her drive away after sex though. For a variety of reasons, after that first time we started going to her place whenever we were planning an intimate evening. I'd like to say it was because I was concerned with the girls catching us, and that is true, but the reality is that I didn't like being in the ghost of Gina. To me, it was still her house. She still hung over it all, and I didn't like having to push her out of my mind. It was easier to relax and just be me in a completely different environment. Besides, we weren't teenagers anymore. We needed a bed and there was no way I was going to be able to do that in what I still thought of as our bedroom.

I know this is going to contradict everything I just said but bear in mind that was what I was thinking at the time. If I were to talk about it now, with a few years of looking back and working through my feelings, I feel like I should have waited longer. Not necessarily the sex, but I probably should have just found someone to have sex with because once you go there with a woman that you're dating, you're attached. That seemed to attach us faster than I wanted to. After that night, she was over almost every day. It was almost as if us having sex gave her the key to my life. I should have slowed it down but with the holidays coming up, I knew that not only was I not going to want to be alone, I was going to need her help. That's not why I slept with her, but it is why I didn't slow things down after.

Yes, you're right. I'm a selfish ass.

61

A REAL HALLOWEEN GRIN

HALLOWEEN WAS NOT FAR off and I wanted it to be celebrated between the girls and me, so I kept Denise at arm's length for this. I had costumes to take care of, as well as scheduling trick-or-treating and have candy handed out at the house. The first thing on this list was obviously costumes. As any two young girls would, they had grand ideas of what they wanted to be. When we went to the store, the whole episode and primarily that conversation with Amber telling me that Denise was not part of our family was still dominating my thoughts, so it was hard for me to say no to them. I bought everything.

I'm sure most of that was my way of overcompensating for the bullshit I put them through, and that was just as wrong as putting them through it in the first place, but that's what I did. Looking back, this is one thing I definitely learned was a mistake in that initial year or so with the kids. Spoiling kids with love is good, but spoiling them with gifts and things never is. No matter what the reason. I set a precedent with them at that point and in many ways, I'm still paying for it.

The girls had a neighborhood kids party to go to the Saturday before Halloween, the same place we have our neighborhood 4th of July shindig. It's pretty fun, with hayrides, games, and a costume parade. I got them dressed in their costumes and as I was looking at them, I was pretty proud of what I was able to accomplish. I still felt the pang of missing Gina. She was always so good with this stuff, adding in her homemade touches and things like that. The girls looked good, but everything was store bought.

We went to the party and left Denise out of the whole event. The more I thought about 'the incident,' the more I thought I should leave her out of it. It was a fun night and to be honest, I felt a lot more like a Dad that night than I did in years past at this event. Even with me bouncing back and forth between the bars and dumping the kids on Nona and all that other stuff, I was so much more involved in the kids' lives now with Gina gone as opposed to before when she handled everything, and I just enjoyed time with them. Even though it was still fairly recent, being the first Halloween since Gina had passed, nobody really addressed it. A couple of people asked me how I was holding up, but outside of that it was just a night that all of us parents had a good time and focused on our kids. Same went for Halloween a few days later. I took the girls trick-or-treating and as we walked through the neighborhood (well I walked, they sprinted from door to door), and I couldn't help but smile as I watched them, feeling like I had finally gotten a grip on this single-dad stuff.

6 2

HOLIDAY FREAK OUT

AS MUCH AS I thought I had a grip, I found out quickly any grip I had was because I had help holding on. As Halloween passed and we started to float towards the holidays, I found out that Nona's plans had changed and she wouldn't be back until after New Years. Even in my proudest moment of thinking I had a handle on things, I was well aware of how much I depended on Nona.

The eighteen-year-old girl I had in her spot wasn't great, but by this point she was already in place, everyone was comfortable (even though her dinners and laundry still sucked), so we just rode her wave until Nona got back.

Outside of the girls, I was petrified of the holidays. Thanksgiving wasn't going to be a big deal. That's kind of a non-holiday anyhow, and my mom takes care of that. Christmas however is a different story entirely. Gina always blew it out and it was a huge deal in our home. Every year it took her about a week to fully decorate the house. Now that it was on me, I felt a tremendous amount of pressure to hold this up for the girls. I knew I didn't have that kind of time, but I still wanted the house to explode with Christmas for them. Plus I was going to have to shop, cook, and organize the day, on top of tending to the decorations. It was early November and I was already freaking out about the holidays.

Speaking of my mom, we were talking a lot at that point. As proud and independent as I am, there's something very soothing about being able to open up to my mom. She gave me a lot of pointers, not just about my emotions and my thoughts, but about getting through the holidays and what to do. I actually created a mantra for myself that year. "Get on Christmas before it gets on you." Not exactly the ho-ho-ho theme most people operate behind, but my anxiety was getting the best of me. I asked the girls for their Christmas lists right after Halloween and once I got them, boom, I was out shopping for gifts that first weekend.

I didn't pay attention to it at the time in part because I was so self absorbed and in part because I was trying so hard to make sure all my tasks got checked off my list, but I found it a little odd that the girls weren't really talking to me much about Gina. They talked to Nona about her here and there, but with her having been out of town for some time and in the midst of one of the most emotional times of the year, they were oddly silent. I should have been worried that the girls were dealing too well with all of it, much better than any kids should have been, but I was too busy managing the house and pleasing my own selfish desires.

I wish I would've asked my mom or my sister for help here. I didn't have the sensitivity and softness they did, and I sure as hell wasn't intuitive enough. I did well with their schedules and my routine caretaking responsibilities, but I was horrible at digging into their brains. It probably didn't help that my mom and sisters 'Monday Morning Quarterbacked' me a lot. They would criticize a lot of my actions or decisions, which caused me to distance myself a bit. Who wants to stand next to a critic? I should have, but my ego often got bruised and my anger tended to flare up. So I declined to ask for help, time marched on, and as a result, the girls suffered.

As Thanksgiving approached, I gave more and more thought about how to handle it. Remember, I was still dating Denise and while we were going to my mom's house like we always do, I didn't know if it was a good idea to bring her into that world yet. I did, however, want her to meet my mom, so we met for lunch at a local restaurant just before the holiday. It was awkward at first, kind of like being a teenager bringing a girl home to meet your folks. Denise had pretty good people skills (usually) and between her and my mom, everyone was at ease pretty quickly.

Denise was fine keeping our Thanksgivings separate. She had her own world as well with her kids and family anyhow.

Leading up to Thanksgiving, things were pretty normal, but once the day arrived, I could feel Gina hanging in the air again. It wasn't caused by anything in particular; it was just one of those things where sadness kind of creeps in and sits in the air. Not for the girls, they seemed fine, but for me. I tried to dress the girls up as pretty as their mom would have and I had apparently done an okay job because nobody made any snide remarks. Even though it was just my family, we did receive a solemn reaction upon our entrance. I think because it was the first major holiday that we had all come together for since Gina died.

That said, by this point it's something I've become fairly accustomed to; I was used to the girls and me walking into the room and everyone giving us puppy dog eyes of hurt, as if we were incomplete. It used to bother the hell out of me but as time went by, I grew to realize there was nothing we could do about it and at the very least, it meant that they cared.

The rest of the day was great. The meal was normal and there was plenty of football on television, the way most other families celebrate Thanksgiving in America. There was no mention of Gina in conversation or in the saying of Grace, so even dinner felt normal. It probably helped that we weren't the kind of family that always sat in the same seats or anything, so there was no real 'hole' next to me at the table.

We also used that day to celebrate Jackie's birthday, since she was born in December a week before Christmas. This way not only did she not get gypped; we could spend it with the whole family. While we all missed Gina, it was definitely a much more celebratory mood than if we would have tried to do something in the Christmas holiday, when I was already scared I would be feeling the pangs of her absence.

When we got home, I went right into normal executive mode. I got the girls ready and in bed and started making lists. In addition to Christmas coming, I had booked a Disney Cruise for us and we were leaving a week after. It was only going to be me and the girls, along with our neighbors Jane and Fred. I opted to leave Denise out of this too because the trip was for me and the girls. I did, however, lean on her pretty heavily to help us get everything ready. It was probably wrong but again, hindsight is 20/20.

As it turned out, Disney cancelled our cruise due to an outbreak of the Norwalk virus. They were going to have to dock the ship for a few weeks to clean and sanitize it. When Jane (who is both our neighbor and travel agent) told me the news I was crushed. I knew how much the girls were looking forward to it. I felt absolutely horrible breaking the news to the girls. The disappointment in their eyes as I told them the news was enough to melt my heart. These kids just could not catch a break. What a damn year for them! I didn't leave them empty handed though; I had made arrangements for us to go to my folks' house in Florida. So when I told the girls, I at least had a replacement vacation for them.

As it turned out, they were happy and it actually ended up better than a cruise. We did some beaches, theme parks, etc. We were able to shake it up and do a lot of things whereas on the cruise, we would have been relegated to the ship. It was a nice week away. More than just a week out of the cold Chicago weather and into the sun, but with no Denise it really seemed to bring the girls and me together.

It was nice and I absolutely recommend it to anyone in my situation who can swing it. It doesn't have to be Florida and it doesn't have to be expensive. You'd be surprised at how much kids like just getting away so even if you can just swing a hotel night or two with a pool, you'd be surprised at what a wonderful thing that is not just for the kids but for your family.

63

CHECKING MY EGO AT THE DOOR

I KNOW THIS SOUNDS selfish as hell, but this was one time when I thanked God that I still had Denise around because she helped me tremendously. Even with things going well with Denise and the closeness I felt with her, I still missed Gina tremendously around this time and Denise and I talked about her a lot. She was really good about that. She was very good about respecting Gina's place and presence in the house. I couldn't understand but always appreciated how she never resented talking about Gina. Maybe it was because she knew even though we were talking about another woman I loved, she was dead and therefore no threat to her. She really did play the role of therapist as well as girlfriend. Now with Christmas coming, she played the role of my right arm as well.

Here's another glaring mistake I made. I was scared that the house would be stark because I knew I couldn't decorate it the way Gina did, so Denise asked if she could decorate the house while we were gone on vacation. I felt a little awkward letting her do that as it such a signature Gina task. She did a great job and while I knew it wouldn't be anywhere near the degree or style that Gina did it, I was happy that the house would look pretty and festive when we got back.

I was really appreciative of her efforts, not just in doing it, but knowing that she was filling the void (and task) of a ghost. But the second we walked in the door, Amber had a problem with it. In my eyes, with Gina gone it wasn't something that was necessarily my job; it was more like a task that had to get done. Lord knows I would have been horrible at it anyhow. In Amber's eyes though, Denise had just crept in on her mother's territory again. I can see that now, but I was pretty oblivious to that back then. I talked Amber off the ledge and explained to her that Denise was just helping us out, so the house would look nice while we were able to take a vacation. That seemed to do the trick and smooth things over pretty well. It probably helped that the house looked the same on the outside, as I hired the same guy to hang the outdoor lights, so there was some consistency they could lean on.

I righted the ship the next year, and from that point on decorating the house became something I did with the girls. It's turned into a tradition and something we all really look forward to now. Let me tell you, it's much better to do that as a family and enjoy the holiday spirit with laughter and love than to get through it as if it were a task.

All the decorations looked great, but they gave the house a little bit of a broken feel to me. I'm sure it's because I was so accustomed to all those years of Gina's work, but still, every so often I would look around and it would prick me in the heart. One night I was sitting by myself on the couch in the living room, just looking at all of the decorations after the girls had gone to bed, and I realized that there was no way I could wake up there on Christmas morning. Amber had gotten to me about letting Denise put up the decorations and while I didn't see it the same way, I completely understood where she was coming from. The more I thought about it, the more I realized that there was no way I wanted to screw up Christmas morning. It was going to be a very emotional and different Christmas morning than any of us had ever had before, and I was terrified of making it any worse.

In a moment of weakness, but also one of complete correctness, I called my mom and told her that I just couldn't handle Christmas Eve at the house this year and asked if it was okay for the girls and me to stay at her place that night. I'm proud of the fact that I was able to recognize that this situation was bigger than pride, and there was no way I could tackle it alone. Lord knows the girls didn't need to have a dead mother and a weeping father ruining their Christmas morning. Thankfully, my mother understood.

Not only did Denise help with the house, she helped me with the madness that is Christmas toy shopping. Other than last year when we did all of the shopping together, most of the time Gina took care of this on her own. If I was there, I was more of a robot along for the ride, soldiering through it. It sounds nice to any guy not having to go out in that craziness, but you find out later that you missed out. Not only would it have helped me know what to do now, it's actually nice and fun if you're doing it with someone you love and for kids you love. There were a lot of good memories that my selfish ass never took the time to make.

As we walked through the parent-crazed aisles, I watched the married couples and wished I would have made more of an effort to be a part of the experience with Gina.

I spent most of December in a funk feeling sorry for myself, and thank God Denise was there to make sure I didn't let myself sink ass deep in it. She let me bob up and down in the pity waters, but she never let me really go under. Not to mention that on top of Christmas, Jackie's birthday was coming up. We had already celebrated it with the family so we had a little cake at the house just for us. That was nice. We all missed her, but it went over better than I had expected. That Thanksgiving celebration really helped.

As Christmas Eve approached, I started to have second thoughts about staying at my mom's. I was embarrassed to be waving the white flag, but every time I started to feel the pangs of embarrassment, I knew deep down it was the right thing to do. Emotionally for me and for the girls, there was no way I could swing waking up Christmas morning in our house. Not after everything we had gone through and surely not after the Christmas we had last year when we gave Gina that video.

When I told the girls about my plan, they were reluctant at first. They wanted to be home and I can understand that. It took a bit of a sell job but in the end, they agreed, and if they weren't happy about it, then they did a good sell job on me too.

64

THE GHOST OF CHRISTMAS PAST

AS MUCH AS I had Denise helping me with Christmas, she wasn't my only elf. In addition to letting us stay the night, my mom was helping me with the gifts. I was picking everything out and buying them, but I would drop them off at her house and she would wrap them for me. As far as I was concerned, this accomplished two things. One, since we were going to be waking up at her house this allowed me to get the kids' Santa gifts under the tree without having to sneak them out of the house and potentially get caught. Second, have you ever seen a guy wrap a gift? No Christmas picture ever shows Dad-wrapped Santa presents under the tree, if you know what I mean.

Before the actual Christmas holiday was our annual neighborhood Kids Christmas Party. We did it every year and the kids always had a blast. Santa comes and takes pictures, the local high school choir sings carols, and there's dancing, games, prizes- the whole nine yards. We went and as usual, the girls loved it. I had a hard time because again, it was one of those things that we always did as a family. I intentionally left Denise out of this one too. The entire time, I had a smile on my face for the girls, but my heart was aching for Gina. This was one of those times when the hole just wasn't able to be filled.

That's kind of the way the whole Christmas holiday was for me that year. Gina was always heavy on my mind. Most of the time I was so busy with my new responsibilities there wasn't a lot of time to miss her, but she floated in and out and at night when I would lay down, it would really settle in. I got through it okay and the sadness didn't really kick in until Christmas Eve, but the ache seemed to always be there.

Christmas Eve was really a chore for me. We got to my folks later in the evening and the girls pretty much went straight to bed. It felt awkward for me to tuck them in at my mom's and without Gina, but I did it. Even walking out of their room that night, I knew that as humbling as it was, I needed it to be this way this year. Our house would have completely beaten me up and in turn my tears would have ruined the girls' Christmas. They were going to notice the hole in the family enough already.

I had a nice talk with my mom at the kitchen table, and that's what really got the sadness flowing for me. This was a moment I always spent with Gina, wrapping the final presents, putting everything under the tree, and then just sitting on the couch together.

Mom and I talked about everything; we talked about how I was doing, my struggles, my relationship with Denise, and the dichotomy between being happy in a new relationship and missing my wife. The memory of Gina made me sad, but Denise brought me back up. The problem was that sometimes this swing would happen every thirty seconds and just go on and on for what felt like days at a time.

6 5

GETTING THROUGH THE FIRST ONE

INITIALLY I TOYED WITH the idea of having Denise over to my folks for Christmas, but I quickly dismissed it. I'm sure it would have gone over like a lead balloon if I would have uttered it out loud, but more importantly, I knew it was too soon for something like that. I learned my lesson with the decorations. Dating was one thing, but this holiday was for the girls and me.

It played out perfectly too. Well, as perfectly as that kind of situation can allow I guess. Up until today, Christmas morning was pretty much picture perfect. Gina and I would wake up with the kids, she would make coffee, and we would sit there in our pajamas with our Santa mugs as the kids tore into their gifts. One thing about that was their gifts weren't just a surprise to them but to me as well, since Gina did the shopping and wrapping. It was almost like watching a live TV show or something for me. This year however, surprise was replaced with anxiety as I sweated my 'santa purchases.'

I did it right. I woke up with the girls and we all went down to the living room for presents. I always loved that part, when they first lay eyes on the tree and it's just bursting with presents. They bolted to the tree and almost did a baseball slide into position to start sorting everything into separate piles. My folks were already in their chairs. I hadn't even considered the fact that this was a real treat for my parents. It had been many years since they got to experience the magic of Christmas morning with little ones tearing into gifts. A smile took over my face when I realized how I had become like my folks. Looking at them, I laughed to myself, thinking that was exactly how Gina and I used to sit on Christmas morning. Actually, it was how I sat in my chair while Gina chased after them with a garbage bag, picking up the wrapping paper. I sat down on the couch and while I was watching their Christmas morning chaos, my mind was focused on Gina. It wasn't overwhelming to the point that it ruined it for me, but it was very obvious.

I knew my parents sensed my feelings, but they didn't acknowledge them, as if they were scared to tap the barrel. I don't know if it showed or not but I got teary at a couple of moments.

That's one thing that kind of shook me as well. After the excitement simmered down, I realized that it was Gina running through my head, not Denise. Honestly, I don't think I ever gave Denise a second thought, until much later in the morning.

Mom and Dad made a nice breakfast that we all ate together after the gifts. That was a moment I will truly always cherish. The kids flew through their food because they wanted to get back to their toys, but we all laughed and smiled throughout the whole thing.

I didn't bring Gina up and oddly, neither did the girls. They were so focused on their presents they didn't give anything a second thought. She would come up though later in the day when we were all at my sister's house. That's where the pity for Tommy came back around. Everyone was asking me how the girls and I were doing and my brother-in-law acknowledged her when he said Grace. I know they were all just trying to help and show their concern, but in reality they were stirring the hurt.

If I could offer any advice in this situation it would be this – throw it out there. Either do it yourself or let someone else be the messenger, but let it be known that you don't want to talk about her. I wish I would've had my mom say to everyone, privately or individually, to not bring up Gina so we could all just have a nice day. They didn't need to shy away from it if the kids brought it up or something, but they also didn't need to initiate it.

In between my folk's house and my sister's, I took the girls to Christmas service, and that was where I most felt her absence. And holy hell (pardon the pun), did I feel guilty about not taking the girls to church more often. My sister Robyn had been nudging me to take them and Denise had mentioned it more than once as well. To be honest, I don't know why I didn't. I imagine that along with a lot of the bad decisions I made then, I was also selfish with my time. For whatever reason, that Christmas service kicked it off for me and I'm proud to say I kept them going until this day.

Denise was going to come by my sister's later in the afternoon, long after the spirit of Christmas morning had worn off. My family was oddly cool with it and treated her very kindly. It felt strange having her there, but at the same time it was comforting. I'm sure the smitten nature of the holiday made it easier for me, and like I've said before, I don't like being alone. As for everyone else, they embraced her in everything. If anyone felt awkward they didn't show it, and they certainly didn't make her feel that way.

That was the great thing about Denise. Looking back I think she really was kind of an angel sent down for me at that time. She gave me something to look forward to and something to work for. I don't know that I actually ever loved her, even though my desperation for romance and companionship mistook it as so. It was almost more of a "friends with benefits" kind of thing. That's not to say she wasn't truly in love with me, because she very much was. She always put us and our house before her own home and even her own kids. But she had been through her 'process' of getting over someone so she was ready and open for something real. I, on the other hand, was as fragile and messed up as you could be.

One thing I didn't think about regarding Christmas was how many presents the girls received. I took things over to my folks in waves, so I didn't have any real idea of how much stuff they got, not just from me, but also from everyone. Let's just say hauling home the load was a bitch! But with all of us working together, we got it all back to the house and through the door. I got the girls ready for bed and tucked them in and that's when the bomb dropped. Jackie wanted to talk about Gina. "Daddy, do you think Mommy had a good Christmas?" she asked me.

Those words tore me apart. I sat down on her bed and we talked about it. It was not long, maybe ten minutes or so, but it really helped us both. It hurt to talk about her and it was hard to be the strong dad without breaking down, but we talked it through without any tears. There was a real longing in the air though. I could see she really missed her mommy. I played with her hair as we talked and that was another one of those moments I'll never forget. After she was talked out and started to drift off to sleep, I slipped out and fell into my own bed, exhausted and relieved. Normally on Christmas night I would lay down, replaying the day's events in my head or talking with Gina, laughing at whatever silly moment played itself out during the day. Tonight the only thought that went through my head was "I got through the first one."

That was a thought I would have quite a few times on almost every other first. The first New Year's. Our first anniversary. Her first birthday. It was always me falling asleep thinking, "I got through the first one…"

66

COUNTING DOWN TO MOVING ON

ON NEW YEAR'S EVE I was in my office downstairs catching up on a few things when for whatever reason I looked over at the tree just in time to see the cat go running up it and bring the whole thing crashing down. The damn thing exploded upon impact. Ornaments shattered and decorations flew. It was a mess. I just shook my head and thought it was so fucking symbolic of the past year.

I kept that New Year's pretty low-key. Denise came by and we hung out at the house with the girls. I grilled some steaks, opened a bottle of wine, and we all had a nice dinner. After dinner, we just watched TV and played games and waited for the ball to drop in New York. I was so looking forward to starting a new year, it's beyond expression. I know it's just a state of mind, but there's a lot to be said for the impact of perspective. Turning that calendar was going to be monumental for me. A lot of people use New Year's Eve as a reflection day to kind of go over the year past, but not me. I was using it as more of a springboard.

It felt good to have Denise there, but like everything else that year with her, it was a yin-yang thing as it felt just as awkward without Gina. Maybe I was caught up in all of the "It's A Wonderful Life" of it all, but I was really missing her. Regardless of all we went through, drifting closer together and further apart, she was my wife of fourteen years. She was my rock, my backbone, my staunchest supporter, and even though she was gone she was very much on my mind. I was happy to have Denise, don't get me wrong, but she was on my arm and in my head…not in my heart. That spot was still very much taken by Gina and try as I might, I couldn't push her out of it.

When the clock struck midnight, she was very much on my mind. As we were counting down, and I know how crazy this sounds, but it was almost like I was counting down to her death again; only this time I was counting down to moving on. Maybe a better analogy is it was like selling an old car. You look forward to getting a new car and getting rid of the old one, but when the time comes to hand over the keys to the new owner once you've sold it, you get that tinge of finality. That's what this was for me. A big tinge of finality as I left the year that I lost my wife behind me.

Denise and I shared the traditional New Year's kiss but it was odd. How could it not be? Have you ever tried kissing one woman while missing someone else? It isn't easy. She spent the night and that was a little weird. It was supposed to be a new beginning but as we lay in bed, all I could think about was what I was going to do with my New Year. You're supposed to have goals or resolutions and yet, even with everything I had been through last year, I had none.

Normally I would have set goals for the New Year, but this year I was just happy to see the last one end. I was still getting my feet back underneath me and to be honest, I felt like a guy on a boat in the middle of the ocean. I was just sitting on top of the water and bobbing with every wave that passed underneath. While I was eagerly anticipating the New Year, I didn't think much past it. Little did I know a big wave was just beyond that calendar-turning day.

67

TURN THE (CALENDAR) PAGE

AFTER NEW YEARS IT really did feel different. Nothing really changed other than the way my family started approaching me. It seems like everyone looked at New Years as a cutoff for me too. From that point on, they took a bit more of a direct approach with me when it came to their thoughts on how I was handling things. It felt like every time I went to my mom or my sister's house, they didn't help me, but instead took the opportunity to tear into me. If I came over sad, my mom would kick me in the ass. "No one said it would be easy," she would say. If I let the girls do something or didn't let the girls do something, they had an opinion. It was pretty frustrating because work wasn't exactly firing on all cylinders yet, which was normal, but when you're in sales and you work on commission, anytime it's not a high point, it's easy to get incensed. So there I was vulnerable, lonely, and struggling, and everyone was nipping at my heels. At the time, it pissed me off but in hindsight, I can acknowledge they weren't entirely wrong.

Denise was still helping me out a lot at that point, so it was easy to just dismiss whomever and leave. I mean she was really getting involved. She drove the girls to and from their sports, picked up groceries, and cooked dinners. Plus Denise turned a blind eye to anything that bothered her regarding me, so that made it easier to tune out my family as well. I was drinking pretty heavily and she was fine with that too. I figured if I had her approval and she was in the mix, what was the problem? Pretty stupid reasoning I know, but in the midst of it all, it made sense.

If I could go back or tell you something here, it would be this. Listen to your family. They will piss you off to no end but nobody, and I mean nobody, is going to be more honest with you. More importantly, they see the whole picture and they have your kids in their thoughts. Neither you nor your new girlfriend do. There are too many other things clouding your judgments at that point.

Not long after New Year's Eve is the Super Bowl and after the last year, that event will be forever linked with Gina's death. As the weeks began to ramp up to the Super Bowl, it got me thinking. It didn't help that not only did I feel unsteady on my legs, but the days were short and the skies were gray. My mind took over and while everyone else seemed to feel renewed with the beginning of a new year, I was swimming in an impending doom. I had never been through an anniversary of this sort. How was I supposed to mark the day? It's not exactly something you celebrate, but how do you acknowledge it? It wasn't just me I was worried about; I had three kids to think it through for as well. I asked a few people but nobody really had any opinions that helped. In the end, I figured we would just go to the cemetery as a family and bring her some flowers. It was as much of a cinematic cliché as you could get.

When the day finally came upon us, I told the girls that we would go right after school. I wanted to get it out there and gauge their reaction to the idea to see what they wanted to do. My heart was heavy, but I didn't know what they would be okay with. It lingered on me all day. I couldn't concentrate or focus to save my life. Yet as much as I was dreading it, I was looking forward to it. Part of me wanted to talk to her and part of me wanted to just get it over with and put this day behind us.

I left work early but before I picked them up, I stopped and got some flowers. Even there though, I was at a loss. What kind of flowers are you supposed to buy for this? Roses? Carnations? Lilies? I had absolutely no clue, so I just told the lady at the counter what I was doing and she handed me some flowers. To be honest, I was so nervous I can't even remember what they were. On the ride over, I made some small talk but it was really just noise from my mouth – nothing of any substance. Just something to break up the silence.

I've driven by the cemetery a lot but I never go in. It was pretty eerie pulling in off the street. We parked and before we got out, I took a deep breath. I looked at the girls and they both did the same. They had this distant, almost empty stare as they looked out the window. I got out of the car and took both of their hands as we walked the short distance to her grave. We were walking pretty gingerly. Not in a tiptoe fashion, but we weren't exactly striding with confidence either. The tears were welling up in all of us before we even reached her. The cold was pretty spot on as well; the weather felt very reminiscent of death.

When we got to her grave, we all had that uncomfortable awkwardness of not knowing what to do. The girls said little things to her, but you could tell they felt weird. How could you not? You're talking to ground. It didn't feel like you were talking to her. It felt very forced, like this was what we were supposed to be doing.

We didn't stick around long. I don't know if it was the cold or the discomfort of it all, but we high tailed it out of there pretty quickly. Nobody really lost it or anything because like I said, it didn't feel real. It was almost like we were actors in a bad play. We got back in the car and I took them to dinner. As we were pulling out of the cemetery, I let out a huge sigh. I was glad that part was over. In honor of Gina, we went to the Village Squire for dinner. That was her favorite place and the four of us went there often.

I did make one major fuck up here; I took Denise with. I don't know what the hell I was thinking. At the time everyone was okay with it, but I should have been smarter and left it as just the girls and me. To be fair, Denise should have been smarter too, and declined my invitation. As you might expect, dinner was served with a Gina hangover. I kept asking the girls if they were okay. Jackie talked about her Mom while Amber bottled it up.

I think that probably had a lot to do with how they had been dealing with everything up until this point. Not only did Jackie talk with Nona quite a bit about her problems (both Gina and other things as well), she always seemed to have this ability to still connect with her mom. She told me more than once that she talks to her Mom and on occasion, she feels like she can see her in her room. Amber just bottles it all up. That night. The day before. Always.

Once we got home the girls got ready and climbed in bed, but as I came in the room, they still had a few things they wanted to talk about. Jackie is very adamant about not forgetting her mom. This day meant a lot to her, then and now. Amber on the other hand tried to block it out and ignore the day.

After we had our talk and our hugs, they snuggled in bed and I was happy to be heading to my own. We dropped Denise off at her house, so I crawled into bed alone just happy to have this day behind me. It's kind of like a baseball pitcher facing the heart of the Yankee's lineup; you're happy to just get through it without too much damage.

As the years go on, I tend to leave it up to the girls as to how we will 'celebrate' this day. It turned out they didn't want to go to the cemetery the next year, so we didn't. I want to let them be who they are with it and deal with it in their own way. It's pretty obvious that what works for Jackie doesn't work for Amber and vice versa. So as the years go by, we almost never go to the cemetery together. I've gone a handful of times on my own, typically in the spring, but even then I only pop in for a minute or two.

68

ONE MORE LAST FIRST

THE THING WITH TIMING is that it often sucks. Right after we got through the anniversary, Gina's birthday was upon us. As the years went on, these types of anniversaries became more filled with reflection than dread, but this first year they were something I did not look forward to. Every year the anniversary socks me between the eyes, and then her birthday is there for the follow-up punch.

Just before her birthday, Lent is on the calendar and while I'm far from a good Christian boy, I was raised Catholic so I like to observe it and take part. Typically I give up booze, so it's a good cleansing process for me as well. Hey, if I've got to give up something I love, why not make it work for me in the process right?

As you well know by now I like to have a few drinks every now and then, but in this last year it really got out of control. I started right after her death and continued it throughout the year. I liked the temporary 'up' it gave me and the way it helped me to crawl inside my sadness. I know I sound like a martyr and maybe for a little while I was. Still. The first year I started thinking about her birthday I didn't know what to do. I was in the habit of thinking about her birthday at the beginning of the month because I always tried to do something special for her, trying like hell not to repeat the past. This was the first year I didn't have to worry about that and it made me feel empty and strange. I still wanted to do something, especially with the girls. We talked it over the week before and I suggested having a birthday cake for Mommy. They liked the idea so we decided to go with that. It spooked me a little but at the same time, it made me feel good knowing we weren't just going to ignore it.

At this point Denise had become a part of almost everything we did. She was incredibly supportive of me and the girls with everything, including all things Gina related. She helped to keep the house up, and I'm guessing unknowingly kept it very much the way Gina had, and

I give her credit for that. Nona did a large part too in making sure that we were all together. I really appreciated that, but a year later and many of miles into the Denise experience, the house still felt broken and empty. Maybe not empty, but there was a definite hole there.

When her birthday finally came around, I went to the grocery store to pick up the cake. Standing there I had a huge question smack me across the face. Do I buy candles? What do I have written on it? I'm guessing we'll sing, but if we have candles, who will blow them out? I got teary eyed, feeling very awkward standing there by the freezer. I ended up asking the lady behind the counter to write Happy Birthday Gina on it. To be honest, even though the cake was my idea, I didn't really want to do this. Not then and especially not now. But I was doing it because I thought the girls would want to. Especially Jackie. She was hell bent on not forgetting her mom. That's a hard balance for me: moving on but not forgetting. At this point it seemed like there was no real moving on (not counting Denise), but more of having Gina as part of our life, just an absent one.

We did an after dinner thing and that seemed to be the best play because nobody really broke down. We sang "Happy Birthday" and there were some tears but no real meltdowns. We talked about her, how much we missed her, and told fun stories. Jackie talked TO her right there at the table, which made Amber and I feel a little uncomfortable, because we didn't possess the same sensory feelings. I don't dismiss Jackie's medium powers and truth be told, I'm even a little envious. Ever since Gina passed away I've had some very vivid dreams of her. Not a ton, only a handful in all the years, but when I do they are enough to jolt me out of bed with the feeling that she was literally right there. Is this a medium thing? Is this Gina figuring out a way to communicate with me from beyond? I have no idea. All I know is that they are strikingly real.

After the stories and cake, we went into the family room to hang out. Denise was still there and while I probably should have had her sit this night out, from a personal standpoint I felt comfortable with her there. I didn't want to feel the hole anymore, and her company made me feel more complete. Plus she was so good at not being jealous or intrusive of Gina's space, memory, or place with the girls, and me I figured it was okay. I will say that when the girls were home, Denise didn't spend the night so I felt like I had been respecting some sort of line. I know now I was fooling myself, but in the middle of the storm you can make yourself see anything that helps you to feel better.

Going to bed alone that night, I felt a strange awkwardness. For the first time, I started really doubting myself for moving forward with Denise. I felt guilty for being happy with her and guilty that I had such good communication with her. I mean that was my biggest problem with Gina, and it was her death that not only pushed me into another woman but a woman that I *could* communicate with. I tossed that shit around in my head for what felt like hours and at some point, I fell asleep in that huge ass lonely bed.

When I woke up, I woke up with a renewed vigor. That was it. We had finally gone through one of everything since Gina died and I was tired of feeling sick. As I went down to the kitchen, it struck me that the house was entirely as Gina had left it. It was filled with her. I had thrown away most of her knick-knacks and shit, but the design, the furniture, and the decorations were all her and I wanted to move the fuck on. Right then, that's when I decided to do it. This house was moving on.

I called Denise and told her what I was feeling. She was willing to help and hell, why wouldn't she? She wasn't pushing for this at all, but at the same time what woman wouldn't want you to move on from a dead wife and past life when she's standing in the on-deck circle? In one of my smarter moves, I ran it past my mother as well. She thought it was a good idea, but she suggested that I use an interior designer friend she had named Liz. I was cool with that. After all, I wanted something new but I didn't know what the hell I wanted. Besides, if you had seen the way I dressed the girls for school more times than not, you'd know that fashion and design are not my forte.

That same day, I told the girls my plan. I didn't ask them or talk it over with them as much as I told them. This wasn't going to be voted on. I wanted a new living room and kitchen eating area. There was too much of a cloud hanging over them. The memories would remain, but the setting had to go.

A few days later Liz and I had a discussion and agreed on the financials, so we got to work with her sending things for me to look at. As things would arrive, I would often go over the suggestions with Denise for her opinion, but that was it. The guidance was coming from Liz. I was so happy to have Liz take the lead because this was the first time I had ever decorated anything. I had no clue what I was doing, so to call it a cluster fuck is an understatement.

I thought there would have been some sort of a plan, but there wasn't. I guess that's how it goes, but that only meant I was going to be shocked from time to time by a variety of things ranging from some of her crazy ideas to timing. She had me looking at things, but she would almost always make me go somewhere to see it. I had to go to stores to see samples. Sometimes she would send catalogs for me to thumb through, but more so she was sending me to various places to look at samples and designs. When we did decide on something, she wanted me to interview and price out her recommended contractors. What the hell was this? I had no problem paying the woman to help me with my design but I didn't want to pay her and still do all the work!

Then came the next insane moment in the brief Liz era. Her recommended painter came over to look at the living room and quoted me $1,300 to paint it. One room! Now I may have never had decorators before, but I'm not stupid. I told a friend of mine who sent over a painter he knew named Tony Pallonti. He took a look at the space, we talked about what was possible, and he quoted the job at about half the price that Liz's guy gave me. It was half the price, so I made two snap decisions right there. First off, I whacked Liz. I was already overwhelmed with moving on, work, and raising the girls. I didn't want to have to watch my back for someone who was taking advantage of my naivety. The second decision I made was to hire Tony.

When it came to carpeting, I just walked into the carpet store and picked out the one I wanted it. I wanted a complete change in the family room, something completely new. A fresh start. So the carpeting went from a burgundy to a tan. I painted the walls lighter and bought new window treatments that let more light in. I bought all new leather furniture and sent the old stuff down to the basement for the girls to play on.

The entire process took about three weeks but when I was done, I stood there looking it over and it was exactly what I needed. It was so much brighter, almost as if we opened up the curtains and the light washed out the darkness of death that hung in the room. It was good for the girls too. It really helped with their transition and it gave them a basement to play in. It was such a mind-freeing thing. One of the reasons I hated the room before was because it was all Gina and what I had lost. This renovation allowed me to live inside the same walls with an entirely new beginning. It gave me a new sense of 'me' and 'us,' as in the girls and me. Ever since that redo, I spend a lot more time in there and even after all these years, there are times I just sit in my chair and look around and smile. It makes me feel good.

A year later, we repainted the kitchen. The laundry room got a remodel too. Same thing, just some fresh paint and a bulletin board to keep the girls' sports schedules so I knew which uniform had to be clean by when. The girls were good with the changes and as we went along, I included them in the process. We would pick out colors together and they would pitch in and help. It became a fun project, not a Gina cleansing. We did their bedrooms and by then, I gave them complete autonomy. You have never heard a little girl shriek with excitement until you take them shopping and tell them they can do anything they want to their bedrooms.

With all of these projects behind me, I felt so much better about myself. I started really flowing with the confidence that I could keep this all together and that I could do this. The whole thing seemed to make my life lighter.

I left my bedroom the way it was. I don't mind it and to be honest, it was still comforting to me. It took me six years to redecorate the master bedroom. As the years peeled off and I went through all of the other changes, it eventually just became my bed. At one point, it occurred to me the bed had had it, and I decided to get rid of it and buy myself a new bedroom set. It wasn't like some of the other things in the house where it was some monumental decision or cinematic moment.

It was just time for it to go.

6 9

BECOMING ONE OF THE GIRLS

I HAD FIGURED OUT the house décor and kept things running, but the biggest everyday issue with me was actually raising the girls. I don't mean getting them through the dark days of losing their mother, I mean actually raising them. I'm a guy and I'm every bit of a guy. I like sports. I like to have a couple of pops now and then. I'm competitive and protective and all of that testosterone-driven stuff.

I know nothing about 'girl' issues. The girls were ten and seven when Gina passed and there was a whole lot more ahead of us than behind us. I was scared as hell that not only did I not know about things like bras and makeup and boys, I was scared I wouldn't be able to give them all they were going to need emotionally. Luckily Nona was still around. Not only was she like family to us, she was a very feminine lady so that helped when it came to some of those things. Some things like fashion and hair the girls figured out on their own. I think like every normal kid these days, school, media, and their girlfriends played the major roles in that, though not right away. The first year I had to dress the girls for their school pictures was one for the ages. I always laugh and say that anyone who saw those two walking down the street knew a single Dad dressed them. Things didn't match or they matched too much. There were days I dressed them so much in one color they might have been mistaken for two of the four Fruit Of The Loom guys walking down the street.

Shopping for clothes was always quite an experience and that never changed throughout the years. You want to have some fun? Wait until you have to learn women's sizes. As guys we have two things – Men's and Boys. Not them. They have Juniors, Misses, Petite, etc. Then there's a million styles, a million stores, a million accessories. Plus the shoes! I can't tell you how many times I was awkwardly the only guy in the women's section at Kohl's or in some boutique, waiting for the girls to try on clothes to come out and show me. That wasn't ever a problem until Amber turned about fourteen or fifteen. At that point, it became more of a struggle getting her to try things on and show me in the store. It was a huge pain in the ass and became a fight every time we walked into a store, but as I've come to find out that's pretty normal, which makes me feel better. Not that we fought, but that every parent has that fight, so that must mean I was doing things normally.

This went on for a few years, but Amber seemed to mature quickly so she took on that role of 'mother' with Jackie. By the time she was twelve, she was pretty much dressing herself and helping shape Jackie with her style. Amber started wearing make up at about eleven or twelve years old and I saw no problem with that. It wasn't a lot, it wasn't as if she was wearing smoky eyes or lip liner. She didn't look like a hooker or anything, but she put on some light eye shadow and lip-gloss. Hell, I didn't know what the appropriate age was for that. Looking back, I should have put the skids on that until about thirteen or fourteen, but what the hell did I know?

That's another area where I wish my mom and sister would have stepped in to help, but they didn't and it was my fault for not asking. About the time Amber was fifteen she started going shopping with her girlfriends and their moms. That was fine with me and I have come to find out that's pretty normal as well, so again, chalk one up for old Tommy.

Bras. Never a dirty word for a guy until you have to buy one for your daughter. Let me tell you, they look a lot different when you're eyeballing them on the breasts of a woman versus seeing them on a clothing rack in a store and buying them for your daughter. The girls and I had pretty good communication so they told me when they needed their first one. I had no idea not only when they needed them, but how to fit them. I spent my whole life trying to take them off, not put them on!

When that day came, I took Amber to the store (Jackie came with of course) and we bee-lined for a sales lady that would help us. I tried to find someone who looked like she would be the least awkward for me to talk to. Once I found one, I explained that my wife had passed away and the girls were going to need help buying a bra. She could not have been nicer and was incredibly helpful. My first inclination was to walk away and let her and Amber take care of business, but I didn't. I hung close, listening to her every word so I could absorb the info and learn how it works. The girls were paying attention too, probably so they could come do this next time without me.

Haircuts were another escapade. At first the girls kept going to the same place Gina used to take them. The stylists there already knew the girls and how they did their hair, so there wasn't much input needed from me. I would pick out a day every eight to ten weeks and we'd do a family trip to the salon. I'm bald. My head is Schick shaved so there was no work for me, but the girls used to love it. After a year or so, Amber wanted to try a new salon, so I let her. By that point, both girls were starting to figure out who they were and what they wanted to do with their appearance. I was pretty much just there to pay and make sure nobody walked out with pink hair.

Looking back, I loved those days of clothes shopping and hair cuts. It was girly stuff but I'm so glad I shared those experiences with them. Had Gina not passed, I honestly don't think I would have ever done any of those things.

On the subject of girly things, I think it's probably time we address the elephant in the room. Periods. Menstruation. Whatever you want to call it. Now I know this might sound odd, but I knew absolutely nothing about menstruation other than that they came around once a month and when they did, that meant your girlfriend (or wife) wasn't pregnant. And of course, I knew to tread lightly with your woman when it DID come around. But seriously, I knew nothing about them. I did a little research before Amber got her first one because when I was freaking earlier about all the things that were going to fall on me after Gina passed, this was one of the things that scared the shit out of me. When I went for my own physical, I asked my doctor and he explained it a little. I also asked Nona, which was uncomfortable but necessary. What other woman could I to ask? As much as I love my mother and sister, it seemed like a line I didn't want to cross with them unless I had to.

When Amber did get her first one at about eleven years old, she came and told me. I had already talked with Nona about it and she was the one who took her to the drug store to teach her what to buy and how to use it. All the explaining in the world wasn't going to teach me either of those things. Have you ever looked down the women's aisle at the store? As Jackie rose through the ranks of womanhood behind her sister, Amber took the reigns and guided her.

The girls' physicals were something else altogether though. With the bras and periods and whatnot, there's a level of disconnect you have even if in the midst of it. I mean I wasn't in the room when the girls were putting on the bra or anything. But with physicals, as the parent of a minor you have to be in the room when they are being examined. It was awkward and uncomfortable going through that at first, but that's part of the deal when you're both Mom and Dad all rolled into one.

70

GUT CHECK

THE TEENAGE YEARS WERE hard to discipline. It's hard to be both the good and the bad cop when you're doing it all on your own. You have no back up and even though you may be fighting with a twelve year old, when they gang up on you it can really get frustrating.

I'll admit, I overcompensated for them losing their mother and that was mistake number one. I spoiled them too much with stuff. Had Gina been alive I would have never paid eighty dollars for a pair of jeans, but when we would be out shopping I would feel bad for them so I'd get them. I let them get away with some other things too, like being mouthy and talking back to me. Instead of cracking down on them like I should have, I chalked it up to them lashing out in anger and getting their frustrations out.

All of this goes back to the grief counseling I should have put the girls through. While I thought Amber was dealing with it all really well, it was really just stirring inside her like a volcano waiting to erupt. She had more of what I call a delayed reaction, as it wasn't until she was fourteen or fifteen when it really hit her. One day she was having a crying fit, really missing her mom, and all of a sudden her fist went flying through the wall. My sweet little angel had punched a hole in the drywall. Now that's something I would expect out of me, but never out of her. It didn't stop there either. She started to go through a rebellious phase. She quit playing basketball, started hanging with a rougher, partying crowd, and ultimately got busted for weed in school. That was later, but it happened.

The weed incident really shook things up. They mandated she see a counselor so she did, but she liked it so she kept going even after her requirements had been met. I let her go and let her quit when she wanted. As it turned out, that helped her tremendously.

My mom was the real treat through all of this. I got a lot of arm-chair quarterbacking from her, which could irritate me more than anything. The last thing I needed was someone criticizing my parental methods and me. I knew I was fucking some things up, but what hurt the most was that the help never came when I needed it. Plus, I was dissappointed with myself for dropping the ball at times. I was sensitive about my situation and her nitpicking only enlarged the magnifying glass. Even when she was right, it caused a lot of fights, especially because she was right.

That led to some of my own problems. I would get furious with my mom and become so incensed that I would drink it down. Then when I was tipsy, the alcohol would fuel my rage more and I would take it out on whoever was in the house. I never hit anyone, but damn could I be mean. Then they broke down, I felt like hell, had another drink, and the cycle began all over again.

One day I sat down with Amber's counselor, and she did the best thing that anyone has every done for me in that period. She told me to back off. Not with the girls, but with everyone. She told me to share less with my mom and sister. She told me to involve them less. She suggested my rage was eating into the girls and she was right. So I did. I backed way off. Where I used to talk to Robyn once a week, I started talking to her once every two or three weeks. I still talked to my mom every day but I kept it surface or at least away from conversations about the girls. If it got to be too much, I got off the phone. And it worked. I still made mistakes and the girls and I still had our issues, but we were together and working through growing up just like any other family.

71

WE'RE GONNA BE OKAY

AS THE YEARS WORE on, schedules were rough. It was easier when Jackie was little because she just went wherever Amber had to be. As she got into her own things, it got much harder. Basketball, soccer, cheerleading, school, birthday parties, shopping trips, doctors…it was so much! Not to mention I had my own work schedule and the things that go into that. I tried the school carpool with the other ladies around the neighborhood but they drove me nuts. I may play the role of Mom, but I'm still not a woman, and those women were nuts. It was easier for me to just do it on my own.

Remember, I'm in sales. As much as it is a 9am to 5pm job, it's also a wining and dining job. At times it got to be too much and I would get overwhelmed. I would feel sorry for myself and blame it on Gina's death, but I came to understand and appreciate that it was no different than with any other single divorced mother or father. The only real difference was that they typically get a break every other weekend, whereas I didn't.

The trick is, you just have to get used to fighting through fatigue. When you're on your own like this, everything has to go through you. There is no 'ask your mother' or 'wait until your mother gets home and she'll take you.' Every decision. Every ride. Every check. It's all on you. It takes some getting used to, but eventually, you settle in. Routines help a lot and you learn to anticipate and prepare for things. Everything from school clothes to septic tanks to Christmas lights. You just have to be aware of your own psychological well-being. You have to know that it's okay to ask for help. I couldn't have made it if I would have tried to be everything. You have to ask someone sometimes to take the kids for you or pick up something from the store if they're there.

The upside for me was that my girls were very self sufficient, responsible people. They were as little kids, they are as teenagers, and they will be as adults. Granted, at times I pushed them too fast, but again, hindsight is 20/20.

That's one important thing you have to accept. You have to accept the fact that you are going to make mistakes.

Sometimes, you are going to make the wrong decisions. Plain and simple. It isn't because you're a widower. It isn't because you went through some horrible tragedy. It's because you're a person. Every parent makes mistakes. What's truly important is how you right those wrongs, the relationships you foster with your kids, and the people you surround yourself with.

Neither of my girls are perfect and neither is Jackson. Lord knows neither am I. But we all know love. I surround them with it and I'm happy to say we've all come out fine on the other end. If you do that, regardless of the bumps along the way or the wrong turns you may make at certain points, you will too.

ACKNOWLEDGMENTS

To my son Michael: you are both my proudest moment & my biggest accomplishment. Always dream big and work hard to chase your dreams down. I couldn't love you more or be more proud of you. You and me buddy...always.

To my mom Debbie: there is no other way to say it than thank you for everything. My entire life it has never mattered if I needed someone to cheer me on or cheer me up, give me a laugh or a kick in the ass; you've always been there. You've always been my rock and you're the reason I'm the man & father that I am. Love you.

To my step dad Big Dave: thank you for being "Sallyamooah" and everything that goes into that. You're the goods.

To my friends who have become my brothers: JB, Paul, Jon, Mark, Michael, David, Joe, Bill, TJ, Ramblin' Ray & Joey: you guys mean the world to me. I can't thank you enough.

To Jeff Schwartz, Wendy Harrison, Deb Heed, Tom Lounges and Bruce Parrot: thank you for taking whatever chance you did on a young journalist / creative mind. Without you both my life and my career would be drastically different.

To Dina Bair, Jane Melvin and everyone at DWCC: thank you not only for your friendship but also for your tireless efforts as "soldiers of another kind." You truly are one in a million.

To Arianne Nardo, Janet Barding, Ron Kittle, Gretchen Wilson, Craig Campbell, Tiffany Bearden, Doug Buffone, Brandy Reed, Holly Gleason, Nancy Russell, Alison Auerbach, Karen Tallier, Scott Stem, Kathy Best, Eddie Robba, Chris Keaton, Pete McMurray, Terry Boers, Dan McNeil, Kevin Matthews, Dan Richman, Ryan Arnold, Mandy Zahn, John Castino, Bernie Glim, Adam Bailey, Dave Rudolf & Jack Adams: I have known all of you for many, many years and whether you know it or not each one of you has often amazed and inspired me and I thank you for of it.

And to anyone I may have forgotten, understand that I have limited space but please feel free to insert your name here: Thank you _____. ☺

ABOUT THE AUTHOR

Ken Churilla is a Chicago-based writer who was first published at the age of 16. A career journalist, Ken's work has appeared in numerous magazines & newspapers all over the nation. He has also authored media kit artist biographies for artists such as Kenny Chesney, George Strait, Martina McBride, Joey+Rory and more. He is also a songwriter in Nashville. *No One Said It Would Be Easy* is Ken's first book.